LAW AND REVOLUTION IN SOUTH AFRICA

just ideas

transformative ideals of justice in ethical and political thought

series editors

Drucilla Cornell

Roger Berkowitz

LAW AND REVOLUTION IN SOUTH AFRICA

UBUNTU, DIGNITY, AND THE STRUGGLE FOR CONSTITUTIONAL TRANSFORMATION

Drucilla Cornell

FORDHAM UNIVERSITY PRESS

NEW YORK   2014

Fordham University Press has no responsibility for the persistence or accuracy of URLs for external or third-party Internet websites referred to in this publication and does not guarantee that any content on such websites is, or will remain, accurate or appropriate.

Fordham University Press also publishes its books in a variety of electronic formats. Some content that appears in print may not be available in electronic books.

Library of Congress Cataloging-in-Publication Data

Cornell, Drucilla, author.
   Law and revolution in South Africa : uBuntu, dignity, and the struggle for constitutional transformation / Drucilla Cornell. — First edition.
      p. cm. — (Just ideas)
   Includes bibliographical references and index.
   ISBN 978-0-8232-5757-7 (cloth : alk. paper) — ISBN 978-0-8232-5758-4 (pbk. : alk. paper)
      1. Constitutional law—South Africa.   2. Respect for persons—Law and legislation—South Africa.   3. Customary law—South Africa.   4. Ubuntu (Philosophy)   I. Title.
   KTL2070.C67 2014
   342.68—dc23

2013037280

Printed in the United States of America

16 15 14   5 4 3 2 1

First edition

for Michiel Bot

Contents

Preface

I first visited South Africa in 2001. It was a fairly straightforward academic trip, to give lectures on my work. South Africa was a particularly important destination to me, because it represented revolutionary possibility in a world that had seemed to have completely forsaken such possibility. Like so many others of my generation, I grew up with the international struggle against apartheid and, therefore, to see revolutionaries—many of them imprisoned for years—come to power in the government was truly exhilarating. Of course, by the time of my visit in 2001, many on the left (including myself) had become extremely concerned that the economic policies of the African National Congress had gone in the wrong direction, and conceded way too much to what has popularly come to be known as the Washington Consensus. But revolutions, particularly the long and bloody struggle to overthrow apartheid, do not succeed within a day. The struggle to transform South Africa was alive in 2001, and it is alive today.

The essays in this book were written not simply by someone on the left who engaged with the struggle in South Africa as if it were an exemplar of what might be, or, alternatively, as a harbinger of the ultimate failure of any meaningful alternative to capitalism. Instead, they were written during a time when I was working on the ground in South Africa to create a project called the uBuntu Project, and I have been deeply influenced by this on the ground work in South Africa. The uBuntu Project was formed in 2002, and its initial projects were interviews in the townships on the Western Cape, addressing the significance of uBuntu for young people in the urban areas. The project was born in the townships, and later, the uBuntu Township Project took over the work of this early pilot project. It has now become a much larger project dedicated both to research and the advocacy of indigenous ideals in the new dispensation. I lived in South Africa from 2007 to January 2010, in part in order to expand the work of the project.

For most of my life, I have been involved in the antiracist struggle within the United States. But like many critical theorists, my academic roots were to be found in German idealism and critical theory. It was only once I was working on the ground in South Africa to build the uBuntu Project, a project that supports research into indigenous ideals and the living customary law, that I came to see the need to begin a long process of education into Africana philosophy. There was no way I could come to grasp the significance of uBuntu in South Africa without completely reeducating myself.

The uBuntu Project as a project-based research group also demanded that I face the complexity of a number of questions that have always haunted leftist and progressive thinking: What does it mean to be part of a collective research project? What does it mean to work on a research project with those who are deeply invested in the indigenous values that the project is researching? In my own case, I became an advocate for the reconstitutionalization of uBuntu, well aware of how such constitutionalization would change the meaning of uBuntu if it were legalized on that level. It would also be a step in "indigenizing" the South African Constitution. I was not simply critiquing uBuntu or researching its meaning—I was fighting for its "re-cognition." Of course, the "re-cognition" of uBuntu also demands a critical engagement with this value. The question of what it means to "retrieve" indigenous values is itself overwhelming in its implications, but clearly it involves acts of imagination, since there cannot be anything like a pure retrieval. Beyond that, questions of theory and practice are raised when one becomes an advocate and not simply a researcher. It demands that we think differently about theory, practice, and advocacy. I have long argued that theory is not only critique—although it certainly involves critique—but also the defense of ideals. Simply put, the project has forced me to rethink some of our deepest assumptions about research, objectivity, theory, and what it means to be a theorist in a collective struggle to fight against the erasure of indigenous values imposed by colonialism. The style of this book, which is indeed reflective, is part and parcel of this long and continuous process of self-questioning that my commitment and practice in the uBuntu Project has necessarily imposed on me.

As the great philosopher and critical race theorist Lewis Gordon has pointed out, Africana philosophy has long been engaging with European philosophy. Africana philosophy critiques neat geographical designations as being inaccurate, but this critique also involves an analysis of how Europe came to be identified as the home of reason and philosophy. Without this context, and how it has profoundly impacted my life and my thinking, it would be difficult to understand how these chapters attempt to grapple not only with the critique of eurocentrism, but also with the important relationship between Africana philosophy and German idealism and critical theory. In other words, it would be way too simple, and certainly against the grain of Africana philosophy, to argue that one must simply walk away from the best European or continental philosophy. Instead, there has to be a critical engagement between these different philosophical traditions—and I mean critical in the best sense of the word—in that we need to see how the relations between the developments of different strands of critical theory both build off and sometimes limit one another.

Thus, the two chapters in Part I attempt to reflect on two of the central debates in contemporary political philosophy. Chapter 1 is a critical engagement with Martin Heidegger to argue that his work can have both ethical and political significance in the Global South, because of his powerful philosophical engagement with the meaning of technology. Chapter 2 engages with both Ernesto Laclau and Chantal Mouffe, who have from the outset developed an important theory of radical democracy by working through some of the most important thinkers of our time, from Antonio Gramsci to Jacques Lacan to Jacques Derrida. The question of the relationship of radical democracy to anything like a socialist future is one that they have not only raised: it haunts all of their work, and as a result, given the burning question of what socialism would mean in South Africa, I felt compelled to engage critically with their work.

In Part II, I turn to the inadequacy of Anglo-American and European debates on multiculturalism and legal pluralism. In these chapters, I tried to think with Jean and John L. Comaroff about the significance of what they call "policulturalism"[1] for law in South Africa. The Constitution is the only law that has direct force in South Africa, and yet what that simple statement means for different sources of law has turned out to be extremely complex, particularly now that indigenous ideals like uBuntu are more frequently used as justiciable principles at the level of the Constitutional Court. These chapters are reflections that seek to challenge the terms of the reigning debates, to open up the way in which the living customary law, indigenous ideals, and their incorporation into constitutional jurisprudence all demand that we see the political challenge to the traditional notion of the nation state as inhering in this complex configuration. This is a challenge, however, which in no way undermines neither the importance of the nation state nor the striving for something like the new nation of South Africa rooted in a substantive revolution.

In Part III, I engage critically with an often heard argument that indigenous ideals like uBuntu are part of a throwback to traditional societies that will be simply overcome as South Africa, and indeed Africa, moves toward modernity. Throughout these chapters, I argue that African modernity is *sui generis*, and therefore ideals like uBuntu, and the whole body of work that has come to be known as Africana philosophy, is thoroughly modern. But like all ideals, uBuntu can be deployed by both conservatives, particularly those who want to conserve what they see as indigenous cultures or intellectual traditions, and those on the left who want to develop them as a challenge to neoliberal capitalism. Chapter 7 explicitly addresses the work of a lesbian *sangoma* or spiritual healer, as she has defended the rights of gays, lesbians, and the transgendered through an appeal to Zulu identity and the living customary law of the Zulus. Her appeal is not done through disidentification, but through a direct struggle with the meaning and significance of being Zulu in the new dispensation. The questions raised in these chapters are complicated indeed, but they certainly demand reflection, and as Jean and John Comaroff have argued, many questions raised in the Global South are now the central questions that critical theory has to engage everywhere.[2]

Chapters 3 and 4 have not been published or presented before. Chapter 1 was first published as "Is Technology a Fatal Destiny? The Relevance of Heidegger for South Africa and Other 'Developing' Countries" in *Refusal, Transition and Post-Apartheid Law* edited by Karin van Marle (Stellenbosch: Sun Media, 2009), 141–52. I presented a shorter version of Chapter 2 at a celebratory conference on Ernesto Laclau and Chantal Mouffe's *Hegemony and Socialist Strategy*, organized by Jacques Lezra in the Department of Comparative Literature at New York University on February 20, 2010. Chapter 5 was first published as "The Significance of the Living Customary Law for an Understanding of uBuntu," in *Constitutional Court Review* 2 (2009): 395–408. Chapter 6 was first published as "uBuntu, Pluralism, and the Responsibility of Legal Academics in the New South Africa" in *Law and Critique* (Winter 2009): 43–58. I presented Chapter 8 at a seminar organized by Stu Woolman in November 2009 at the South African Institute for Advanced Constitutional, Public, Human Rights and International Law. This seminar was published with comments by Emeritus Justice Yvonne Mokgoro and Stu Woolman in *Is This Seat Taken? Conversations at the Bar, the Bench and the Academy*, edited by Stu Woolman and David Bilchitz (Pretoria: Pretoria University Law Press, 2011). A shorter version of the conclusion was published in *The Thinking Africa Newsletter* of Rhodes University, June 2012, 2–4. The conclusion will also appear as "uBuntu and Subaltern Legality" in *Ubuntu: Curating the Archive*, edited by Leonhard Praeg and Siphokazi Magadla (Pietermaritzburg: UKZN Press, forthcoming). I would like to thank all publishers for their permission to republish.

As always in producing a book manuscript, there are many people to thank. John Comaroff has over the years I have been working in South Africa played a crucial role in my own intellectual development. He has given me critical comments on almost every chapter in this book. He has played a major role in the uBuntu Project and helped me rethink its direction on many occasions. His encouragement, as well as his criticism, has been a major force in my life over the last ten years. I am in his debt, and of course all the mistakes I continue to make are my own. His wife, Jean Comaroff, has also played a major role in participating in the uBuntu Project. I am grateful for her support. Jane Gordon and Lewis Gordon have read many of the chapters in this book and have given me incisive criticism on them. I am thankful for the time and attention they have given to my thinking. Lewis Gordon has played a major role in my reeducation in Africana philosophy, a project, of course, which I am still undertaking.

Emeritus Justice Yvonne Mokgoro, the patron of the uBuntu Project, has been an important critic of my own thinking on uBuntu. She has been an indispensable source of inspiration to the project as a whole, and has regularly participated in seminars and events since we first met in 2005. She has also played a central role in developing uBuntu as a justiciable constitutional principle while she was on the court. I am grateful both for her participation, for her dedication to the project, and, more importantly, for her inclusion of indigenous ideals as central to the new dispensation. Emeritus Justice Albie Sachs has been an indispensable critic and friend of the project since its inception. He has generously participated in a number of seminars, workshops, and conferences, and has been an excellent critic of many of the chapters in this book. With Emeritus Justice Yvonne Mokgoro, he has also played a crucial role in the development of the uBuntu jurisprudence of the South African Constitutional Court. I owe him my profound thanks for his support, criticism, and encouragement. Emeritus Justice Lourens "Laurie" Ackermann has also been a friend to the project, and has regularly participated in seminars, workshops, and conferences. He has constantly pushed me to critically analyze the relationship between uBuntu and dignity. He has also throughout my time working in South Africa served valiantly as my "Dutch uncle," to use his phrase, advising me at every step through the difficulties of developing a project like the uBuntu Project. His advice has always informed my decisions about the project, and his friendship has been crucial to my own decision to move to South Africa and pursue the work in more depth.

Karin van Marle has played a central role in the uBuntu Project and worked as my collaborator in almost every event the Project has organized since 2004. We started this project at a time when it was controversial, if not downright unpopular, and she stayed with me throughout some of our most dire times, when the project was publicly criticized. Her courage and commitment always helped me to continue. Her friendship has been a source of sustenance for many years now. Jaco Barnard-Naude also became a supporter of the project at its inception, and is engaged in all the uBuntu events since the project was first started. He has also been a major critic of my work, and has given me much valuable feedback on many of the chapters in this book. During our time when we were professors at the University of Cape Town, we spent long hours discussing some of the theoretical issues that tie this book together. I am grateful for his friendship and his critical engagement with my own work. The former dean of the University of Pretoria Faculty of Law, Duard Kleyn, supported the project with one of its most important resources, money. He generously gave to the project for two major conferences in 2004 and 2009. He has also remained a dear friend and a supporter of the project after he stepped down as dean. Chuma Himonga was a codirector of the project from 2005 until 2011, when we both stepped down to be members of the board of directors. She has played a crucial role in the project, and her scholarship is at the cutting edge in work on the living customary law in South Africa. Her critical mind has been very important to the development of a number of the pilot projects related to the uBuntu Project. She conducted a project on gender, uBuntu, and the living customary law in 2007 and 2008. Nyoko Muvangua and Hylton White are also important members of the project. Nyoko is the co-editor of the recent publication, *uBuntu and the Law: Indigenous Ideals and Post-apartheid Jurisprudence.* As my research assistant, she played a major role in compiling the cases and working on the summations of each case. Hylton

White has done foundational work in Zululand funded by my National Research Foundation Chair in Dignity Jurisprudence, Indigenous Values, and the Living Customary Law. He is a regular participant and supporter of the project. His unsurpassed skill as an anthropologist has been crucial to an analysis of how the living customary law operates outside of state institutions. His work is central to rethinking how the living customary law is a form of subaltern legality. Dean Annette Lansink has been a supporter of the project from its inception. In the last several years, she has held regular events at the University of Venda Law School to support the group's research goals. Her enthusiasm and unwavering commitment to indigenous values has played a central role in pushing forward the project into new areas of research. I am grateful for her friendship and support.

Sampie Terreblanche, whose work *A History of Inequality in South Africa* is foundational for anyone who wants to understand the strengths and weaknesses of the transformation that has taken place in South Africa, has also been an important critical force in the project. He has brought his economic insight into a number of seminars that have allowed for provocative suggestions about how uBuntu could be used both legally and politically to challenge the dire results of the African National Congress's capitulation to neoliberal capitalist policies. Amartya Sen has long been an important supporter of the project, and played an important role in helping me shape the project as a working research effort into the significance of indigenous values in the new dispensation. I am in his debt for his support.

I also need to thank my assistant Sam Fuller for his research help, which has helped me throughout and which led me to ask him to co-write the introductions of the two casebooks that the project has produced and will be publishing with Fordham University Press. I also need to thank the National Research Foundation of South Africa for awarding me the chair in Dignity Jurisprudence, Indigenous Values, and the Living Customary Law, which I held in the years 2008 and 2009. This funding was indispensable for the development of all the different aspects of the project. My students on this side of the ocean have also been indispensable for their research assistance and document production. I also want to thank Richard Falk, who graciously agreed to review the book for Fordham University Press. I am in debt to him for his remarks and critical analysis of the book. I also want to thank the anonymous reviewer for her or his in-depth review of the manuscript.

My daughter, Serena Cornell, has lived with me in South Africa throughout the development of the Project. Once we had moved to South Africa, she participated as a photographer and an interviewer in the uBuntu Township Project. I thank her for her generosity of spirit, which led her to embrace South Africa as her second country.

It has become a popular expression to use a phrase that without a particular person, "there would be nothing." In this case, this person is Michiel Bot. Michiel is one of the most brilliant young minds that I know, and I have been fortunate enough to have him as my research assistant since 2010. He has an incisive mind plus the kind of analytical precision that never lets me get away with a sloppy formulation. His attention to detail is extraordinary, and mistakes that might otherwise have gone unnoticed have been picked up and corrected because of his attentiveness. As a critical theorist, comparatist, and lawyer, he has been able to follow the more technical chapters and give me critical feedback. He has been part of almost all of these essays as a research assistant, editor, and critic. He has influenced the shape that many of these chapters took. He has certainly kept me on the "straight and narrow," and I am forever in his debt because of his combination of rigor and creativity. As a result of all the hours we spent together working on this book, I am dedicating it to him with my profound thanks for his effort and for his commitment. Of course, any remaining mistakes are my own.

Drucilla Cornell
New York City, March 2013

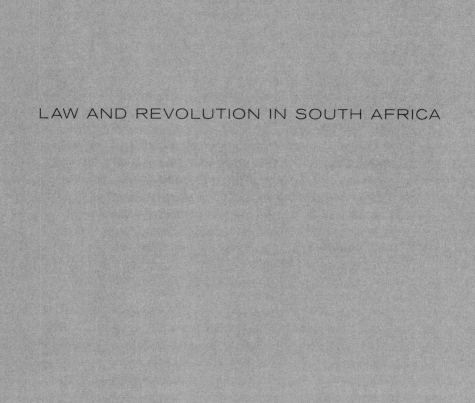

LAW AND REVOLUTION IN SOUTH AFRICA

Introduction:
Transitional Justice versus Substantive Revolution

The defeat of apartheid and the establishment of the "new South Africa" were hailed throughout the world as a miracle. A country ripped apart by the worst kind of racialized violence, the brutalization of the majority popu- lation by the apartheid state, and even the very idea of apartheid as a militant state-enforced degradation would hardly have seemed the likely candidate for such a miracle. Indeed, perhaps the very use of the word "miracle" is an insult to the heroic struggle in which millions of people sought to assert their dignity as human beings and their political rights as citizens.[1] It was so- called ordinary people who made the government ungovernable, to quote one of the African National Congress's famous slogans. These so-called ordi- nary people were not just a few leaders who endured imprisonment, torture, and exile; they were thousands of people. South Africa was a country torn apart by civil war within the country and a war on the border, after the ANC had no choice but to create an armed wing and declare the armed struggle as the only possibility left to the majority. To refuse to grapple with the reality that is to negate the history of South Africa and the truly heroic effort to bring down apartheid. But how do we understand what went on in South Africa? And how do we understand the effort to transform a society rooted in racialized capitalism? Has it succeeded? Has it failed? Can we even think in those terms anymore? All these questions and many more are raised by what I am going to term, following Emeritus Justice Lourens "Laurie" W. H. Ackermann, the substantive revolution in South Africa. The issues raised by the transformation in South Africa are complex, but I will suggest in this introduction and throughout this book that we will never understand what South Africa offers all of us who hope for a better world unless we use the now much contested vocabulary of revolution, emancipation, and transformation.[2]

Since the fall of the Berlin Wall, there has been a growing body of litera-ture on "transitional justice" from authoritarian regimes to liberal democ-ratization. Obviously, much of this literature focuses on what was viewed as previously "communist" governments, as these governments had to deal with the domination of a one-party system. In most of the literature, the focus was on classic democratic proceduralism and the attempt to quantify whether or not a country was actually making the transition. This literature focused on procedures such as the right to vote, the development of a thriv-ing civil society, the establishment of basic civil rights, and of course the shift from a planned economy to a so-called market economy. In a certain sense, there were criteria, then, if formal and procedural, for when the tran-sition had been completed and the country had been successfully removed from its authoritarian past and launched into its democratic future.

Of course, a number of books have been written on the possibility of a democratic South Africa within the democratic proceduralist framework.[3] All of these works assume the hegemonic view that what is sought in a transitional period is a new social contract. The question becomes, then: is such a new foundational social contract possible in a society deeply divided by purportedly racial and ethnic conflict? For example, a great deal of this literature focuses on the battle between the ANC and the Inkatha Freedom Party, often explored as an example of the remaining ethnic tensions that led to extreme violence between 1992 and 1994. This understanding of the conflict is itself one-sided, because it reduced a political battle to one of ethnicity. There were in fact Zulus and Xhosas on both sides of the struggle. But for now I want to focus on some of the assumptions that were made through an appeal to certain hegemonic concepts of political theory such as the social contract. To quote Timothy T. Sisk on the question of whether or not such a contract is possible, given his own use of these hegemonic concepts:

> But not all political players will be willing to reach agreement. It is more reasonable for them to sit on the sidelines and await (and, if possible, bring about) the failure of moderation and negotiation. Those who perceive the situation in zero-sum terms outbid those who moderate for the support of the communal bases on which political parties in divided societies in conflict ultimately rely. The outbidders in the South African conflict, ethnic nationalists and the black radical left, demonstrate this point directly. The challenge of transition is to create sufficient incentives to make participation more beneficial than self-imposed exclusion. Moderation gives centrist actors a common incentive to cooperate in fighting the forces of outbidding and to *eschew identity politics*. An incentive to cooperate is also an incentive to converge on a new set of democratic political rules, a result that protects against the extremists and marginalizes appeals to ascriptive solidarity.[4]

It is impossible to summarize even the literature on South Africa when considered as a matter of transitional justice in the limited framework of a democratic proceduralism. But we can at least point to two basic lessons contained within this literature. The first is: eschew identity politics, and the second is: adhere firmly to "moderation," which of course in the context of the 1990s and the beginning of the twenty-first century meant that the African National Congress had to step away from its long-term commitment to the development of a socialist economy, and allow itself to be subjected to the mandates of the economic and legal institutions of what is called neoliberal capitalism. Again, to quote Sisk: "The challenge ahead will be to use that legitimacy to create a set of permanent postapartheid institutions that perpetuate the moderation, borne of necessity, that arose during South Africa's transition from apartheid to democracy."[5] The main concern of this literature is not only identity politics, but also that important word, *moderation*. Moderation meant something very specific in the context of South Africa. The ANC had long been a socialist party committed to the ideals of the Freedom Charter. The Freedom Charter explicitly called for the nationalization of the primary resources and many large corporations. Of course, the Freedom Charter was written in 1956, and the question of what kind of economic transition was necessary in South Africa was a huge one, given the failure of legal nationalization alone to lead to the kind of society which could hope to aspire to the great ideal of "From each according to her ability to each according to her need."[6] But the proponents of moderation were not interested in the complex question of how one might organize a socialist economy, or indeed deal with the overwhelming economic devastation of the actual lives of the majority-black population. They were instead interested only in whether or not the ANC would get on board with the Washington Consensus and eschew socialism altogether. Not surprisingly, then, much of that literature focuses on just how much inequality is compatible with the transition to democratic proceduralism, particularly since this includes the move to a "market system" dictated by the mandates of neoliberalism.[7]

Revolution was defined narrowly and completely rejected as antithetical to democracy. Therefore, the absolute key to whether or not South Africa could be democratized was that the ANC give up on all of its revolutionary goals and commitments, and become a party of moderation. Those who hung on to the ANC's revolutionary commitments were condemned for their nostalgia and warned against "the perils of wishful thinking."[8] To quote Donald L. Horowitz:

> It is natural to think that it detracts from the revolutionary goals of the struggle to plan for the future. Planning may mean playing at least a hypothetical role as a future "insider," and this may seem contaminating. But that is exactly the sort of "contamination" required for democracy to emerge. It is sobering to reflect that, at least since 1789, hardly ever, if at all, has revolution alone "produced a stable democratic regime in an independent state."[9] Revolutions require the use of undemocratic methods and the consolidation of undemocratic leadership. Both are inimical to the development of democracy later. If a democratic South Africa is desired, a future orientation is required.[10]

Revolution and democracy were thus opposed to one another, and the question was whether in negotiations the ANC would forsake its former revolutionary aspirations. I will return shortly to what it has meant that the ANC did capitulate to the demands of neoliberal capitalism. For now, I want to emphasize that even the richer literature on transitional justice, which tries to challenge the hegemonic model of democratic proceduralism that dominates political science in the US academy, still holds on to two basic ideas: first, that we are now in a postrevolutionary era, and second that there is some consensus on the meaning of democratization, even if it cannot be reduced to a set of procedural components.

Ruti G. Teitel has challenged the notion that transitional justice can be reduced to democratic proceduralism. She replaces democratic proceduralism with what she calls a constructivist approach, which would allow us to grapple with the key normative aspects associated with transitional justice. And yet she continues to focus on the shift from an authoritarian one-party state to forms of democracy, even if they now include a much richer spectrum of democratic institutions, such as Truth and Reconciliation Commissions, reforms in administrative justice, as well as context-sensitive notions of the criminal law which would allow for pardoning of those who participated at least on lower levels of the previous authoritarian regimes. To quote Teitel:

> The thesis of this book is that the conception of justice in periods of political change is extraordinary and constructivist: It is alternately constituted by, and constitutive of, the transition. The conception of justice that emerges is contextualized and partial: What is deemed just is contingent and informed by prior injustice. Reponses to repressive rule inform the meaning of adherence to the rule of law. As a state undergoes political change, legacies of injustice have a bearing on what is deemed transformative. To some extent, the emergence of these legal responses instantiates transition. As the discussion proceeds, it will become evident that the law's role in periods of political change is complex. Ultimately, this book makes two sorts of claims: one, about the nature of law in periods of substantial political change and, the other, about law's role in constituting the transition. For, contrary to the prevailing idealist accounts, law here is shaped by the political circumstances, but, also challenging the prevailing realist accounts, law here is not mere product but itself structures the transition. The association of these responses with periods of political change advances the construction of societal understanding that transition is in progress.[11]

However, even Teitel's richer framework insists on two things that make it distant from the revolution in South Africa. (And as I will shortly explain, we should think of the transition in South Africa as a revolution.) First and foremost, Teitel, like so much of the literature on transitional justice, accepts that we are now in a postrevolutionary period.[12] The second feature, related to the first, is that even though this richer phenomenology of transition assumes that we are in a postrevolutionary period, Teitel tends to generalize from the transitions out of what she accepts were authoritarian communist regimes to regimes such as the new dispensation in South Africa. The problem with such over-generalization is that it decontextualizes the South African revolution, and therefore loses the specificity of its challenge to the reigning hegemony of the role of capitalism in this so-called transition.

Indeed, as Sampie Terreblanche has powerfully argued, there can be no democracy in South Africa until there is a break from the neoliberal consensus, and an attempt to develop an economic order that can effectively break up the hold on the country of a powerful capitalist ruling class. To quote Terreblanche:

> The compromises reached at those negotiations determined the power relations between the "democratic" and "capitalist" components of the new politico-economic system in the post-apartheid period. It was also decided that neoliberalism (or the ideology of liberal capitalism) would determine economic policy, and that post-apartheid South Africa would have a free market economy. The terms of this settlement were such that the poorest half of the population has, over the last eight years, become entrapped in a new form of oppression: a state of systemic exclusion and systemic neglect by the democratically elected government and the modern sector of the economy respectively. It is therefore not surprising that the situation of the poorest half of the population has deteriorated during the past eight years.[13]

Terreblanche argues that without an economic transition that democratizes economic relations, there can be no long-term democracy in South Africa in which the ideal of rule by and for the people is anything but a mockery. Indeed, in his book, Terreblanche argues that the transition—which he agrees with other critics was an "elite" transition—was incomplete, precisely because it did not democratize the economy. He has now argued that the transition has failed, because there can be no democracy when close to 50 percent of the people live in dire poverty.[14] Of course, this implies a very different definition of democracy than the democratic proceduralism that is hegemonic in the debates about transitional justice. What this failure might mean has dire implications for the future of South Africa.

In Part I, I explicitly defend the need to think through what constitutes democratic socialism as opposed to radical democratic theory in my critical engagement with the work of Ernesto Laclau and Chantal Mouffe. As I write, the Economic Freedom Fighters (EFF) have become an officially registered party in South Africa with an openly socialist agenda that begins with the expropriation of all the major resources in South Africa. The question of whether or not the EFF represents a return to notions of the dictatorship of the proletariat and therefore rejects the substantive revolution in South Africa is beyond the scope of this introduction. But what is evident is that the call for the overthrow of capitalism and a return to the socialist politics of the ANC is gathering great momentum. Thus, it seemed important to address the issue embodied in the name of their party: economics. Of course, the EFF is by no means the only new organization that is formed to present a direct challenge to the ANC's neoliberal economic programs. The Association of Mineworkers and Construction was formed after the 2012 gold miners strikes, and has an explicitly anticapitalist agenda. The Shack Dwellers Movement is now a major presence in South Africa, and has called for a politics of revolutionary uBuntu. It is clear that the ANC no longer holds hegemony over the revolutionary struggle in South Africa. What is clear is that we must think and struggle for economic alternatives to capitalism in the name of socialism; whether or not the EFF or any of the other alternative organizations that have been formed can effectively challenge the ANC of course remains in the hands of the struggle on the ground.[15] Chapter 1 may seem a long way from the on-the-ground struggle for an economic alternative to capitalism. Heidegger undoubtedly would have dismissed such a struggle as one that would inevitably be captured by the reign of technological reason. My reason for including a chapter on Heidegger is his continuing relevance—despite his own distance from socialist struggles—to those of us who want to think through what it might mean to think the economic without having the economic completely overcome the ethical and the social. In other words, his work continues to be an important warning to socialists about the dangers of economism. Of course, the two chapters in Part I challenge the hegemonic idea in certain academic circles that we are in a postrevolutionary age, and that any thinking of revolution, let alone socialism, is nothing but mistaken nostalgia. But as I argue in Chapter 6, we also have to take account of how hegemonic academic models, particularly those that foreclose revolutionary possibility, actually undermine the kind of thinking that has to go on if we even begin to think about what the process of true decolonization might entail today.

However, for the purposes of this introduction, I want to focus on an aspect of South Africa that may make its attempted revolution relevant beyond the current economic and political crisis that is undoubtedly endangering the "new" South Africa. So far the literature on transitional justice accepts that we are in a postrevolutionary period, and that all theories of transitional justice argue that the process of democratization demands that new regimes must forsake revolution. The irony is that some of the great thinkers of the South African transition, even those who were justices on the Constitutional Court, have defended the idea that there was and must be a continuing revolution in South Africa, and that that revolution should be considered substantive.

But what is a substantive revolution? In his pathbreaking article, Emeritus Justice Laurie Ackermann attempted to define the transformation from apartheid to the new South Africa as a substantive revolution.[16] Of course, Ackermann did not appeal to the miracle of the negotiations, nor to their peacefulness. He was only too well aware of the prolonged violence and indeed war on the borders of Angola and Namibia that went on for almost twenty years and killed thousands. So if it was not a miracle peaceful transition, why return to the idea of revolution? Ackermann does not speak much of revolution, concentrating instead on the word *substantive*, but I want to focus on revolution. Famously, Hannah Arendt associated the great revolutions of the twentieth century and the previous revolutions in the United States and France, as having always two prongs: violence in the overthrow of the old order, and the aspiration to freedom of the new revolutionary government or nation state.[17] Does South Africa have these two prongs? Here is where it gets interesting. The revolution in South Africa that Ackermann refers to as "substantive" demands the complete overthrow of the nonethical relations between human beings that lay at the basis of South African society, in the name of the great ideals of the new constitutional dispensation: dignity, freedom, and equality. The creation of the possibility of an ethical relationship between human beings, institutionalized by law, which would end the exclusion, the subordination, and the exploitation of the black population, was the dream of the Freedom Charter.

Note that already we have moved away from the model of the social contract. The Freedom Charter demands an end to subordination and exploitation, and these demands challenge even the most radical notions of the social contract. Could we then redefine revolution as a legal institutionalization of a nation that grounds the state in the great ideals of freedom and dignity, and therefore transforms society, here understood as the ethical relations amongst human beings, in the "direction" of those ideals?[18] The revolution, in this sense, would imply emancipation in terms of the recognition of the sovereignty of all citizens of South Africa to create democratic control over every walk of life. It would also imply transformation, as Terreblanche argues, of the conditions of subordination and super-exploitation imposed by apartheid. The project of South Africa seemingly remains within the modernist aspiration to create a new nation state, but it is one in which the connection between nation and state was not taken for granted. The new nation is inseparable at least from the promise of both emancipation and transformation. The state is to be grounded in those ideals, and therefore was to be a unique African version of the *Rechtsstaat*. There are two senses in which the complex demands of decolonization in South Africa challenge Hegel's own notion of the *Rechtsstaat*. The first is that forms of ethnic, tribal, and religious belonging cannot simply be overcome—that is, sublated in a new nation state that recognizes, in Hegel's sense, a complex notion of citizenship, but still turns on a conception of the person as always beyond any of those "earlier," purportedly pre-modern forms of belonging. As John and Jean Comaroff have long argued, these forms of belonging are not multicultural; they are "policultural" in that they involve challenges to the domination of the new nation over traditionally conceived fundaments of the nation state such as control over violence, overarching state law, and the conception of citizenship that would attempt to create a notion of a homogeneous population and identity.[19]

For example, other sources of law were recognized by the new dispensation, including the living customary law and the Roman Dutch Law, as long as these other sources of law were rendered compatible with the great ideals of the radical change in the substance of human relations called for by the revolution. Throughout this book I discuss what a thoroughgoing recognition of politically as well as culturally defined difference actually means for law and the substantive revolution in South Africa. This revolution is complicated indeed.

Could there be a revolution (not just a rebellion) that did not involve the seizure or remaking of the new nation state? That question is way beyond the introduction of this book. But I do want to at least suggest that the notion of the substantive revolution in South Africa that grounded the ideals of the state in the aspirations of a new nation committed to the transformation of society, and one that was to proceed legally in the broadest sense of the word, was at least an important innovation on the thinking of revolution. And why so? Because it attempted to recouple revolution and law, even at the level of the Constitution.

As Boaventura de Sousa Santos has argued, revolution and law had been decoupled in the twentieth century, and this of course helps us at least understand the hegemonic opposition between democracy and revolution. I agree with de Sousa Santos when he argues the following:

> If liberal political and legal theory had expelled revolution from the legal constellation, Marxism, particularly in its Marxist-Leninist version, expelled law from the revolutionary constellation. If it highlights the sharp contrast between liberalism and Marxism, this symmetrical opposition also betrays the underlying complicity between the two. In both liberalism and Marxism, the dialectical relation between law and revolution is lost. At the most, we might say that it stands frozen on one of its legs by political fiat. When Lenin and, later on, Wyschinsky say that "law is one category of the political," they are in fact doing nothing more than pushing the liberal conception of law to the utmost, since for both of them, as indeed for liberal theory, politics (and hence, law) is the realm of the state. It is not the Russian Revolution but rather the postrevolutionary state of the nineteenth century that brings the modern Western legal tradition to a collapse. The Russian is a symptom or an effect of that collapse, not its cause.[20]

One crucial aspect of the South African Revolution is the attempt to recouple revolution and law, and this at least should be noted as an important paradigm shift away from what de Sousa Santos describes as the idea that revolution itself is always illegal in terms of the order it is to overthrow. After the broad range of organizations considered revolutionary were unbanned and allowed to participate in the negotiations, including the Communist Party, there is an original challenge to the idea that revolution is outside the current state. Of course, in a very real sense, during the negotiation process, the nation state was under erasure. It was to be utterly transformed in the course of the negotiations, in accordance with what Ackermann calls the substantive revolution. Therefore, this is the second sense in which law and revolution were recoupled, because these organizations did not have as a formal mandate that they relinquish their revolutionary commitment. If they did relinquish those commitments, it was not because there was any legal demand that they do so, nor, obviously, were explicitly revolutionary organizations like the Communist Party rejected from the negotiations. This alone would make South Africa different from societies in "transitional justice," many of which outlawed the Communist Party or took other steps to demolish its political legitimacy. Here it is the recognition of formerly banned organizations with revolutionary aspirations as part of the negotiations that has been designated the miracle. But a more precise way of examining the importance of this move is that it played a major role in bringing law back into a relationship with revolution, because it was revolutionaries who were negotiating with their enemies for a new government. What is missing in the transitional justice literature is the insistence of many of the negotiators from these revolutionary organizations that South Africa needed to engage in some kind of revolution that would thoroughly transform the society, the long-stated goals of the ANC.

Ackermann himself relies on the distinction between substantive and procedural revolution, terms used by the great legal theorist Hans Kelsen.[21] Kelsen defines procedural revolutions very much along the lines of Hannah Arendt. Kelsen defines a procedural revolution as the violent overthrow of the entire legal order and all of its government institutions, to be replaced with a completely new set of laws and institutions. We have already defined substance from a political and ethical perspective, as it means a complete undoing of the color bar and all its manifestations. But for Kelsen, "substantive" means something a little more limited. His definition emphasizes that the new substance of the ethical order that would be the basis of right, in the German sense of *Recht*, would not abolish all the laws on the books and would not fire all of the current justices and administrative officials. It would instead insist that the substance of the revolution, the very meaning of right or *Recht*, would be the only justification for the force of law. Simply put, no existing law on the books could be enforced unless they were consistent with the principles of right or *Recht* that undergird and give significance to the meaning of the transformation from the old order to the new order. If we interpret section 39 of the South African Constitution to mandate that all law must appeal to its constitutionality in any judgment, then we see that this ideal of the substantive revolution has been taken seriously indeed.[22] Simply put, the force of law is now identified with the elaboration or interpretation of the significance of the substantive and ethical change mandated by the new Constitution. The term *transformative constitutionalism* has often been used to describe the kind of constitutionalism that has been practiced by the South African Constitutional Court, particularly in its first seventeen years.[23] Such a phrase has often been ridiculed as being against the idea of constituting a government. But if we take the idea of substantive revolution seriously, then it is not to be ridiculed at all. The role of law is to live up to the ideals of the new nation; the nation is inseparable from those ideals. The state has enforcement power only to the degree that it attempts to enact those ideals in all of its laws and government institutions, and society, or what has come to be popularly known as "civil society" has to be transformed in accordance with those ideals. This of course takes us to one of the most controversial provisions of the South African Constitution, section 8, which argues that the Constitution will have horizontal application between individual members of society. Critics of horizontal application have argued that this ideal of horizontal application is not law at all, because it attempts to regulate directly relations of social "actors" who must be left in their freedom to engage in their relationships with one another without any infringement by the state, unless the state is directly implicated through state action. But under the understanding I have just elaborated of a substantive revolution and its rethinking of the notion of the nation state and society, horizontality is not only a coherent ideal, it is mandated by the very idea of what this revolution entails.[24]

Therefore, in a deep sense, the South African Constitution, understood as a substantive revolution, does indeed challenge certain Anglo-American conceptions of law, which reduce constitutionalism to vertical relationships between individuals and the state. It is not surprising that the Constitution has been accused of being chaotic and for having antipositivist underpinnings to the point that it no longer seems to be law at all. But what made the South African "transition" significant is that it at least began the process of recoupling revolution and law, and that this recoupling needs to be further examined and developed for thinking the meaning of rights and revolution in the twenty-first century.

Part of the substantive revolution is what Boaventura de Sousa Santos has called "interlegality."[25] To quote de Sousa Santos on this point: "Interlegality is a highly dynamic process, because the different legal spaces are non-synchronic, and thus result in uneven and unstable combinations of legal codes (codes in a semiotic sense)."[26] Many of the chapters in this book grapple with the importance of interlegality, and with what we called, with Jean and John Comaroff, policulturalism, for ethics, politics, and law in South Africa. The South African Constitution is notable in that almost all of the so-called multicultural provisions that have been advocated by Anglo-American and European political theorists have indeed been incorporated into that constitution. But what makes the South African Constitution particularly interesting is the ways in which it has been challenged to struggle with other formal and informal orders of law, including indigenous ideals such as uBuntu.

uBuntu itself shows why interlegality best describes the rich dynamic process of law and law-making in South Africa, precisely because it is not, strictly speaking, an indigenous value in a simple sense at all. uBuntu is a Zulu word which is sometimes translated with the Tswana word *botho*, and remains untranslated when it is referred to either as a value or now as a justiciable principle. uBuntu is not justified because it is Zulu or Tswana but because it provides us with an ethic of what it means to be an ethical human being. Therefore its justification does not lie in its indigenous roots.

How is uBuntu related to the substantive revolution in South Africa? There are at least two important points to be made here. The first is that uBuntu implies a form of belonging together that is not based on a social contract, and is certainly not rooted in any notion of national homogeneity. South Africa has over eleven languages, and a number of different tribal affiliations, and even peoples who claim sovereignty over part of the territory of the country. Therefore, part of the substantive revolution implies a different conceptualization of what it means to belong to the new South Africa, one that takes us beyond some of our current thinking about the basis of a national legal system in which law is primarily rooted in the state.

Related to this is of course the fact that the so-called indigenous values, as well as the living customary law itself, were either completely distorted in the so-called written law that was organized first by the British and then the Afrikaners, and was purportedly only to apply within the so-called homelands of the black majority, the "Bantustans." The recognition that there are African values in South Africa, as well as a living customary law that may have little or nothing to do with what the British organized as indigenous law, is part of the process of decolonization. But what is particularly interesting for our purposes here is that the living customary law is not now being interpreted as only having reach within the former Bantustans, but instead has pervaded all of the arenas of law. In other words, uBuntu is not simply a value or ideal to be applied in the customary courts: it has become a justiciable principle at the level of constitutional law.[27]

Of course it was disputed whether uBuntu could be a justiciable principle in a modern legal system, because of the hegemonic notion of what a justiciable principle was in a positive system of law. Again, returning to de Sousa Santos's notion of interlegality, the notion of justiciability itself has been broadened and challenged, as well as the relationship between ethics and law as these two must be combined in the notion of the substantive revolution.[28] Justiciability has usually been reduced to a ruler principle that has been legitimated as part of the formal legal system of a nation state, and therefore can inform the resolution of disputes by justicial organs, again, as these are defined by the foundational laws or rule of recognition of any particular nation state. The importance of this definition of justiciability is that the definition of what can be a legal rule or principle is what is formally separated from a moral or ethical principle, and this separation in turn means that there are special organs or third parties, and only those that can resolve disputes. This notion of justiciability has been challenged and expanded by the incorporation of uBuntu. uBuntu is an explicitly ethical value or ideal, and therefore rejects any neat separation between law and ethics. Indeed, some would argue that law should be completely integrated into the ethical reach of humanness that uBuntu demands. Therefore, in its most radical understanding, we would think of law as "law in the uBuntu of South Africa," rather than "uBuntu in the law in South Africa."[29]

The expansion of the notion of justiciability challenges the positive notion of law, which says that there needs to be a connection between rule and legal consequence, that uBuntu, as an explicit ethical value, would seem too vague to work as a conventionally defined legal rule. But if the South African Constitution, through the notion of the substantive revolution, is an ethical project, then its founding value is, not surprisingly, one of what it means to belong together in an ethical relationship that in turn implies a fundamental challenge to apartheid and, more broadly conceived, the color bar. Thus, uBuntu, as I will show in the chapters in this book, has been defined as a justiciable principle, even at the level of the Constitutional Court, both as a grounding ideal and value and as a principle that mandates particular legal consequences.

But there is another point that needs to be emphasized here. The broad notion of justiciability means that it is not simply the courts that are the only third party to enforce the law, broadly defined, in South Africa. As Hylton White has emphasized in his ethnographic work in KwaZulu-Natal, the court structures or the courts of the living customary law are not even the primary sites for the "justiciability" of values like uBuntu. White's work involves the way in which one particular *izinduna*, a spiritual leader, defined one of his primary tasks as bringing law to the people. And what is the content of this law? As White emphasizes, it is precisely the creation of normative spaces in which human beings can hope to realize their nonalienated forms of freedom through the creation of domains of mutual recognition, understood as a struggle to create a way of being human together that of course has to completely undermine the difficult conditions of liberation under neoliberal capitalism. Thus, law practiced through all of these different local leaders is explicitly performative of the normative space, indeed of complex realms of normativity, and uBuntu is one of the ways in which these realms of normativity are judged, in terms of an ethical way of belonging together that is crucial to the very notion of the substantive revolution. Here we are returned to the pathbreaking work of John and Jean Comaroff, who argue that the questions posed by the Global South are becoming *the* questions most relevant to political philosophy.[30]

For example, the question is often asked: is South Africa a *Rechtsstaat*? But as I have argued elsewhere, a *Rechtsstaat*, for Hegel, demanded the actualization of right at the level of the nation state, which in turn, although it allowed for differentiation of spheres of right, deliberately broke down other forms of prenational belonging. Here I am suggesting that what belonging means is being created on many levels of local and community life, which are as important for the substantive revolution as is the creation of a constitutional jurisprudence of right. Indeed, the latter must be informed by the former, and a good deal of the work of the uBuntu Project has been precisely to argue how the living customary law itself may help enrich the very notion of law, so as to allow for the flourishing of constitutional jurisprudence.

The uBuntu Project was begun as a pilot project in 2003, funded by the Stellenbosch Institute for Advanced Studies.[31] From the beginning, it was not simply conceived as a research project into indigenous ideals, but as part of the struggle to recognize different intellectual heritages, which is part and parcel of any meaningful effort at decolonization. It has therefore been activist and participatory from the beginning, and its research has never been separate from its emancipatory aims. This has affected who participates in the project, which not only includes academics, lawyers, and justices, but also many activists. And this explains the similarities with some of the research projects conducted by de Sousa Santos and many others working with him, in that the project did not only seek to give voice to those formerly disenfranchised, but also sees itself as conducting research as an emancipatory practice.[32] Therefore, the uBuntu Project has never conceived of itself as a "neutral" project conducting an "objective" research program. In a deep sense, the uBuntu Project sees itself as pedagogically inseparable from what de Sousa Santos calls the reinvention of social emancipation beyond the limits of the modern project conceived of as a European project, in which the failure of modernity to realize its aspirations has led to a sweeping

theoretical pessimism in the hegemonic discourse in law and the social sciences in Europe and the United States. Thus, the turn to the Global South
is not simply one of intrigue and exoticization. Instead, it is here that we
see developing new manifestoes and narratives of emancipation. To quote
de Sousa Santos:

> To my mind, this alternative globalization, in its confrontation with neo-
> liberal globalization, is paving a new path toward social emancipation.
> Such a confrontation, which may be metaphorically characterized as a
> confrontation between the Global North and the Global South, tends to
> be particularly intense in countries of intermediate development, or, in
> other words, semi-peripheral countries. It is, therefore, in these countries
> that the potentialities and limits of the reinvention of social emancipa-
> tion manifest themselves most clearly. This is the reason why four of
> the five countries in which the project was conducted are countries of
> intermediate development in different continents. The five countries in
> question are Brazil, Colombia, India, Mozambique, and South Africa.[33]

One aspect of the uBuntu Project has been to create an interview book
conducted, translated, and transcribed by people in the townships as to the
meaning and significance of uBuntu. That project was conducted under a
subgroup of the uBuntu Project called the uBuntu Township Project. All the
questions, all the choices of interviewees, were done collectively by the project, with the idea of giving voice to those who were closest to the value of
uBuntu in day-to-day life. But the project has also conducted and supported
ethnographic work in a number of the rural areas of South Africa, as well as
advocating for the justiciability of uBuntu as a constitutional principle. The
assemblage—to use Gilles Deleuze's word—of the complex and diversified
research is due to its attempt to reformulate itself as part of a pedagogi-
cal grappling with the meaning of emancipatory practice. It also attempts
to challenge, as part of such a project, the hierarchy between theory and
practice, researchers and activists. In other words, it implicitly challenges
one received notion of the division of activism and research, or theory and
practice. Often, the division of theory and practice, to paint it with a broad
brush, is conceived as follows: theory is a form of critique, and practice or
activism is a political, legal, or ethical struggle for hegemony.[34] A complex
research assemblage such as that of the uBuntu Project conceives itself as
serving the emancipatory project not only by restructuring how research
agendas are defined and who participates in them, but also in explicitly

advocating for new ideas as these are actually being formulated and practiced in revolutionary struggles. One of those struggles has been to advocate
uBuntu as a value that must be incorporated in all levels of law, as well as to
underscore the significance for decolonization of what de Sousa Santos calls
interlegality and orders of legal plurality.

The chapters in Part II of this book work through the complex relationship between constitutional law and uBuntu. The chapters in Part III also
show the ways in which law-making—understood through the prism of
Hylton White's ethnography—also points to on-the-ground practices that
inform day-to-day struggles, from the battle for gay and lesbian rights to
movements such as the movement of the poor and the Shack Dwellers, who
advocate that revolutionary uBuntu presents a serious challenge to some of
the conventional legal understandings associated with capitalism, particularly the right to property.

De Sousa Santos has argued that if there is to be a subaltern legality, we
need to—and by "we" I mean those who have been raised educationally in
the modernity of "the West"—recognize that there are other intellectual
heritages and epistemologies that must inform our emancipatory practices,
including law-making construed as the ethical and normative domains of
being human together. To quote de Sousa Santos:

> Transnational Third Worlds of people are also transnational Third
> Worlds of knowledges, and they feed on each other. Learning from
> them, learning from the South, is one of the epistemological prerequi-
> sites of a cosmopolitan politics. Indeed, as I will argue in Chapter Nine,
> the view that results from such learning is the epistemological condition
> for engendering practices of counter-hegemonic globalization. Competi-
> tion among different knowledges is a prerequisite to the transformation
> of the history of the modern world system into a tribunal to determine
> culpability and liability, grant entitlements to compensation, and estab-
> lish the criteria for burden sharing. it is also an epistemological condi-
> tion to distinguish among differences that do not generate legitimate
> or occult subordination, and differences that do. Without alternative
> knowledges within the same hermeneutic constellation, it is not possible
> to sustain multicultural pluralism within the same territorial time-
> space.[35]

The uBuntu Project began with the profound acceptance of de Sousa Santos's ethical call for us to learn from other epistemologies and intellectual

heritages, if we are to truly develop an ethical way of thinking beyond what he refers to as "localized globalism" or "globalized localism." The project began with the attempt to understand the epistemological roots of uBuntu, as well as its role in day-to-day life.

Jean and John Comaroff have made an even stronger point. They have argued that not only is there theory from the Global South, not only is there a *sui generis* African modernity, but the ways in which the Global South challenges us to rethink basic questions actually demands that we subvert the relationship between north and south. To quote the Comaroffs:

> But what if, and here is the idea in interrogative form, we invert that order of things? What if we subvert the epistemic scaffolding on which it is erected? What if we posit that, in the present moment, it is the global south that affords privileged insight into the workings of the world at large? That it is from here that our empirical grasp of its lineaments, and our theory-work in accounting for them, is and ought to be coming, at least in significant part?[36]

Throughout this book, I attempt to take very seriously the significance of the Comaroffs' basic point, that it is in the South that some of the most pressing questions of law, politics, and ethics are being raised, and what this means in turn for Euro-modernity. Indeed, the attempt in these chapters is not, of course, to displace theory from the North with theory from the South, as if there could be such a neat divide. The Comaroffs always remind us that there can be no such neat divide, because Europe has always been a presence in the Global South, and the Global South is both literally and metaphorically a presence in the Global North. The question is precisely to think this exchange through the mandate of a notational equality of different intellectual heritages, and what they might mean for a different way of thinking about law, politics, and ethics. Complexity is oftentimes pitted against any kind of emancipatory agenda. But it is through the work of many thinkers, including the Comaroffs, that we find in complexity itself spaces of hope that allow us to continue to invest time and energy in projects that keep alive the ideas of emancipation and transformation in a time of neoliberal capitalism.

Should Critical Theory Remain Revolutionary?

Is Technology a Fatal Destiny?
Heidegger's Relevance for South Africa and Other "Developing" Countries

In recent years we have all heard of the dire fate we will endure if we do not do something about global warming. And the steps that we must take, we are advised, are not small—a little recycling here or there will not solve the problem. We must change our way of living in the world with all of our electronic toys and horrifically wasteful oil-burning devices such as the massive SUVs that crowd our roads and highways. Of course, we must do something big to grapple with the problem of industrial waste. More generally, industrial consumption and destruction of the environment in the frantic effort of industrial capitalism, which always expands at a rapid rate of growth, must be curtailed if we are to save our planet. The documentary *An Inconvenient Truth* draws out, in graphic detail, the fate of our planet if we do not, together, do something drastic to save it. For example, Al Gore shows us through solid documentation that most of Europe and a good part of South Asia will be under water within the next 150 years.

At the same time, we are confronted with the horrific reality of massive impoverishment in the Global South. As we know, neoliberal models of "development" have become so hegemonic in economic thinking that they are rarely challenged in the literature of development economics, with few notable exceptions. These programs are always the same—driven by a supply-side conception of economic growth, with all that this entails: fiscal conservatism, stable taxes on corporations and the wealthy classes of society, and the restriction of all direct delivery systems to the poor. The problems in the Global South such as lack of education and the resulting deficit in skill levels are often addressed by the dominant economic institutions of the Global North such as the IMF and the World Bank, as if the people in these countries were difficult adolescents, who either simply refuse the inevitability and good sense of capitalist development, or worse yet, simply cannot live up to the demands of a well-functioning capitalist economy. Hence they are called to "develop." This refusal, of course, is most evident in the truly obstinate "adolescent" countries that not only refuse capitalism as their fate but also insist on institutionalizing socialism as a serious economic, social, and ethical alternative to capitalism. The celebratory ripping down of the Berlin Wall may have ended the so-called socialist states of Eastern Europe, states that suffered under the domination of the Soviet Union after World War II, but it has not kept leaders like Chavez in Venezuela from declaring themselves socialists and seeking to institutionalize a socialist state. And Chavez is not the only leader to defend and seek to realize the possibility of a socialist alternative to capitalism.

Yet the question remains: what is the connection between socialism and the crisis of global warming? For some, the problem of technology *is* ultimately just a problem of Western-style capitalism and can be solved by economic and social reorganization. At the same time, we have the 1997 Kyoto Protocol, which is a groundbreaking agreement at least insofar as it imposes limits on "developed" countries concerning the burning of oil. The United States did not sign this agreement, complaining of the unfairness of allowing countries in the Global South to be released from the restrictions that were "imposed" on the United States. The Kyoto Protocol was a significant moment in the recognition that nation states would have to unite to solve problems that were truly of a global nature. However, what was not challenged was the basic conception that development inevitably involved some destruction of the natural environment if the poorer nations were to get on their feet.

Indeed the first socialist state, the Soviet Union, pursued modernization programs, and a case in point here is the collectivization and industrialization of farms, which cost millions of lives, but were still considered a necessity. The defense of this program was rooted in an idea that held much sway in Marxist circles at the time. Simply put, the idea was that a peasant-based economy such as that of the Soviet Union must go through an inevitable stage of capitalism before it can reach the ultimate "goal" of becoming a socialist society. The price was high indeed. Thus, even those countries that aspired to socialism in the first fifty years of the twentieth century were entangled in the "logic" of capitalist development.

It is therefore not surprising that what was not challenged at Kyoto was the idea of development as modernization and industrialization, and the idea that a country's wealth and success in development was to be measured by its gross national product.

Amartya Sen has bravely challenged that measurement of development as the sole or even primary one.[1] He has defined development and the test for it through a different measure. This measure directs us to study what Sen calls the functionings and capabilities that human beings are actually able to achieve as they define their own aspirational goals. Development becomes integrally tied to the solidification of freedom as human beings aspire to realize their capabilities and achieve basic functionings. This definition of freedom, then, becomes the basis of how one judges "development"—a standard that exposes the lie that countries of the Global North are the most developed in the world. Sen's definition is explicitly a reform program as well as a theoretical measure by which to study development. Of course, the question of what would constitute postapartheid development is of burning political, social, economic, and ethical significance in South Africa.

HEIDEGGER'S RELEVANCE

As 50 percent of the black population remains in desperate poverty, it might seem obscene to worry about Heidegger's warning that there is an integral connection between development, modernization, and our ensnarement in what he calls *Gestell*. *Gestell* in Heidegger is not a chosen relationship we have to technology. Instead, it entails an essence of modern technology that is rooted in a world of nature that science can effectively put to use. For Heidegger then, the danger in modernization and development is that these ideas are themselves expressions of our entrapment and, therefore, cannot help us in building a more just world worthy of our human dignity. Given the dire state in which so many human beings find themselves, is it not ethically problematic to worry, with Heidegger, about the question of technology? Should we not, instead, simply get down to the business at hand and do everything we can to end the horrific suffering that is endured by millions of people every day?

Before even beginning to answer that question, let us briefly review Heidegger's turn away from Kant. For Heidegger, we are ensnared in a technology that cannot but fundamentally undermine our destiny as the shepherds of the Being of the world. The more we try to get out of our entrapment by our efforts to reform, the more entangled we become. For Heidegger, it is precisely the idea that we are the makers of the world and give value to all things that is the problem in the first place. Of course, in Heidegger our ensnarement is not the result of an idea, or not in the way we usually think about it. The great Kantian achievement was to reconceptualize knowledge as *Gegenstand*, that which "stands against" in scientific objectivity. This reconceptualization was, of course, thought of by Kant as an idea of critical reason. Kant's great critical insight was that the space for our human freedom and the explanation of scientific objectivity were two sides of a critically revised conception of reason. According to Heidegger, this critical insight was not wrong. Kant's critical philosophy is how Being reveals itself to us in the scientific age. He had it right as the "spokesman" of Being, but his thinking was embedded in the Newtonian universe of his age, which brought forth a specific sense of the mathematical.

For Heidegger, the mathematical changes the way in which nature presents itself to us. We explore nature as an abstract set of relationships; thus, we no longer engage with the specificity of things. Nor can we just take notice of how we are approaching nature, see what the problem is, and fix it. We are not in charge of how Being presents itself to us. Thus, energetic attempts at development through technological rationality can take us only further and further away from our destiny as the shepherds of Being. For Heidegger, nature is now revealed to us as a "setting upon" in which we dominate it. This "setting upon" challenges nature in two ways: it both unlocks and exposes nature's resources in the name of achieving some further goal. Heidegger uses the example of a hydroelectric plant as it is set in the current of the Rhine River to show vividly the violence in this challenge to nature. To quote Heidegger:

> The hydroelectric plant is set into the current of the Rhine. It sets the
> Rhine to supplying its hydraulic pressure, which then sets the turbines

turning. This turning sets those machines in motion whose thrust sets going the electric current for which the long-distance power station and its network of cables are set up to dispatch electricity. In the context of the interlocking processes pertaining to the orderly disposition of electrical energy, even the Rhine itself appears to be something at our command. The hydroelectric plant is not built into the Rhine River as was the old wooden bridge that joined bank with bank for hundreds of years. Rather, the river is dammed up into the power plant. What the river is now, namely, a water-power supplier, derives from the essence of the power station. In order that we may even remotely consider the monstrousness that reigns here, let us ponder for a moment the contrast that is spoken by the two titles: "The Rhine," as dammed up into the *power* works, and "The Rhine," as uttered by the *art*-work, in Hölderlin's hymn by that name. But, it will be replied, the Rhine is still a river in the landscape, is it not? Perhaps. But how? In no other way than as an object on call for inspection by a tour group ordered there by the vacation industry.[2]

Is there no way for us to challenge this "monstrosity" that turns the Rhine River into a mere waterpower supplier? For Heidegger, if we try to intervene to improve our relationship with technology, we can do so only as "inspectors," as he sarcastically refers to those that come to view the Rhine now dammed up in its use as an electrical power station. We are left to examine the river as power supplier either so as to make sure that it is functioning properly or to admire our ability to control the powers of nature. And why is it that we can be only "inspectors," even as we want to pay attention to the power of this river? The answer for Heidegger is as follows:

The unconcealment of the concealed has already propriated whenever it calls man forth into the modes of revealing allotted to him. When man, in his way, from within unconcealment reveals that which presences, he merely responds to the call of unconcealment, even when he contradicts it. Thus when man, investigating, observing, pursues nature as an area of his own conceiving, he has already been claimed by a way of revealing that challenges him to approach nature as an object of research, until even the object disappears into the objectlessness of standing-reserve.

Modern technology, as a revealing that orders, is thus no mere human doing. Therefore we must take the challenging that sets upon man to order the actual as standing-reserve in accordance with the way it shows itself. That challenging gathers man into ordering. This gathering concentrates man upon ordering the actual as standing-reserve.[3]

Thus, are we caught in and by this ordering of nature? And are we, as a result, to sit back and do nothing? Heidegger's answer is: yes. At least, if we think of doing something as an activity that we take up as subjects, who can change their world and our relationship to technology. Still, we are called—or some of us who are thinkers are called—to think the profundity of our ensnarement as *Gestell*. If there is courage here it is to bear witness to the full force of the danger to ourselves and the world around us. In this thinking the danger, we might allow a glimmer of a different destiny to open up before us. Heidegger's thinking is not nihilism. In a deep sense the opposite is the case. He calls us to think the nihilation of Being as commanded by our disenchanted world that has lost all of its poetry. But that is what is left to us: to think.

Like so many others who live and work in South Africa, I am not one satisfied to be a bystander, even a thoughtful one, in the face of overwhelming human suffering. That said, do we simply reject Heidegger? Do we insist that he be rejected as one who advocates a mere excuse that "gets us off" the ethical "hook" so that we are not obliged to do anything to alleviate suffering and promote justice? Or is there a warning in Heidegger that even the most dedicated activist must continue to heed?

THE WHALE CALLER

I offer an interpretation of Zakes Mda's novel *The Whale Caller* to aid us in thinking about the foregoing question. In this novel, the Whale Caller was pulled into his destiny to dance and sing with the whales when as a young man he was anointed as the chief horn player in a church aptly called the Church of the Sacred Kelp Horn. The Bishop of this church had initially been part of a more conventional Christian church with traditional Christian music, that of the harp and tambourines. But the Bishop held his ground against the protest of the Elders that he was taking his church into the realm of the Prince of Darkness: "A kelp horn, he said, was a natural musical instrument that took the congregation back to its roots. It was an instrument that celebrated the essence of creation. God would lend a sharper ear to the prayers of those who praised Him to the accompaniment of an instrument that was shaped by His own hand through the agenda of the seas."[4] The Whale Caller loves his church and his kelp horn. But it is only when a whale interrupts a baptism in which the Bishop is interpreting the story of Jonah as a prophesy that a new whale will come to swallow up the evildoers of Cape Town, that the Whale Caller's true destiny is revealed. The whale that has disrupted the baptism seems to be on a mission of his or her own. As the kelp horn blower (who is to become the Whale Caller) blows his horn ever more vigorously, the whale seems to be actively involved in the ceremony, such that even as it sails away it lob-tails to the sound of the music. And it then dawns on the kelp horn player who he truly is—the Whale Caller. Note that in Mda's novel the Whale Caller is transformed from the kelp horn player into who he becomes, but never has what we think of as a regular name. Who he *is* is inseparable from his destiny as someone whose meaning in life is to care for the being of the whales. Here we hear a Heideggerian echo in that the Whale Caller's destiny comes to him as a gift from the whales. He does not set upon the whales with his kelp horn (to use Heidegger's words) but instead responds to their music.

For the next thirty-five years he listens attentively to the whales, learning to distinguish each whale's unique voice and song. He learns and listens. He continues his wandering all the way up to Walvis Bay in Namibia. He dedicates his entire life to talking to whales who called him to them: "He was listening to the songs of the southern right, the humpback and the Bryde's whales, and learning to reproduce them with his horn. He also learnt to fashion different kinds of kelp horns: big horns with deep and rounded tone colours and small horns that sounded like muted trumpets."[5] Each horn is carefully crafted from the gift of the sea, and is shaped to sing to a particular kind of whale, to send the tremors through the ocean so as to join with the whale's own music. Of course, there is what Heidegger calls foreknowledge in building a kelp horn. There has to be a plan in advance in building the horn. That plan comes from vigilantly listening to the whale, and then figuring out what kind of horn would best produce the tremors that would sing to that particular whale. This kind of foreknowledge is what Heidegger attributes to the Greek understanding of the mathematical.[6] But this kind of foreknowledge is not a Newtonian principle which abstracts from the specificity of things to give us the law, for example of how every body, if left to itself, moves uniformly in a straight line. The kelp horn is a classic example of what Heidegger means by a thing that is respected in its accordance with its unique capacities to engage with the whales as they are in their peaceful coexistence with each other and with their music. In a Heideggerian sense, the Whale Caller dwells with the whales. Heidegger writes: "To dwell, to be set at peace, means to remain at peace within the free, the preserve, the free sphere that safeguards each thing in its essence. *The fundamental character of dwelling is this sparing.*"[7]

The kelp horn player gathers together a gift from the sea to shape it in accordance with the songs of the whales. Its purpose is to sing to a specific kind of whale. In the case of his beloved Sharisha, her special kelp horn plays a song just for her, because, unlike other southern rights, she can sing like a humpback, something that she was taught in the back and forth between her and the Whale Caller: "He has owned hundreds of kelp horns since his first. But this one that he holds so lovingly against his chest is the best of them all, for it is the horn that first introduced him to Sharisha. He closes his eyes and is sucked by a whirlpool into a dreamless sleep."[8] Once, the Whale Caller was compared to Irish shark callers who could woo the sharks into the nest so as to make a kill. The Whale Caller was horrified. He sings to the whales for their mutual joy in the dance. Nothing more.

When the Whale Caller returns to his original village of Hermanus he finds it completely changed, eaten up by tourists who come to see the whales as a holiday thrill. There is even a whale crier who makes money by alerting the tourists to where the whales are. The Whale Caller wants nothing to do with this new tourist hot spot, insisting on the old name of Hermanus-pietersfontein. He stays away from the tourist business, living for his whales:

> He was not a showman, but a lover. Since returning to Hermanus he
> has hardly any privacy because the place is always teeming with tourists
> during the whale season. He has, however, been able to continue with
> his conversations and singalongs with the whales unobstructed by the
> activities of the village and its whale watching culture. And has managed
> to stay out of the way of the official whale crier.[9]

When Sharisha does not return as expected, the Whale Caller turns to his one confidant, a magical figure, Mr. Yodd, who lies tucked away in his grotto. To Mr. Yodd and to him alone he confides his worries. But Sharisha does return. The Whale Caller has the joy of having her for a whole year as she stays in the waters of Hermanus with a new calf. His existence as the Whale Caller is disrupted by Saluni, the village drunk, who refuses to leave him alone. Slowly, she winds herself into his life and into his heart. Prior to her relationship with the Whale Caller, Saluni's life revolved around the taverns and the Bored Twins, children of workers in the vineyards who have no choice but to leave their children adrift. They have nothing to do and no direction in life, hence their name. They stray through the countryside, sometimes playing vicious tricks, particularly on Saluni. Her relationship with them started with the hope of obtaining wine from their parents, but it grows into what the Whale Caller refers to as a euphoric relationship, in which she is mesmerized by their angelic voices.

She introduces the Whale Caller to their "cleansing rituals," their secret name for sex. They begin an existence together in which each tries to participate in the rituals of the other, the Whale Caller learning how to shop with his eyes and Saluni joining him in his dance with whales. But Saluni becomes obsessively jealous of the Whale Caller's love for Sharisha, wanting to be the only female in his life. She begins a war with Sharisha, mooning her behind the Whale Caller's back, much to the horror of Sharisha. Indeed, her jealousy leads her to defy the sun by refusing to put on the glasses made for her to watch an eclipse. Her blindness is meant to be a kind of revenge. The Whale Caller does indeed feel guilty and leaves his whales behind to take Saluni out of Hermanus where they can be together without him being pulled by his other love. When her sight returns, she learns about his little lies done to protect them, pretending the candle was still burning to assuage her fear of the dark, yet blowing it out to keep wild animals from being attracted to the flame. Her rage knows no bounds, and when the Whale Caller accuses her of ugly behavior, she hears only that she is ugly. Their return to Hermanus finds the village in ruins from a storm, and the two cannot return to any kind of peace. The Whale Caller runs to the sea in hopes of finding Sharisha, in despair of his relationship with a female human:

> His eyes are tightly closed as he blows Sharisha's song that he has now adapted into jeremiads. For some time he is not aware that Sharisha herself has come to save him from the death he is hankering after. As he blows the horn furiously and uncontrollably she comes swimming just as furiously. She has been longing for the horn. She has not heard it for a long time. All she wants is to bathe herself in its sounds. To let the horn penetrate every aperture of her body until she climaxes. To lose herself in the dances of the past. She is too mesmerised to realise that she has recklessly crossed the line that separates the blue depths from the green shallows. When he opens his eyes from the reverie of syncopation she is parked in front of his eyes, so close that he thinks he can almost touch her if he stretches out his hand. She is not quite that close though. But

certainly she is less than a hundred metres from the shoreline. Perhaps less than fifty. Her stomach lies on the sand. He stops playing.[10]

Sharisha is beached. The Whale Caller often imagined himself in days gone by, in the Dreamtime of the Khoikhoi, when the beaching of a whale was celebrated as a gift from the gods.

> He can see even deeper in the mists, before there were boats and fisher-men and whalers, the Khoikhoi of old dancing around a beached whale. Dancing their thanks to Tsiqua, He who tells His Stories in Heaven, for the bountiful food he occasionally provides for his children by allowing whales to strand themselves. But when there are mass strandings the dance freezes and the laughter in the eyes of the dancers melts into tears that leave stains on the white sands. The weepers harvest the blubber for the oil to fry meat and light lamps. They will ultimately use the rib-bones to construct the skeletons of their huts, and will roof the houses with the baleen. Other bones will become furniture. Or even pillows and beds. Nights are slept fervidly inside variable whales that speckle the landscape.[11]

But this was in Dreamtime. The Whale Caller shouts for help and the rescu-ers respond immediately. The technicians and scientists take over. As they try to solve the problem of how to get the whale back in the ocean, the Whale Caller returns to another legend of Dreamtime. He prays to the Strong Man of the Ramindjeri tribe. Legend had it that the Strong Man could sing to make a whale and her calf escape from the shallow waters. His prayers and his attempts to reach Sharisha are in vain. "He can't reach her. He can never acquire the powers of those whose totem is Kondoli ngatji. Perhaps he should just leave everything to the experts from Cape Town. They will save Sharisha. They will surely save her."[12] The scientists and the technicians diligently keep the whale wet to keep her from dying. They try everything they can to get her back out to sea, even tying her tail to a boat so as to pull her. But to no avail. The politicians arrive, making the most of Sharisha's suffering. The tourists rush to pose for photos. Finally, the deci-sion is made by a scientist to blow her up, or dynamite her to give her a quick death. The Whale Caller despairs of what he has done to her, for in his own frenzy he was too self-involved to heed the danger to Sharisha. He was out of sync with her. He did not take care, needing to assuage his soul. In a profound sense, he imposed himself upon her, rather than letting her be with him as he had before. He refuses to protect himself to take cover as the dreadful deed is done. His imposition closed down the open region of their dance in which the two of them could be together. Heidegger writes: "To let be—that is, to let beings be as the beings which they are—means to engage oneself with the open region and its openness into which every being comes to stand, bringing that openness, as it were, along with itself."[13] The Whale Caller's failure to "let her be" has dire consequences, and he holds himself responsible: "The Whale Caller sits silent and still as blubber rains on him. Until he is completely larded with it. Seagulls are attracted by the strong stench of death. They brave the black smoke and descend to scavenge on the tiny pieces that are strewn on the sand and on the rocks. The sea has become very calm."[14] Saluni watches her lover's horror and grief, wanting to hold him, but she does not approach him. Her remorse takes her back to drink and to the Bored Twins who once again play a vicious trick on her, locking her in the dark cellar—her worst nightmare—to be enclosed in the dark. In response to her screams they let her out, and her only thought is to run to the Whale Caller. The Twins try to slow her down, at first concerned with her safety, worrying that she might fall. One throws a rock to slow her down and the rock throwing takes on a life of its own. One more aimless game. But this time they actually kill her. Their apologies fall on dead ears, and in panic they run away only to return later to cover her exposed body in tulips. The Whale Caller, having lost Sharisha to a ghastly death, longs for Saluni. He plays his song for her on his kelp horn, but of course there is no response. But there is a response from the sea. Sharisha's calf starts to sail towards him. And the Whale Caller stops playing: "He must not enslave the young one with his kelp horn. Softly he says: 'Go little one. You do not want to know me.' The wind will carry his words to Sharisha's child."[15]

He seeks out Mr. Yodd for flagellation, now determined to give up his horn as an offering to Mr. Yodd. But the grotto is blocked by sand and sea-weed. He cannot find the mortification he needs. He leaves Hermanus, no longer the Whale Caller: "He will walk from town to town flogging himself with shame and wearing a sandwich board that announces to everyone: *I am the Hermanus Penitent*."[16]

Is *The Whale Caller* a kind of Heideggerian allegory of how we are fated to lose the Whale Caller's enchanted universe in which a human being can dance with the whales for the sake of the dance only? The novel opens with the following sentence: "The sea is bleeding from the wounds of Sharisha." Can we get back to a different relationship to nature, as before the explosion of technology? As we have seen, Heidegger's answer is: certainly not by any kind of reform activity that tries to change our relationship to technology, make it serve us better. The Whale Caller becomes Hermanus the Penitent, left to mourn his own failure to care for Sharisha and his lost life as a Whale Caller. Could there be another, or is such a calling gone forever?

CONCLUSION

Of course, *The Whale Caller* is a novel. It neither presents solutions nor tells us that there is no solution possible. But one cannot read this novel without confronting Heidegger's questioning of technology. There is, of course, specificity to that question in South Africa and, indeed, in Africa. Can and have indigenous ideals, rituals, and ways of life survived the horror of colonialism, apartheid, and, more generally, the aftermath of national development? It was a popular slogan in Marxism during the heyday of the Marxist movements in Africa that "the tribe must die for the Nation to live." Of course, Heidegger himself would not put it that way. But the Heideggerian question does demand that we ask the question more broadly: must the "tribe" die under the force of technology?[17] If Being is always slashed precisely because it is what gives things to be and, as a gift from elsewhere, eludes our grasp, then we cannot know that "only the gods can help us now," to paraphrase one of Heidegger's famous statements. A philosophically grounded pessimism cannot excuse us from ethical responsibility. And yet part of that responsibility is to think the question of technology. Certain cruder forms of Marxism clearly became part of that problem in the frantic effort to modernize in order to stand up to the Global North and, in particular, the United States. As I have written over and over again, I remain a socialist and take seriously the famous line, "from each according to her ability, to each according to her needs!"[18] But what does it mean to aspire to institutionalize this ideal, even as we grasp that all attempts at institutionalization will fail to meet the ideal fully? Socialism as an ethical ideal calls us to negotiate with different forms of social and economic organization; socialism clearly should not be reduced to a set of slogans to nationalize, modernize, and industrialize.

As we have seen, the novel allegorizes a way of life in which nature is not "set upon." Of course, in the novel, the Whale Caller loses his destiny to a moment of frenzy and self-involvement. But is that life as a whale caller now completely lost? Is the open region between this man and his whale now lost in that last explosion? My suggestion here is that these questions should be thought against the Heideggerian warning, without succumbing to paralysis or the easy way out of "we are screwed and there is nothing for us to do about it." If we are not simply to mourn and embrace nostalgia as we read the allegory of *The Whale Caller*, we must confront the "bleeding of the sea." But even if we think against a certain Heideggerian pessimism, we must still ask the question of technology as we continue the struggle for a more just world—one that would respect, rather than seek to obliterate, the difference of other ways of life that continue to survive—as other to the onslaught of advanced capitalism.

Socialism or Radical Democratic Politics?
On Laclau and Mouffe

When Ernesto Laclau and Chantal Mouffe's *Hegemony and Socialist Strategy: Towards a Radical Democratic Politics* appeared in 1985, many committed socialists like myself hoped to find new insights into the meaning of socialism and its continued relevance to any notion of democracy.[1] Twenty-five years later, we are still—and by "we" I mean radicals on the Left—profoundly in their debt, for their searing critique of the economism of the European Marxist parties, and, more specifically, for their fundamental insight that the struggle for socialism is always a political struggle, and not one that is in any way determined by a given set of forces of history. Some of their insights— for example into how subordination must be politically activated so that it becomes a site of oppression to be resisted and a form of domination to be changed—remain as enlightening to us today as they were then. Certainly, their critique of the Left for turning over questions of so-called culture to the Right because they were an aside to class politics is still a powerful warning. I want to focus on the relevance of *Hegemony and Socialist Strategy* to a radical political project today, while putting into question Laclau and Mouffe's insistence that the time of emancipation and transformation is over, and with it, the overthrow of capitalism and the transition to socialism. I want to suggest that much writing in the Global South concerns exactly the question of how popular struggles rooted not only in the industrial working class but also in movements of "the poor"—as those movements identify themselves in South Africa—are explicitly against capitalism and for socialism, even if the meaning of socialism is part of the political struggle.[2]

I want to begin with two quotes, and with what I see as an important corrective to many readings of Laclau and Mouffe's text: I do not read *Hegemony and Socialist Strategy* as only a defense of radical and plural democracy—although it is that—but, more importantly, also as a deepening of the understanding of socialist practice. Here are the two quotes:

> Of course, every project for radical democracy implies a socialist dimension, as it is necessary to put an end to capitalist relations of production, which are at the root of numerous relations of subordination; but socialism is *one* of the components of a project for radical democracy, not vice versa.[3]
>
> . . . if the subversive moment of the logic of democracy and the positive moment of the institution of the social are no longer unified by any anthropological foundation which transforms them into the fronts and reverse sides of a single process, it follows clearly that every possible form of unity between the two is contingent, and is therefore itself the result of a process of articulation. This being the case, no hegemonic project can be based exclusively on a democratic logic, but must also consist of a set of proposals for the positive organization of the social.[4]

Although in these two quotes there remains a lingering commitment to some kind of connection between social and economic change—and by change, I mean change away from capitalism—and their project of radical democracy, Laclau and Mouffe seem to have moved away from their position elucidated above toward one that replaces socialism with radical democracy. In order to demonstrate that this is the case, I need to challenge them to answer four questions about their continuing commitment to socialism as it is necessarily connected to any radical democratic project. My questions will be seeking clarification from Laclau and Mouffe about the significance of a socialist project, including projects of global transformation. My questions will be based on South African struggles, to help ground my theoretical discussion in analyses of the ongoing battles in the name of a socialist project that pervade the political landscape and discursive field of the new South Africa.

I begin with Laclau's argument of how a particular section of society comes to be identified with the general emancipation of the society as a whole. In his dialogue with Judith Butler and Slavoj Žižek, Laclau argues that a particular sector of society comes to represent—albeit imperfectly—the universal, because it names its own oppression as the result of a general crime. Laclau here is elaborating the first dimension of the hegemonic relation, which is unevenness of power:

> We have, in the first place, the identification of the aims of a particular
> group with the emancipatory aims of the whole community. How is this
> identification possible? Are we dealing with a process of *alienation* of
> the community, which abandons its true aims to embrace those of one
> of its component parts? Or with an act of demagogic manipulation by
> the latter, which succeeds in rallying the vast majority of society under
> its own banners? Not at all. The reason for that identification is that this
> particular sector is the one which is able to bring about the downfall of
> an estate which is perceived as a *"general* crime." Now, if the "crime" is
> a *general* one and, however, only a *particular* sector or constellation of
> sectors—rather than the "people" as a whole—is able to overthrow it,
> this can only mean that the distribution of power within the "popular"
> pole is essentially uneven.[5]

But returning to *Hegemony and Socialist Strategy*, my question to him and to Chantal Mouffe is this: is it the naming of a general crime that allows a particular sector's oppression to represent the universal, or is it instead the representation of universal ideals that would overcome the conditions of oppression that allows a sector of society to stand in for the promised universal of a free and equal society? Famously, the African National Congress (ANC) did not generalize racist oppression by condemning apartheid as the Antichrist. Instead, in 1956, the ANC did indeed establish itself as the leader of the oppressed (and note that this is before the establishment of apartheid), through the elaboration of a Freedom Charter,[6] which, to use Laclau and Mouffe's own phrasing, sought to articulate management of the positivity of the social and the articulation of diverse democratic demands, so as to achieve, again in Laclau and Mouffe's phrasing, a "maximum of integration."[7] The Freedom Charter did indeed call for nationalization and socialization of the means of production and all basic resources, and therefore profoundly challenged the right to private property as basic to freedom.

My second question is related to the first. Laclau and Mouffe never deny that we need a vision of what kind of society we are fighting for. It is never enough for them simply to name a frontier and to call out an adversary, although, as we know, both of those last aspects are crucial to what they defend as radical democracy. Throughout, they argue that the great democratic revolutions provide us with those ideals, which Étienne Balibar has called "equaliberty,"[8] which is why they have completely rejected the Jacobin current in Marxist heritage, and have argued that we must deepen liberal democracy, and not overthrow it. The problem in the Anglo-American context is that liberal democracy and all notions of liberal freedom, not just the neoliberal, accept that freedom is inextricably associated with the right to private property, broadly construed. Certainly, neoliberals have extended that right to patent and copyright, to areas of nature and genetic manufacturing that were once seen as simply beyond property, because they were either natural or part of the shared knowledge of humanity. So neoliberals have undoubtedly extended property rights beyond what was once conceived as their proper reach. That said, left-leaning liberals, including John Rawls, never fundamentally challenge the right to private property, but simply regulate it in the name of redistribution. Thus at least in the Anglo-American context, a certain socialist project is legally foreclosed. And so it would seem that we would need not only a deepening but a reconceptualization of democracy and the tradition of liberal constitutionalism for a socialist project. At the very least, we need to set up a profound *tension* between the right to private property and other socio-economic rights, such as the right to housing, education, and so on. Of course, in the United States we do not have constitutionally protected socio-economic rights, and this is in part because the protection of private property is foundational and because the negative vertical nature of the Constitution does not impose social obligations on the state. This tension, however, is embodied in the South-African Constitution in sections 25 and 26 of the Bill of Rights which protect the right to housing and the right to private property, respectively.[9] This tension has indeed been productive in the creation of what Seyla Benhabib and Robert Cover have called "jurisgenerative transformations" of the right to private property in South Africa.[10] In the words of Justice Albie Sachs, an Emeritus Justice of the South African Constitutional Court, the question of ownership of land is only the beginning and not the end of an investigation about whether or not shack dwellers should be evicted from lands they occupy.[11] A subsidiary question, then, to Laclau and Mouffe, is: how far will we have to move in any given society or indeed global social ordering to a notion of social rights, and therefore some kind of socialist project, in order to allow the space for the challenge of the foundations of the right to private property as conventionally understood in liberal philosophy and jurisprudence? It is important to note here that for Laclau and Mouffe, workers' struggles for their rights should be recognized as only one more democratic movement in the chain of equivalences in which all of the movements have only a relative universalization. Famously, for both Laclau and Mouffe, the universal is an empty and yet necessary signifier, because we can only define the context of differential relationships in any society, relationships that are constitutive of that society, through the struggle for hegemony. The return to politics is precisely that the universal is always at stake, in that the struggle for hegemony demands it, but also because no context can be self-delimiting. Each attempt to draw lines around an identity will always appeal to something beyond it, and that something is the space of the empty signifier. If there is a moment of philosophical reflection, or role for theory, it is in emphasizing that no group can ever truly represent the fullness of society. As they argue, Marxism tried to defend the proletariat as the truly universal class. There can be no truly universal class, only particular struggles that seek relative universalization, and, momentarily, in any particular context, may achieve it by uniting diverse groups in a chain of equivalence. But what is clear is that their notion of radical democracy is equally as compatible with capitalism as it is with any other form of economic organization, because to argue otherwise would make economic organization in some way hegemonic over other movements in the chain of equivalence. In *Emancipation(s)*, Laclau summarizes the theoretical foundations they share when it comes to the elaboration of the significance of the universal:

> As far as the function (as different from the content) of the "universal" is concerned, we have said enough to make clear what it consists of: it is exhausted in introducing chains of equivalence in an otherwise purely differential world. This is the moment of hegemonic aggregation and articulation and can operate in two ways. The first is to inscribe particular identities and demands as links in a wider chain of equivalences, thereby giving each of them a "relative" universalization. If, for instance,

feminist demands enter into chains of equivalence with those of black groups, ethnic minorities, civil rights activists, etcetera, they acquire a more global perspective than is the case where they remain restricted to their own particularism. The second is to give a particular demand a function of universal representation—that is to give it the value of a horizon giving coherence to the chain of equivalences and, at the same time, keeping it indefinitely open. To give just a few examples: the socialization of the means of production was not considered as a narrow demand concerning the economy but as the "name" for a wide variety of equivalential effects radiating over the whole society. The introduction of a market economy played a similar role in Eastern Europe after 1989.[12]

I began this chapter with two quotes from *Hegemony and Socialist Strategy* which indicated that the category of the social and the idea of social revolution remained inscribed in that book. But in their later work, it is becoming increasingly evident, as I have written, that workers' struggles or the struggles for radical change in economic relations are only one struggle in the chain of equivalence. What this means is that although they would never argue that capitalism is necessary for democracy—far from it, because that would claim some kind of true universal in the realm of economic organization—they also would never argue that without the overthrow of capitalism, there could never be radical democracy. But isn't the whole point, broadly construed, of the Marxist tradition that capitalism is per se antithetical to democracy?[13]

My next question involves a view of the ethical, which has been defended by both thinkers, but has been explicitly defended again by Laclau in his exchange with Butler and Žižek. Let me just stress that to a certain extent, I agree with Laclau that there is an unstable relationship between the ethical and the normative, but I disagree with, or want to put into question, the idea that the ethical is a moment of madness, or it cannot even briefly represent the desire for the impossible unreachable fullness of society which—and I again agree—no social order can hope to achieve. To draw out my question, I want to use the example of the uBuntu electricians in South Africa. The uBuntu electricians have reinstalled electricity in homes and shacks where it had been turned off because people could not pay their bills. They have done this relentlessly, to the point that the ANC has tried to move to prepaid meters in order to counter the effectiveness of their actions. And how do they articulate their struggle? The struggle as they see it is that everybody in South Africa has electricity, regardless of wealth, and they do this in the name of uBuntu. It is of course beyond my comments here to offer anything like an adequate articulation of uBuntu. The closest we can get to it in the English language is that it is an activist ethic of virtue in which what it means to be a human being is ethically performed, on a day-to-day basis, in a context, in which how we are supposed to live together is constantly evoked and at the same time called into question. It is irreducible to our own liberalism/communitarian debate, because uBuntu carries with it a strong commitment to individuation and the realization of each person's capabilities, even if understood as a social project. Now in some ways the uBuntu electricians seem to exemplify Laclau and Mouffe's socialist activists, since they are not fighting for any given interests, and most of them count themselves among the lucky ones who are employed in the new South Africa. Instead, they see themselves as a moment (using Laclau and Mouffe's vocabulary deliberately) in a discursive field and set of movements explicitly fighting for a people's commons as integral to any definition of socialism. My question here, then, to return to the ethical as a moment of madness, is whether movements like that of the uBuntu electricians, might not be better understood through Michael Hardt and Antonio Negri's conceptualization of a dialogue between local intellectual heritages and habits, which articulate an ethical practice that does indeed have content, if not that of prescribed rules and principles.[14] Another way of putting this, to use Seyla Benhabib's formulation, is that uBuntu itself undergoes a "democratic iteration" as it becomes part not only of the explicit struggle against the unequal distribution of electricity, but also of the socialist praxis which, right now, tries to turn a resource like electricity into a common good.[15] Whether or not that can be done is a whole other question that is beyond the reach of this chapter. My point here is to underscore that the uBuntu electricians are acting out of a profound ethical call to bring electricity to those who desperately need it.

The uBuntu electricians are so effective that on the drive from the Cape Town airport into Cape Town you will see sign after sign reminding the population that it is a crime to turn on electricity when someone has been unable to pay the bills, and that citizens are all obligated to turn in the uBuntu electricians if they find them engaged in such work. So my question to Laclau and Mouffe is: do other ethical practices, indeed, non-European practices, signal a different relationship between the ethical and the political?

If they do not undermine antagonism understood as a limit to any fullness of symbolization, might they not undermine the necessity of the friend/enemy opposition as the form of that antagonism in all circumstances? Of course, the uBuntu electricians do have an enemy, namely the unjust distribution of electricity, but the practice of uBuntu would reject the universal friend/enemy formulation of antagonism as integral to their ethical and political practice.

Another on-the-ground movement in South Africa, the Shack Dwellers, raises the following questions: is there a logic of capitalism that is more than a given conjecture in a specific setting—in Laclau and Mouffe's terms—that is an effective limit on hegemonic projects and therefore must be overcome?[16] Do we need something like a critique of capitalism as fundamentally against forms of democratic control over the economy that have historically been associated with socialism and communism? And related to both questions: is that limit imposed by capitalism in any way determinative of how the struggle for socialism and a just radical democracy should proceed now? Again, the Shack Dwellers and the movements of the poor more generally seem to point us to exactly the argument Laclau and Mouffe want to emphasize, that the struggle for socialism is political, and not determined in advance by given interests. And indeed, to a large extent, that is the case. But following Rosa Luxemburg, whose work has become crucial to thinking about the relationship between the so-called first and second economy of South Africa as well as the enclosure of the commons, the poor should be recognized as included in the logic of capitalism.[17] Any adequate discussion of Luxemburg's contribution to current South African debates is beyond the scope of this short chapter; instead I will summarize Luxemburg's central argument in *The Accumulation of Capital.* Her argument was that primitive accumulation is not a historical stage in capitalism but inheres in the very logic of capitalism, and therefore the expropriation of the commons will be endless: it will last as long as capitalism does. Thus, under South African readings of Luxemburg, we would expect more and more of the commons, common good, and publicly owned entities to be appropriated by capital.[18] Needless to say, South African natural resources such as diamonds and gold have long been appropriated by capital, indeed almost exhausted. But the point here is somewhat different. If capitalism generates its own outside—both as a surplus population (the poor) and a surplus of products of a productivity that it cannot contain—it always also seeks to recontain what it has produced as outside. Therefore, the Shack Dwellers, as well as leftist economists and other organic intellectuals—such as S'bu Zikode, who once was the president of the Shack Dwellers—have argued that the struggle for a people's commons, which reappropriates for the poor what has been taken out of the commons (water, land, and so on on) is an essential moment of socialist praxis now.[19] In this way, then, a certain logic of capitalism at least feeds the socialist imagination that seeks to answer the question: "What is to be done?" This struggle for a people's commons now is irreducible to the Anglo-American debate that speaks of redistribution versus recognition as a way to comprehend current activist struggles. Indeed, the Shack Dwellers explicitly argue that they are not seeking better service delivery or better forms of redistribution: they are seeking to reappropriate common goods such as land and water as belonging to all of the people.

In Laclau's debate with Žižek and Butler, Žižek worries that Laclau has disavowed the possibility of global transformation.[20] Laclau's response is that he no longer knows what socialism might mean, and that the demand to socialize the means of production is peculiar. Obviously, any complex discussion of what socialism is and might demand in terms of an end to capitalist relations of production is beyond the scope of this chapter. But Laclau cannot so easily excuse himself from the project of how capitalism blocks any attempt to achieve radical democracy, unless one entirely excludes the question of democratic control over the economy as crucial to what democracy means. In a certain sense, then, democracy in both Laclau's and Mouffe's sense, is a paradox that cannot be solved.[21] Indeed, it is a particular formulation of a paradox inherent in universality that makes radical democracy in their sense possible. To quote Laclau:

> My answer is that this paradox cannot be solved, but that its non-solution is the very precondition of democracy. The solution of the paradox would imply that a particular body had been found, which would be the *true* body of the universal. But in that case, the universal would have found its necessary location, and democracy would be impossible. If democracy is possible, it is because the universal has no necessary body and no necessary content; different groups, instead, compete between themselves to temporarily give to their particularisms a function of universal representation. Society generates a whole vocabulary of empty signifiers whose temporary signifieds are the result of a politi-

cal competition. It is this final failure of society to constitute itself as society—which is the same thing as the failure of constituting difference as difference—which makes the distance between the universal and the particular unbridgeable and, as a result, burdens concrete social agents with the impossible task of making democratic action achievable.[22]

If we take this quote seriously, Laclau has given up any integral connection between the fight for radical democracy and the struggle for socialism, if we understand it very broadly as democratic control over the means of production. Therefore, there is no fundamental contradiction between radical democracy and capitalism, and it is precisely this formulation that on-the-ground movements in South Africa reject. They argue that there *is* such a fundamental contradiction.

I now want to mention some of the issues that are raised by the movements of the poor. First, there is the fight to mobilize around the protection of a people's commons in the form of taking back such resources as land and water. Second, there is the question of what to do about the state, and whether or not it will be necessary to overthrow the ANC, or, alternatively, to infiltrate it and bring it back to the Freedom Charter with its articulation of the socialization and democratic control of the means of production. Third, how can the struggle for a people's commons be turned into a much broader conception of something like a democratic socialist government, in which questions of economics would not be left to the side of politics? These are real questions that are asked on a day-to-day basis, and organic intellectuals are challenged to join with such movements in thinking about such questions and providing at least tentative answers. In *Moral Images of Freedom*, I argue that we must dispel the idea that socialism is an impossible dream: "We may not be able to tell grand stories that will guarantee the ultimate success of socialism, but it is precisely because we cannot tell such grand stories that doom it to failure that leaves it up to us to make the 'truth' of the ideal of socialism something that cannot be beaten out of this world."[23] I began by arguing that *Hegemony and Socialist Strategy* defends a socialist practice. But as is apparent in their definition of radical democracy, Laclau and Mouffe move further and further away from any integral connection between radical democracy and democratic control over the economy which would be crucial to any definition of socialism. Indeed, I would go so far as to say that they have replaced socialism by their definition of radical democracy, and this at the very time when capitalism is in a severe crisis. Sadly, then, a book such as *Hegemony and Socialist Strategy* does not deliver on its promise to help us rethink the complex relationship between democracy and socialism. It is left for those of us who do not believe that democracy is possible under capitalism to continue to think that project.

The Legal Challenge of uBuntu

Dignity Violated:
Rethinking *AZAPO* through uBuntu

In 2006 I was asked to contribute to a volume on the legacy of the *AZAPO* case.[1] The *AZAPO* case was then, and remains today, one of the most controversial cases in the new South Africa, because it upheld that in certain circumstances, the Truth and Reconciliation Commission could grant conditional amnesty, and that this would override the rights of citizens of the new South Africa to seek both criminal and civil redress from the courts. I will discuss the legal arguments surrounding this case shortly. When I was first asked to write this essay, I was critical of *AZAPO*, because of its failure to grapple adequately with the recent developments of international law that insist on the criminal prosecution of those who participated in acts of violence to forward the aims of a state later declared to be dictatorial. I was also critical because *AZAPO* did not go far enough in upholding an ideal of restitutional equality and a detailed program of reparations that would make the overriding of the constitutional right in the South African Constitution to redress from the courts justifiable on any principle that I could uphold. During the last few years, however, I have come to see that my two arguments were contradictory, and therefore, I had to change my mind about *AZAPO* in the broadest sense of the word. I have come to see that although *AZAPO* got the direction of international law wrong on the question of prosecution, the judges were right in their basic understanding that what was demanded by the two overriding ideals of the new dispensation, dignity and uBuntu, was sweeping socio-economic reform.

Part of my dilemma was that I was still operating under the idea that South Africa could be included as a "transitional" society, and therefore, judged by the now voluminous literature on "transitional justice."[2] I will return to some of the questions raised by the literature on transitional justice later in this chapter, as these apply or do not apply to South Africa. Since I first considered the *AZAPO* case, I have become increasingly convinced that constitutionalism in South Africa should be understood against the South African intellectual heritage of uBuntu/botho. uBuntu demands that we criticize *AZAPO* not from the standpoint of the direction of international humanitarian law, but as it runs against the full demands of uBuntu itself.

I had to come to terms with what I had already learned about uBuntu and its significance over many years to rethink my position on *AZAPO*, and why South Africa should not be considered through the literature on "transitional justice" at all, but as a substantive revolution, with all its fragility, and all the demands implied by the words *substantive* and *revolution*. These demands put South Africa in the context of the history of revolutions in Africa, as opposed to some much more general scheme that can encompass countries as diverse as Lithuania and Iraq, as if there were some overarching truth to the march of civilizations in the direction of liberalization. We all know the coda of the literature on "transitional justice": authoritarian societies are moving in the direction of liberalization and democracy under such criteria as the move to a market economy, the right to vote, the right to certain basic civil rights, and so on. I am for all those rights—though not the market economy—and all those rights are embodied in the South African Constitution, again with the exception of the "right" to a market economy. To review *AZAPO* from the standpoint of the ideals that have dominated South African jurisprudence, uBuntu and dignity, will take us to a very different kind of critique than the one that has often been offered from the liberal perspective or even the international humanitarian perspective, although I will review both.

My basic conclusion is as follows: the two grounding ideals of the new jurisprudence in South Africa, and the possibility of a new dispensation itself, can be understood as dignity and uBuntu. Together, these two ideals can help us take a different approach to *AZAPO*, and indeed to reparations, and finally, to how we grasp our debt to the millions who have fought and died for a communal way of living, which some have called socialism and others have addressed recently as "the idea of communism."[3]

For many on the left it was once taken for granted that if dignity were to be taken seriously as an ideal it would demand socialism, understood as the aspiration to a society in which the organizing economic and social principle would be "from each according to her ability, to each according to her needs!"[4] Ernst Bloch underscored the importance of returning dignity as a moral and ethical ideal to the Marxist tradition, and to do so as part of a reconceptualization of the rights of man broadly conceived:

> Happiness and dignity, the concerns emphasized on the one hand by social utopias and on the other hand by doctrines of natural law, for so long marched separately and sadly never stuck together with the priority of human care and support, and the *Primat* of human dignity: It is more than ever necessary that along with the concrete heritage of social utopian thought, and equally concrete even the differences in the intentional fields finally be recognized as functionally related and practically surmounted. This thanks to the certainty that there can be no human dignity without the end of misery and need, but also no real happiness without the end of old and new forms of servitude.[5]

However, because of the discrediting of socialism in the late 1980s and early nineties, the attempt to think dignity and socialism together faltered. The Berlin Wall was then hailed by many as the end of the socialist nightmare. The ideal of liberal democracy has come to be identified with liberalization and thus privatization of the markets, regardless of whether there was or is true privatization in the world of state-supported finance capitalism. But the integral connection between the privatization of markets and liberal democracy is espoused in all the major economic institutions that are a controlling force in our globalized world.

The famous Freedom Charter of 1955 took for granted the connection between dignity and the ideal of socialism.[6] The ANC has now moved away from this connection, endorsing—through the neoliberal Growth, Employment and Redistribution (GEAR) strategy—capitalist supply-side economics.[7] By relinquishing their commitment to socialism, has the ANC given up on the ideal of dignity and undermined the notion of responsibility that, as I will argue, is inherent in uBuntu? And if so, what does this mean for a constitution grounded in the ideal of the respect for the dignity of all others? Grand Apartheid was a total system of socio-economic organization, and because of that, certain human rights models of dignity that focus on victims and perpetrators cannot adequately address the form and the violation of dignity.[8] The staggering toll on the dignity of the black and "colored" populations demands that we ask seemingly old-fashioned questions about the relationship between socio-economic organization and the ideal of dignity. And that is all to the good.

In this chapter, I will examine the relationship between violations of dignity and redress, especially the ideal of restitutional equality. By now, volumes have been written on the Truth and Reconciliation Commission (TRC), including on how the organization of the TRC was established so as to minimize the need for socio-economic redress and reorganization. I could not possibly answer all those criticisms in one chapter. But under the rubric of the two ideals of dignity and uBuntu, I want to first address Mark Sanders's insightful argument that the TRC mobilized itself through an ethical dispropriation of law that appealed to uBuntu as fundamental to the restoration of the dignity of the persons who testified before the TRC.[9] To my mind, Sanders has made the most important theoretical contribution to understanding why the South African TRC is unique, in that it was rooted in an African ideal that urges all the participants and the population in general to move away from a more convenient and liberal notion of the individual person that is self-constituting and recognized in its individuality because of its self-constitution. But if we are to take seriously Sanders' argument that condolence, as he defines it, is what was the ultimate ethical call of the TRC as a form of reparations,[10] we still need to address the economic question of reparations, and even what is owed to the dead who lost their lives in the struggle for a new South Africa. In other words, we need to criticize *AZAPO* not for upholding the need for social repair, so as to override individuals' rights to redress in the courts, as a form of bad utilitarianism that cannot be justified in any of the better notions of the ethical basis of criminal law, but rather, for its failure to connect its ultimate conclusion to the ideals of both dignity and uBuntu.

My discussion of international law has to be seen within the following context. In the late 1950s and throughout the 1960s, one African country after another rose up in massive liberation struggles that were forced into the course of armed struggle after all avenues of protest had been brutally repressed. The retaliation by the colonial state apparatus against such movements has become legendary for its indifference to the international strictures on the conduct of war. The apartheid government did not want to have its hands tied in its total onslaught against the liberation movement in South Africa by the niceties of international conventions. Thus, the government refused to sign Protocol I of the Geneva Conventions, which was deliberately set up to extend the protections and the mandates of the Geneva Conventions of 1949 to wars of liberation against colonial domination.[11] By the time of the development of Protocol I, the struggle of the African National Congress against apartheid had gained wide-ranging international support. We will return to the significance of the history of apartheid's relationship to international law when we discuss the judgment of *AZAPO* in its conceptualization of the role of international law in the new South Africa. For now, we need to turn to the broader question of how the new dispensation had to grapple with a socio-economic system that had itself been judged a crime against humanity, as that has come to be understood in the humanitarian literature of international law.

How can and must a new constitution address the seemingly endless violations that follow from a system that was itself considered a crime against humanity? Traditional legal redress based on individual claims hardly seems adequate for such a daunting task, since all members of the black and "colored" population can be considered to be within the ambit of the violation. To at least partially address this difficulty, the Parliament of South Africa established a Truth and Reconciliation Commission that was unique in that it offered those who had suffered violation public hearings in many different languages. Such a commission, at least in theory, can allow for a much broader forum of redress and reparations than that offered in a modern system of criminal law, with its strict procedures for evidence and its roots in a concept of individual violation and individual responsibility. To quote Justice Mahomed DP:

> Most of the acts of brutality and torture which have taken place have occurred during an era in which neither the laws which permitted the incarceration of person or the investigation of crimes, nor the methods and the culture which informed such investigations, were easily open to public investigation, verification and correction. Much of what transpired in this shameful period is shrouded in secrecy and not easily capable of objective demonstration and proof. Loved ones have disappeared,

sometimes mysteriously and most of them no longer survive to tell their tales. Others have had their freedom invaded, their dignity assaulted or their reputations tarnished by grossly unfair imputations hurled in the fire and cross-fire of a deep and wounding conflict. The wicked and the innocent have often both been victims. Secrecy and authoritarianism have concealed the truth in little crevices of obscurity in our history. Records are not easily accessible, witnesses are often unknown, dead, unavailable or unwilling. All that often effectively remains is the truth of wounded memories of loved ones sharing instinctive suspicions, deep and traumatizing to the survivors but otherwise incapable of translating themselves into objective and corroborative evidence which could survive the rigours of the law. The Act seeks to redress this massive problem by encouraging these survivors and the dependents of the tortured and the wounded, the maimed and the dead to unburden their grief publicly, to receive the collective recognition of a new nation that they were wronged, and crucially, to help them to discover what did in truth happen to their loved ones, where and under what circumstances it did happen, and who was responsible.[12]

But to defend a truth and reconciliation commission in South Africa, since there had been various types of these commissions throughout the world, does not necessarily mean that this kind of commission has to have certain specific terms and limitations. Such a commission, for example, would not necessarily have to grant even conditional amnesty or foreclose prosecution. In what was undoubtedly one of its most difficult decisions, the South African Constitutional Court upheld the Promotion of National Unity and Reconciliation Act 34 of 1995, which established the terms of the TRC.[13] I offer only a brief summation of the court's argument here, because I will return to the criticisms that have been made of the terms it upheld as the basis for the commission. As already indicated, one of the primary goals of the TRC was to restore the civil dignity of the majority black and "colored" population, first by giving them the chance to tell their own stories in a public forum, second by recommending "reparation measures" in respect of such violations, and third by compiling a comprehensive report in respect of all its functions, including recommendations of measures to prevent future human rights abuses. One of the chief goals of the commission was to give victims who had no idea of what had happened to their loved ones the "truth," including, where possible, access to information about the remains of the dead so that they could at last be given a proper burial. Many of the requests for information on the dead also included a demand for proper burials to be paid for by the commission.[14] These demands were often made in the African languages of the majority population, and appealed to the uBuntu of those who were listening to them, to understand the profound need to respect the dead and their restoration to the status of humanity. The commission did indeed pay for many burials and exhumations, and I agree with Mark Sanders that the responsiveness of the commission to that request is best understood through the ethic of uBuntu.

To return to my discussion of the structure of the TRC: three committees were set up as part of the commission. The first was the Committee on Human Rights Violations, established primarily to give a public venue to the victims of apartheid (narrowly defined as those who had suffered gross human rights violations at the hands of someone pursuing a "political objective").[15] The second committee was the Committee on Reparation and Rehabilitation, which was given power to gather information and receive evidence so as to make recommendations to the president as to what might be suitable reparations for the victims. This committee had no power to provide reparations, but only to make recommendations to the president. The third committee was the Amnesty Committee, which had to be chaired by a judge. It had the power to provide amnesty as long as there was full disclosure of all relevant facts, and the act of the perpetrator was committed in the pursuit of a political objective associated with the conflicts of the past history of apartheid. There was no requirement that the transgressor acknowledge that the act was wrong or make an apology to the victim, although many perpetrators did make such apologies. Clearly, differential powers were allotted to both the Committee on Reparations and Rehabilitation and the Committee on Amnesty. The former could only make recommendations to the president, the latter could actually grant amnesty. After amnesty was granted, the person was to be free from criminal prosecution and civil liability. Not only was the person cleared from any possible criminal and civil liability, but the state itself was also freed from such liability.[16]

A number of organizations—including the Azanian Peoples Organization (AZAPO), which arose out of the Black Consciousness movement—and persons, including the widow of renowned activist and theorist Steve Biko, challenged the constitutionality of the amnesty provision in the Promotion of National Unity and Reconciliation Act. They argued that it violated section 22 of the Interim Constitution of 1993, which ensured the right of citizens of the new South Africa to seek redress from the courts for justiciable disputes.[17] The challenge also invoked the Geneva Conventions of 1949 and subsequent protocols as mandating that the new state pursue criminal prosecutions of the perpetrators of gross human rights violations.[18] The moral heart of this argument was that if the apartheid state had removed itself from the conventions of international law that regulated war, it was desperately important for the new dispensation to recognize the significance of international law on these points. The court argued that even if the Geneva Conventions could be successfully invoked, they could not override the constitutionally mandated demand for the Truth and Reconciliation Commission. The court found such a constitutional mandate in the final clause of the Constitution:

> In order to advance such reconciliation and reconstruction, amnesty shall be granted in respect of acts, omissions and offences associated with political objectives and committed in the course of the conflicts of the past. To this end, Parliament under this Constitution shall adopt a law determining a firm cut-off date, which shall be a date after 8 October 1990 and before 6 December 1993, and providing for mechanisms, criteria and procedures, including tribunals, if any, through which such amnesty shall be dealt with at any time after the law has been passed.[19]

The epilogue was read as having equal constitutional weight to section 22 of the Interim Constitution, and then interpreted so as to provide a constitutional mandate to establish the Truth and Reconciliation Commission to provide a justifiable constitutional limitation on that right to seek legal redress in the courts. It is important to note here briefly that both the Interim Constitution and the 1996 Constitution of South Africa has a limitations clause so that no freedom in the Constitution is absolute, but can be overridden in certain circumstances, as these circumstances can in turn be interpreted so as to respect the ideals of the new constitutional dispensation.

Not only was the limited amnesty clause found constitutional, its ramifications for civil liability were also found constitutional. Thus, the court rejected the applicant's argument that even if the amnesty provision was to be held constitutional, other civil remedies must remain viable. In the case of the civil suits against individuals, Justice Mahomed returns to his two central arguments: the need to provide the conditions that will encourage truth and the overarching spirit of uBuntu as the basis of reconciliation underscored in the epilogue. He writes:

> There is nothing in the language of the epilogue which persuades me that what the makers of the Constitution intended to do was to encourage wrongdoers to reveal the truth by providing for amnesty against criminal prosecution in respect of their acts but simultaneously to discourage them from revealing that truth by keeping intact the threat that such revelations might be visited with what might in many cases be very substantial claims for civil damages. It appears to me to be more reasonable to infer that the legislation contemplated in the epilogue would, in the circumstances defined, be wide enough to allow for amnesty which would protect a wrongdoer who told the truth, from both the criminal and the civil consequences of his or her admissions.[20]

Justice Mahomed recognizes that even if one accepts that the release from criminal prosecution leads to release from civil liability, at least in the case of individuals, this does not necessarily mean that the state must also be released from liability. The argument that "truth" would somehow be foiled if the state was offered freedom from liability seemed implausible to Justice Mahomed.[21] Here, then, the appeal to the need to provide conditions to encourage the "truth" to be told by the wrongdoers does not seem convincing to the court. Indeed, Justice Mahomed recognizes:

> I think it must be conceded that in many cases, the wrongdoer would not be discouraged from revealing the whole truth merely because the consequences of such disclosure might be to saddle the state with a potential civil liability for damages arising from the delictual acts or omissions of a wrongdoer (although there may also be many cases in which such a wrongdoer, still in the service of the State, might in some degree be inhibited or even coerced from making decisions implicating his or her superiors).[22]

Here, of course, Justice Mahomed is implicitly recognizing that many "wrongdoers" are hostile to the new ANC government, and therefore would be only too happy to try to financially drain it in some way. They might also well be willing to lie. Given that the need to provide conditions to tell the "truth" could not be the sole basis of release from state liability, Justice Mahomed turns to what he sees as the heart of the argument. The real problem for Justice Mahomed in terms of the release of both individuals and the state from civil liability lies in the serious dilemma of how to achieve meaningful social equality with the resources available to a new government inheriting a dreadful past of systematic racial exploitation.

It is clear that the court recognized the fragility of the negotiated settlement that established the new dispensation. The court explicitly states that without some form of amnesty, the negotiated settlement might not have been possible, and that indeed, the National Party of South Africa had wanted unconditional amnesty. The ANC militantly refused to grant such amnesty.[23] As Justice Mahomed eloquently argues, despite the narrow definition of victim, for the purposes of the TRC, the majority of the black and "colored" population suffered gross violations of their dignity and gruesome exploitation under apartheid. Indeed, the violation of apartheid, let alone the hundreds of years of racialized capitalism that had preceded it, is so overwhelming that it does not easily yield to the one-on-one redress implicit in traditional notions of civil liability.[24] Too many people have suffered in a vast sea of agony and human degradation. Justice Mahomed argues:

> The families of those whose fundamental human rights were invaded by torture and abuse are not the only victims who have endured "untold suffering and injustice" in consequence of the crass inhumanity of apartheid which so many have had to endure for so long. Generations of children born and yet to be born will suffer the consequences of poverty, of malnutrition, of homelessness, of illiteracy and disempowerment generated and sustained by the institutions of apartheid and its manifest effects on life and living for so many. The country has neither the resources nor the skills to reverse fully these massive wrongs. It will take many years of strong commitment, sensitivity and labour to "reconstruct our society" so as to fulfill the legitimate dreams of new generations, exposed to real opportunities for advancement denied to preceding generations initially by the execution of apartheid itself and for a long time after its formal demise, by its relentless consequences. The resources of the state have to be deployed imaginatively, wisely, efficiently and equitably, to facilitate the reconstruction process in a manner which best brings relief and hope to the widest sections of the community, developing for the benefit of the entire nation the latent human potential and resources of every person who has directly or indirectly been burdened with the heritage of the shame and the pain of our racist past.[25]

With rhetorical flourish, Justice Mahomed recognizes that very hard choices had to be made, at the same time that he sees the difficulty of translating the horror of apartheid into effective methods of individual legal redress. Many commentators have discussed the difficulty of ever translating the loss of a loved one into a monetary loss, of trying to tell stories of trauma in a public forum, even one that tried to loosen the traditional rigor of a trial situation.[26] But as we will see shortly, there is another understanding of the ethical significance of these claims under uBuntu that demands what Mark Sanders has called an "ethic of condolence" that grows out of responsiveness to hearing a loss that is so devastating that it demands that we all mourn together for what can never be again.

To return to the judgment, Justice Mahomed's point goes to the immensity of the suffering and the violation which seems in his words here to demand systematic reconstruction, a reconstruction that could override the need for retribution and individual financial redress. He worries about how reparations are to be made, for example, to people who seemingly have suffered the same wrong when one is now in dire need and the other now has a lucrative job. Should they be paid the same amount? Again notions of individual redress seem to flounder here. Addressing himself to the hard choices made by the leaders of the new government, Justice Mahomed writes:

> They could have chosen to direct that the limited resources of the state be spent by giving preference to the formidable delictual claims of those who had suffered from acts of murder, torture or assault perpetrated by servants of the state, diverting to that extent, desperately needed funds in the crucial areas of education, housing and primary health care. They were entitled to permit a different choice to be made between competing demands inherent in the problem. . . . They could have chosen to saddle the state with liability for claims made by the insurance companies which had compensated institutions for delictual acts performed by servants of the state and to that extent again divert funds otherwise desperately needed to provide food for the hungry, roofs for the homeless and blackboards and desks for those struggling to obtain admission to desperately overcrowded schools. They were entitled to permit the claims of such school children and the poor and the homeless to be preferred.[27]

As Justice Mahomed underscores, this preference was made in the name of the reconstruction and the transformation of society that justice demanded, and this demand was precisely what mandated a wider conception of "reparations and redress."

I began this chapter by recalling one of many reasons why rethinking what justice demands of postapartheid society turns us to one of the oldest tenets of the socialist left: that dignity and its violation demand a transformative economic reconstruction of society, so that lives no longer be buried under systematic deprivation and degradation.[28] Understood in this manner, the powerful claims of those who have undergone horrific human rights violations for legal redress in the courts can only be answered by the struggle to institutionalize a society that aspires to justice. I will return to this argument later, but put in this manner, the debate is not over justice understood as a moral or legal right to retribution and redress and some wider consequentialist notion of the good called either peace or reconciliation. The question is how justice can ever hope to be done, given the seeping and systematic nature of the violation. On this reading of these pages of Justice Mahomed's judgment, the "preference" for all of those who have suffered the systematic violation of apartheid is a moral and indeed a constitutional mandate for reparative or restitutional equality.

After the above-quoted words, Justice Mahomed returns to the desperate need for a mechanism providing for amnesty and release from civil liability for both the state and individuals, because without such measures the "historic bridge" itself might never have been erected. Justice Mahomed argues:

> For a successfully negotiated transition, the terms of the transition
> required not only the agreement of those victimized by abuse but also
> those threatened by the transition to a "democratic society based on
> freedom and equality." If the Constitution kept alive the prospect of
> continuous retaliation and revenge, the agreement of those threatened
> by its implementation might never have been forthcoming, and if it had,
> the bridge itself would have remained wobbly and insecure, threatened
> by fear from some and anger from others. It was for this reason that
> those who negotiated the Constitution made a deliberate choice, prefer-
> ring understanding over vengeance, reparation over retaliation, ubuntu
> over victimisation.[29]

The situation in South Africa at the time of *AZAPO* was undoubtedly precarious. There was the profound concern that if the Commission did not go forward, the negotiations for a peaceful transition would be derailed and the country could easily return to the bloody conflict that had plagued its history. Those who have the advantage of critically rethinking *AZAPO* now are doing so without the same responsibility that was placed on the shoulders of the constitutional judges when *AZAPO* was decided. But the deeper point is that Justice Mahomed constantly returns to uBuntu. As I argue throughout this book, uBuntu underscores an activist ethic of virtue and responsibility, in which who and how we are as human beings is not only relational but also turns us back to how we can try to create an ethical relationship that was rendered impossible by the brutality of colonialism and apartheid.

I will now turn to a brief history of post–World War II international law, to put *AZAPO* in the context of those developments.

THE CONSTITUTIONAL COURT'S INTERPRETATION OF INTERNATIONAL LAW IN *AZAPO*

The atrocities of the Nazi regime led to the legal and ethical reconsideration of how crimes against humanity should be punished, particularly those that were perpetrated against its own citizens. The Holocaust shook the conventional wisdom of the limits of international law. The inclusion of crimes against humanity by state authorities against their own nationals, under the jurisdiction of the International Military Tribunal at Nuremberg, fundamentally challenged the long-standing deference of international law to state government as the locus for the punishment of its own citizens. How a government treated its own citizens had long been viewed by international law as a sovereign prerogative. Rules of war had been reserved for crimes committed in interstate relations. The Nuremberg trials treated crimes against humanity as a subsidiary to the traditional war crimes that were covered by the most important source of humanitarian law available at the time, the Hague Regulations of 1907.[30] Thus in a certain sense the nexus requirement, which distinguishes wars against "foreign" nationals from crimes against inhabitants of a sovereign nation state, was kept in place. Crimes against humanity remained linked to either war crimes or crimes against peace.[31]

The four Geneva Conventions of 1949 were drafted in part to codify and further develop the substantive law of the Nuremberg trial. Basic to this development was the grim acceptance of the central premise that crimes against humanity warrant, and indeed mandate, criminal punishment. The four Geneva Conventions attempt to specify gross violations of human rights: "willful killing, torture or inhumane treatment, including biological experiments, willfully causing great suffering to body or health, unlawful deportation or transfer or unlawful confinement."[32]

The Genocide Convention of 1948 further substantiated the law of what constituted a crime against humanity and how the violators of the basic codes of humanity must be punished.[33] It is this convention that first contemplates an international penal tribunal, which was finally set up in 1998.

For the purposes of my argument, it is necessary to focus on how the "nexus requirement" has been effectively undermined and finally dropped altogether with the establishment of the International Criminal Court. In 1991, for example, the Security Council of the United Nations established the Criminal Tribunal for the Prosecution of Persons Responsible for Serious Violations of International Humanitarian Law Committed in the Territory of the Former Yugoslavia, or ICTY.[34] The resolution of the Security Council to set up the tribunal invoked Chapter VII of the UN Charter, so that the action to establish the tribunal was seen as one to maintain international peace, which could be backed by the United Nations' coercive authority.[35] The reliance on Chapter VII provided the overcoming of state sovereignty.

The purpose of my review of international law and the argument that the Geneva Conventions can and should apply in certain cases of internal war does not necessarily lead me to disagree with Justice Mahomed's uBuntu-inspired decision in *AZAPO*. But it does demand an important corrective or clarification of what the role of international law has been in South Africa, a clarification that was made by the Constitutional Court in *State v. Makwanyane*.[36] In *AZAPO*, the Constitutional Court makes two arguments as to why the Geneva Conventions did not apply to the case at hand. The first has to do with a controversial set of statements about the relationship of international law to the constitutional and municipal law of the new South Africa. I will return to this argument shortly. For now, I want to continue focusing on the nexus requirement. By 1994 there was clear evidence that international law had extended the nexus requirement to include internal conflicts. To quote the court's review of its second argument that appeals to the nexus requirement:

> Whatever be the proper ambit and technical meaning of these Conventions and Protocols, the international literature in any event clearly appreciates the distinction between the position of perpetrators of acts of violence in the course of war (or other conflicts between states or armed

conflicts between liberation movements seeking self-determination against colonial and alien domination of their countries), on the one hand, and their position in respect of violent acts perpetrated during other conflicts which take place within the territory of a sovereign state in consequence of a struggle between the armed forces of that state and other dissident armed forces operating under responsible command, within such a state on the other. In respect of the latter category, there is no obligation on the part of a contracting state to ensure the prosecution of those who might have performed acts of violence or other acts which would ordinarily be characterised as serious invasions of human rights.[37]

The court goes on to argue that even if Protocol II to the Geneva Conventions, on the Protection of Victims of Non-International Armed Conflicts, did apply, it would go in the opposite direction. Justice Mahomed at least interprets this protocol to promote his position:

> On the contrary art. 6(5) of Protocol II to the Geneva conventions of 1949 provides that
> "[a]t the end of the hostilities, the authorities in power shall endeavor to grant the broadest possible amnesty to persons who participated in the armed conflict, or those deprived of liberty or reasons related to the armed conflict, whether they are interned or detained."[38]

This interpretation of this provision is itself somewhat problematic, because it is primarily aimed at the participants in the National Liberation Movement, and not its foes. As Nthabiseng Mogale has rightfully argued: "The context, drafting, and history and subsequent interpretation by the International Committee of the Red Cross (ICRC) all indicate that this provision was never intended to shield violators of international humanitarian law, despite the Constitutional Court's attempt to use it in that way."[39] The court concluded that it did not apply because the ANC and Spear of the Nation were not legally recognized as a National Liberation Movements for purposes of Protocol II. The Constitutional Court, in this judgment, refers to the Cape Supreme Court's decision that the struggle in South Africa did not fall with this extension of Protocol II and its definition of a National Liberation Movement. There are two points to be made against the court's argument. First, the ANC clearly did think it fell within this extension. In 1980, Oliver Tambo, then the president of the ANC in exile, deposited a declaration with the president of the Red Cross and not the Swiss Federal Council, which was the body that the declaration should have been deposited to in order to be binding under Protocol II. To quote John Dugard on what was at stake in how the ANC was viewed by the apartheid government:

> The extension of the privileges of the Geneva conventions to NLMs [National Liberation Movements] by Protocol I of 1977, coupled with the ANC's purported acceptance of the obligations under Protocol I, gave rise to expectations on the part of NLMs that their forces would be accorded privileged treatment as prisoners of war. The South African Government, which had refused to sign the 1977 Protocols, rejected this development in humanitarian law and continued to treat the escalating conflict as an internal war to which common article 3 of the Geneva Conventions at most was applicable. Consequently those members of NLMs captured in border conflicts or apprehended for acts of violence in South Arica were treated as ordinary criminals and not as prisoners of war. The issue was raised before the courts of South Africa and South West Africa (Namibia) on a number of occasions.[40]

Some courts did find that humanitarian law was applicable to the ANC and that it could be used in mitigating punishment precisely because the ANC and its armed wing, Spear of the Nation, believed themselves to be part of an international armed conflict. The courts that accepted this use of humanitarian international law were able to save members of the ANC from execution.[41] The stakes were high indeed.

The Cape Supreme Court of Appeals thus took a controversial stance when it argued that the struggle against apartheid did not count as a National Liberation Movement. This controversial decision should not have been simply accepted by the Constitutional Court. Both courts turn their decision on the fact that Oliver Tambo deposited his declaration to have the ANC recognized as NLM under Protocol I with the Red Cross and not the Swiss Federal Council. To determine the status of the ANC on a legal technicality is surprising in this Constitutional Court, and disturbing given the history of what was at stake in past South African court decisions on this matter. Of course, the apartheid government did not sign either of the two protocols. It would have stayed their hand in the total onslaught against the ANC. The Constitutional Court wrote in a footnote: "This Protocol was never signed or ratified by South Africa during the conflict and no such 'declaration' was deposited with that Council (that is emphasized in the original) by any of the parties to the conflict,"[42] as if this was determinative of the status of the ANC. This footnote is, at best, a sleight of hand on a very serious matter. However, the protocols were signed in 1995.

John Dugard reviews why the armed struggle in South Africa might have considered an international conflict for the purposes of the Geneva Convention. He writes:

> The Angolan conflict, particularly in its initial phases when the South African Army advanced to the outskirts of Luanda in 1975, could be described as an international armed conflict. The war in northern Namibia and southern Angola, on the other hand, probably qualified as a non-international armed conflict to which common article 3 of the Geneva Conventions was applicable. The low intensity conflict on South Africa's own northern borders, on the other hand, probably failed to meet the threshold of article 3. The South African government consistently treated members of SWAPO arrested in Namibia (and southern Angola) and members of the ANC and PAC arrested in South Africa (or neighbouring territories) as "terrorists" and criminals who were not entitled to treatment as prisoners-of-war.[43]

Nthabiseng Mogale has argued that the struggle was internationalized, taking place on battlefields throughout Southern Africa.[44] The ANC made history in 1973 by effectively pressuring the United Nations to take a position condemning apartheid, in the International Convention on the Suppression and Punishment of the Crime of Apartheid.[45] Indeed, one of the most effective strategies of the ANC was effectively to isolate the apartheid government in many different campaigns, ranging from media condemnation to massive withdrawal of foreign investments. There is yet another ironic manner in which apartheid internationalized the struggle by its own definitions of the Bantustans. The majority of blacks were rendered "outsiders" or "aliens" in their own land (I am using the word *land* deliberately). As Sampie Terreblanche explains, "The two native affairs acts of 1952 differentiated between two categories of Africans: a minority who were 'detribalised,' and thus permanently urbanised, and the majority, who retained their "tribal" identities and should only be allowed temporarily into urban areas."[46] Much has been written about the racist hypocrisy in calling these "homelands" nations with the corresponding political and legally imposed conclusion that blacks were not citizens of South Africa.[47] However, for the purpose of my discussion I simply want to underscore that under its own terms apartheid "internationalized" the struggle.

Moreover, the direction of international humanitarian law is clearly away from the nexus requirement, and goes further than simply broadening the meaning of that requirement to include civil wars and internal conflicts. The TRC did not precisely define the conflict in South Africa for the purposes of humanitarian law, although it made clear that it was guided by the Geneva Conventions in its thinking about what constituted a gross violation of human rights. Indeed the TRC explicitly notes the move away from the Nuremberg definition of the nexus requirement: "The distinction between international and internal armed conflicts is less relevant today, as the laws of war have evolved to regulate more closely the use of force in all situations of armed conflict."[48] The ANC stated that its struggle was a just war, but that did not give the blanket of justice to all acts carried out in its name. "Just war theory" was to guide the ANC in assessing its own responsibilities in the course of the conflict.[49] The TRC accepted that apartheid could be legitimately conceived as a crime against humanity. Thus the "war" against it was a just war. The TRC further distinguished between a just war and justice in war, a distinction fundamental to just war theory itself.[50] The TRC also went on to recognize that the situation of national liberation movements needed further international attention and further development of international humanitarian law. Renewed international consideration should be given to the way in which liberation and civil wars are conducted, and to the treatment of participants in armed conflict in the circumstances of war, civil war, revolutions, insurgency, or guerilla warfare.[51]

The spirit of these recommendations is that the range of applicability of humanitarian law be extended and further developed to deal with conflicts that do not have the markings of a conventional war between states. They are in accord with the spirit of the direction of international law, while the *AZAPO* consideration of the applicability of the Geneva Conventions is clearly out of the accord with that spirit. Perhaps most importantly, the TRC recommendations recognize the wars no longer have the familiar look of two easily identifiable nation states fighting against one another. Most of the "wars" being waged throughout the world do not fit this pattern. In a very basic way the neat and tidy paradigm of war has been undermined, and with it corresponding notions of what constitutes "a people" and "a nation" for purposes of humanitarian law. The TRC recommendations are clearly a call to recognize the significance for humanitarian law of these fundamental changes.

And yet in the case of South Africa it may be politically and ethically important to call the long struggle to end apartheid—and the other earlier forms of legally enforced racial colonialism and capitalism—a war. Names matter here, and not just for the purposes of the applicability of the Geneva Conventions. To argue that the struggle was not a war minimizes the effects of the violence done in its name, the numbers of people involved in the conflict on both sides, and the profound trauma that has been endured. This minimization, I will argue shortly, has had dangerous implications for the very idea that the "book of the past" could be closed without a well worked–out program of reparations and a further commitment to restitutional equality. Indeed, acknowledging that it was a war and a war against both internal and external colonization can help us grasp ethically and politically why prosecution of the perpetrators could not be the *only* option in a country ravaged by the increasingly violent effort to maintain apartheid and the determined and relentless effort to put an end to it. But in spite of my remarks here, we need to return to how the court rejected the direction of international law away from the nexus requirement and thus slid out of the profound argument the Geneva Conventions could, and should, be applied. Fortunately, the court corrected the relationship between international law and the new constitutional dispensation shortly after the *AZAPO* judgment.

THE RIGHTS CRITICISM

So far we have at least reviewed the argument that the direction of international law seems to be in favor of persecution. However, there are arguments that have been made against prosecution from within the literature on what has come to be known as "transitional justice." Before turning to a discussion of the concept of transitional justice in the new dispensation, I want to review the rights criticism of *AZAPO*, so that we can understand the seriousness of overriding an individual's claim to redress for criminal action against them, even if such action was taken with political objectives.

Within South African scholarship, both Darrel Moellendorf and Richard Wilson have written powerful critiques of *AZAPO* for breaching the fundamental rights of the victims of human rights.[52] Moellendorf relied heavily on Ronald Dworkin, who has argued throughout a life's work that strong rights such as the right of a victim of a crime to have a fair hearing should not be overridden in terms of social goals.[53] The justification for both the conditional amnesty and the overriding of claims of delict against either individuals or the state was done in the name of the recovery of truth and, more importantly, to my mind, the achievement of social justice.

Truth, defined as a social goal inseparable from uBuntu, had at least two dimensions. The first was that individuals needed to find out what had happened to their loved ones, so that they could begin to come to terms with their loss and, if needed, give the dead their long-awaited proper burial. I will return shortly to the significance of how many of those who testified before the TRC were to ask for help with burials. For now, I want to emphasize that this first dimension of truth allowed people to release themselves from the hell of false hope, and take the steps both metaphorically and literally to lay the dead to rest.

The other form of truth was acknowledgment of just how grotesque and pervasive the human rights violations were under apartheid. Thomas Nagel first defined the distinction between knowledge and acknowledgment because this distinction could help delineate the moral education sought by truth commissions.[54] In the course of the public hearings recorded on radio and television, the denied reality was thrown in the face of the "public" and particularly the white minority who all too often hid from how bad things were and what was done in the name of their security. This creation of a "truthful" public record that acknowledges the extent of the violence done to individuals carries the hope that the cry "never again" can be given content and not remain an abstract moral indictment. It is the public record that is to provide acknowledgment of the extent of human rights abuses, because at least in the case of South Africa, the individual perpetrators did not have to acknowledge that they had done wrong in their petitions for amnesty. To remind the reader, the petitioner only had to claim that their act was done for a political motive and that the petitioner had made a full disclosure.

Moellendorf does not find either of these definitions of "truth" worthy as a basis for overcoming the rights of the claimants in *AZAPO*. Moellendorf remains unconvinced that there is enough of a relationship between conditional amnesty and "truth," in either sense, to forego prosecution. He also questioned Justice Mahomed's assertion that without at least conditional amnesty, the negotiated settlement would not be possible, citing examples from South America. Truth commissions in South America were often created to find facts in order to enhance the possibility of prosecution and not to foreclose it in certain circumstances.

Moellendorf does not explicitly rely on a theory of retribution. Wilson does. Wilson relies on Kant who, like Hegel after him, argued strongly for retribution as fundamental to a constitutional republic. Kant makes his argument in the strongest possible terms:

> The principle of punishment is a categorical imperative, and woe to him who crawls through the windings of eudaemonism in order to discover something that releases the criminal from punishment or even reduces its amount by the advantage it promises, in accordance with the pharisaical saying, "It is better for one man to die, than for an entire nation to perish." . . . Even if a civil society were to be dissolved by the consent of all its members (e.g., if a people inhabiting an island decided to separate and disperse throughout the world), the last murderer remaining in prison would first have to be executed, so that each has done to him what his deeds deserve and blood guilt does not cling to the people for not having insisted upon punishment; for otherwise the people can be regarded as collaborators in this public violation of justice.[55]

Kant's stern injunction goes straight to the heart of his argument that retribution is the only theory of punishment consistent with respect for the dignity of all others. We relinquish our "mad freedom"[56] when we leave the state of nature and enter into an ideal social contract with others, so that we can harmonize our freedom with the freedom of others. This is what respect for the humanity of others demands and we have a duty to accept the realm of external freedom, law, because it is what respect for our humanity necessitates. As Kant tells us in the opening paragraphs of the *Metaphysics of Morals*, without this relinquishment of "mad freedom" we could not form a constitutional republic. The criminal violates his own humanity at the same time that he clearly violates the humanity of the one he or she victimizes. Retribution is demanded by respect for the criminal. We respectfully recognize that he or she could have done otherwise because, like us, doing the right thing was a possibility for him or her. But Kant's surprising statement that even if civil society were to be dissolved, punishing the wrongdoers would still be the last injunction of those dissolving their bond.

The basis of the uprightness of law—or, more precisely, *Recht*—is that uprightness is rooted in the respect of the dignity of all others. Thus, even if a specific social contract is dissolved, respect for the possibility of the reconstitution of "Right" is maintained as long as the dignity of humanity is respected through the enactment of retribution. Note that what is stake here is not just individual rights but the condition of "Right" itself. The relevant Kantian point is that right cannot be constituted through its violation, even when an actual legal order has come undone. It would be the duty of the last man or woman after a dissolved social contract to enact retribution in the name of the rightfulness that still might be restored if the dignity of our humanity is respected. Neither Moellendorf nor Wilson fully draws out the significance of Kant's point, which is not just that the only way to respect individual criminals is to enact retribution. The heart of his argument is that rightfulness can only be constituted through the full respect of the dignity of our humanity, which, in Kant at least, is the very basis of a constitutional republic that can command its citizens' respect and thus their obligation.

Hegel further develops the restorative aspect of criminal law.[57] The criminal, by breaking the social bond, has created a rift in the ethical order in which law is grounded. Law can only be put right again if the ethical order based on mutual relations of reciprocal symmetry are respected. The criminal acts against the ethical bond by asserting his privilege of self-assertion. Retribution signals public recognition of the rift of the ethical bond, which begins with the recognition that you are a human being, just as I am. Thus, in Hegel retribution not only restores the condition of rightfulness, as in Kant, but allows a return to the ethical relationship which was disrupted by the violent acting out against the other that denies her otherness as human. In both Kant and Hegel, retribution is not only rooted in respect for the individual criminal and victim. It is, if in different ways, fundamental to the constitution of a rightful constitutional order. In Hegel, retribution is necessary for the restoration of the ethical relationship in which rightfulness is embedded. In Kant, retribution is integral to the respect of the dignity of all others. And that respect, even when the actual state is in a condition of dissolution, holds out the possibility of the reconstitution of a rightful order. Hence, the relevance of both thinkers to South Africa at the time of *AZAPO*.

Wilson further argues that the majority of people, both white and black, were morally committed to retribution and that the Constitutional Court went against the people. Of course, the Kantian and Hegelian point runs deeper. At the time of *AZAPO* there was not a "people," but only a deeply fractured society in which the ethical relationship, as defined by Hegel, had, as Steve Biko reminds us, been brutally pulled apart by the subjugation of the black majority under racialized capitalism.[58] So the reconstitution of a just state becomes a burning question, as does the question whether there can even be such a thing as a nation figured as the new South Africa. The ending of apartheid was not, as in Kant's imagination, a voluntary dissolution, but a state of nongovernability rooted in the inability of either side to "win" the war. The negotiated settlement took place in conditions of a fragile cease-fire in which the threat of civil war was a real and pressing danger. This recognition of the fragility of the cease-fire, of course, is in part what underlies the desperate call for reconciliation that is echoed in the *AZAPO* decision. Wilson gets himself in trouble when he advocates that the Constitutional Court should not rule against public opinion rooted in opinion polls. At the heart of this Constitutional Court's responsibility was, and is, the duty to uphold the principles that signaled the possibility of a new nation. Their fundamental point here is that an order of right must be constituted by respecting rightfulness, not by compromising it, let alone violating it. But is this view of rightfulness the only conception of justice that could underlie the reasoning of the *AZAPO* decision, and indeed, justify it?

THE CRITIQUE OF THE NECESSITY OF PROSECUTION:
TRANSITIONAL JUSTICE, RESTORATIVE JUSTICE

Throughout this book, I have spoken of the relations between uBuntu and dignity, and I want to return to it now. The *AZAPO* decision is rooted in uBuntu in two ways. I will not repeat my longer discussions of uBuntu made throughout this book. But I want to emphasize that the value of uBuntu underscores two aspects of our ethical being-human. The first is that none of us can become a unique human being, individuated with our own road and destiny, without the constant support of others. The second is that what it means to be a human being is profoundly ethical, in that what makes us human is not just the reality of our social connectedness, but the way in which each one of us lives up to the obligations to those who have supported us, and to the broader world in which we live. But this living up to obligation is not altruism or sacrifice, because the other side of it is that others must live up to their obligation to us, so that we can live out our "capability freedom," to use Amartya Sen's telling phrase.[59] uBuntu is not a communitarian ideal in any of the senses used in Anglo-American literature, because that literature often appeals to a community as if it were a pre-given reality. The ethical relatedness that is brought into being by each one of us acting in and through uBuntu is the work of all of us together. It is not some ontological shared reality, but something we struggle to bring about together.

Mark Sanders has made a careful linguistic analysis of the well-known Zulu phrase *umuntu ngumuntu ngabantu*. To quote Sanders:

> The Zulu phrase *umuntu ngumuntu ngabantu* has, in its tropic move-ment, an economy of singular and plural not captured in the banal "people are people through other people." *Umuntu* is the singular form of *–ntu*, or human being. The prefix *–ngu* is copulative. *Nga-* is a noun prefix for forming instrumental adverbs and combines with *abantu*, the plural of *–ntu*, to form *ngabantu*. A preliminary translation might thus be: a human being is a human being through human beings; or the being-human of a human being is realized through his or her being (human) through human beings.[60]

Thus, uBuntu so understood is not antithetical to individuation or indi-viduality rights. Again, to quote Sanders:

> If we preserve that moment of singularity we do not simply reduce *ubuntu* to group solidarity and loyalty (management's "organization man" or "woman"). The kind of dispropriation figured by *ubuntu* implies that being human, in an ethico-political sense, means that one does not enter the public sphere with ready-made rights and duties— any rights and duties have to be claimed and exercised. Making the claim to a right transforms the claimant and the one upon whom the claim is made. Both parties are exiled from their "proper" selves. Once one engages *ubuntu*, there is no going back to a more "fundamental sense," which would ground the subject of rights and responsibilities in prescribed duties and responsibilities, let alone do so within a predeter-mined communal hierarchy. *Ubuntu* implies radical dispropriation— that is why it has the transformative potential that all these writers sense and seek to appropriate and manage.[61]

For Sanders, if we read the TRC through uBuntu, we can understand that the public hearings were reparative in a very specific sense. Sanders explores the significance of the demands for information on where murders took place, where body parts could be found, and for help from the commission for exhumation and then proper reburial. Sanders argues that the TRC actu-ally figured itself as a body responsible to enact a kind of public mourning.

Obviously, the vast majority of those who were narrowly defined as perpetrators did not come forward to testify or even to request conditional amnesty. Thus, under the understanding of uBuntu that I have defended throughout this book and that Sanders also endorses, the TRC's configuration of itself as in the place of the wrongdoer is part of the demand of uBuntu that would allow for condolence to be conducted in a public manner. Sanders defines condolence as a "mourning with" that turns on the recognition that the one who has been murdered was indeed a human being, and needs to be buried as such. In this way, for Sanders, condolence is a form of reparation, and indeed, one that is specifically important to the agents or beneficiaries of apartheid, in that they are allowed to have a projection of themselves as persons who are also restored to their humanity by joining in the public mourning of all those who have been lost. For Sanders, condolence opens up a space for joining in with those who have been wronged to imagine an ethical relationship of uBuntu that is not forsaken by the fact that one has been a beneficiary in apartheid. This, for Sanders, is the significance of the closing of Antjie Krog's poem:

> I am changed forever. I want to say:
>> forgive me
>> forgive me
>> forgive me
>
> You whom I have wronged, please
> take me
>
> with you.[62]

Krog here is clearly writing of how the demand for reparations is reparative for both perpetrators and beneficiaries, in that it is the only way that whites can expect to be taken into the new dispensation, because their humanity could be restored by this very act of repair.

Steve Biko long ago argued that the struggle against antiblack racism was never undertaken in the name of blacks alone. Racism, for Biko, was never understood narrowly as the political exclusion of blacks from political life, although of course it included that. Biko always argued that apartheid also included the systematic subordination of the black majority to racialized capitalism. Black consciousness was for Biko explicitly a call for a new humanity:

Some will charge that we are racist but these people are using exactly the values we reject. We do not have the power to subjugate anyone. We are merely responding to provocation in the most realistic possible way. Racism does not only imply exclusion of one race by another—it always pre-supposes that the exclusion is for the purposes of subjugation. Blacks have had enough experience as objects of racism not to wish to turn the tables. While it may be relevant now to talk about black in relation to white, we must not make this our preoccupation, for it can be a negative exercise. As we proceed further towards the achievement of our goals let us talk more about ourselves and our struggle and less about white.

We have set out on a quest for true humanity, and somewhere on the distant horizon we can see the glittering prize. Let us march forth with courage and determination, drawing strength from our common plight and our brotherhood. In time we shall be in a position to bestow upon South-Africa the greatest gift possible—a more human face.[63]

Repair can be seen as a form of condolence undertaken by those who were perpetrators and beneficiaries in shared gestures of mourning with those who have been wronged. This mourning can be seen as the work of uBuntu that pays a debt to the loss of humanness of those who were killed in the struggle and those who killed them. But as I showed in reference to Justice Mahomed's judgment, the demand for uBuntu also underscores the decision of the parliament to forego prosecution in very particular circumstances. In order to justify that decision, there had to be another sense of uBuntu, to which Justice Mahomed appealed. That was the need to bring about meaningful social justice—if not the socialism that the Freedom Charter advocated—so that capability freedom would no longer be an empty dream of the black population.

The TRC itself did advocate a whole series of reparations, most of which were not taken up by the government. In a powerful article, Mahmood Mamdani argued that part of the core problem of the TRC was that it focused on perpetrators and victims, therefore allowing the vast majority of white beneficiaries of apartheid to get themselves off the hook.[64] The problem, of course, for a white beneficiary of getting themselves off the hook, at least if one takes uBuntu seriously, is that one cannot engage in the repair that restores an individual person or group to their ethical connectedness to other human beings. So it is a loss in a profound sense, ethically, to be released of one's responsibility for wrongdoing. Another problem for Mamdani is that questions of economic social justice were downplayed by this focus, and therefore, it was not an aside or a coincidence that serious reparations in the name of restitutional equality were not undertaken. In 1998, Mamdani and Sampie Terreblanche called for the creation of a Commission of Justice and Reconciliation in order to develop a full program of restitutional equality that could begin to take serious measures to counteract the devastating reality of 354 years of racialized capitalism.[65] In 2008 I joined with Mamdani and Terreblanche to make a second call for a Justice and Reconciliation Commission, in light of the uprisings in the townships that took place in the spring of that year.[66] That commission was to have a three-fold program. First, to hear testimonies of those who have suffered from economic injustice. Second, to hear, advocate, and pass programs for reparations, such as those developed by the organization *Khulumani*.[67] Third, the development of an economic program not rooted in the neoliberal GEAR, which has failed terribly to provide anything like a decent life to a vast portion of the black population. Such a commission has never been more necessary.

But I want to return to the question of rightfulness, and an uBuntu justification for *AZAPO* that has led me to change my own mind about whether the judgment was rightfully decided. As I have argued, under the tradition of German idealism, retribution lies at the very heart of rightfulness and the respect for the dignity of both the perpetrator and the one who was wronged. Critics of *AZAPO* often assumed that the judgment disregarded rightfulness in the name of some form of utilitarianism or consequentialism more broadly construed. Social goals, in other words, were used to undermine individual rights. But what I have suggested, instead, is that uBuntu is a different understanding of rightfulness, one, as the epilogue of the Interim Constitution reminds us, that cannot be vindicated through vengeance or retribution. In a profound sense, it is much more demanding, because it insists that those who have been the beneficiaries of injustice must seek to restore their own ethical human being again through acts of reparation, and that those who have been terribly wronged must be publicly mourned in acts of condolence that demand a shared humanity that in fact has not existed in a colonial situation. Here, humanity, even understood as an ethical ideal, is not something that simply exists. It is ethical work, and part of this ethical work is the undoing of the economic inequalities that mark the privilege of the few as being based in the horrific subordination of the many. Thus, the demand for social justice is part of a struggle to undo the colonial relationship, which is itself a horrific form of violation. It is not surprising, then, that apartheid was condemned as a crime against humanity. But that crime cannot be resolved by killing a few perpetrators. Indeed, in South Africa, it can only be resolved if the new state moves away from the idea of retribution of the few under the value of uBuntu.

South Africa is often included in the now vast literature on transitional justice.[68] Transitional justice includes regimes throughout the world that are undergoing shifts from authoritarian governments to "liberal nation states." It should be noted that in the new dispensation of South Africa, the communist party is not only not outlawed, it is also one the three parties that constitute the alliance of the government. Much of the transitional justice literature addresses regimes that were moving from what that literature sees as a transition from "communism" to liberalism.[69] A full critique of this literature is well beyond the scope of this chapter. My argument is a stronger one, that South Africa, and indeed the complex lessons it has to teach us, should be squarely placed within Africa, and, more provocatively, what Africa and the struggles within the context of Africa have to teach us about the future of justice more generally.[70]

If there is going to be a new South Africa, it must be one in which this very demanding ethical work must be taken on by every individual who remains within the borders of the country. uBuntu, then, can be understood to underwrite a different conception of rightfulness, one that, as I suggested in my introduction, can undertake the complex work of reuniting social justice with dignity. Therefore, in a profound sense, I have changed my mind that the *AZAPO* decision was wrongly decided.

4

Which Law, Whose Humanity?
The Significance of Policulturalism
in the Global South

In this chapter, I will address one of the most pressing questions of our time: how can we respect the fact that there are widely divergent ontologies and ways of life that must be articulated in international law, within the constitutions of nation states, and ultimately in continental communities such as the European community and the African community? In *The Law of Peoples*, John Rawls boldly argued that recognition of ontologically different world views (particularly in relation to religion) would necessarily entail that a law of the peoples could not be rooted in liberal principles, particularly in a specific conception of moral individual agency.[1] Famously, Rawls's respect for pluralism led him to reject a global veil of ignorance, precisely because such a hypothetical experiment in the imagination implicates what Rawls himself viewed as a liberal representation of personhood and justice. I begin with Rawls's attempt to envision what a reasonable Islamic state might look like, as part of his effort to develop a law of the peoples that would truly respect pluralism. I agree with Seyla Benhabib's many powerful criticisms of Rawls's own conception of the law of peoples, particularly as it is insensitive to the devastation of empire and the horrific realities of colonialism.[2] Indeed I will endorse Benhabib's notion of democratic iterations and *jurisgenerative* politics as both descriptively accurate and ethically encompassing of the struggles around legal pluralism and policulturalism in South Africa (I will return to the Comaroffs' concept of policulturalism below). Within legal systems influenced by Roman law, including Roman Dutch Law in South Africa, *ius gentium is* the law of the other. In Roman law the civil law covered the citizens of Rome, the customary law—*ius gentium*—was the law for those outside the reach of the civil law—all of Rome's conquered peoples. Of course John Rawls is not talking about the peoples' law as if it could be divergent within a nation state, due to the separation of citizens from subjects.[3] Rawls is speaking on an entirely different level. Yet the irony of course is that within apartheid, the black majority was treated as if blacks were outsiders in their own country, and their law was other to the governing law of South Africa. Under the apartheid system the peoples' law (*ius gentium*) was the customary law of the majority black population. Indeed, the peoples' law as the customary law in all its diversity remains a source of law in the postapartheid constitution.

As Benhabib has reminded us, "'the other' is not elsewhere."[4] Nor is the law of peoples, at least not in the constitution of the new South Africa. The status of customary law, and indeed what constitutes customary law, remains a burning question in South Africa. Rawls's attempt to respect pluralism, then, has a broader reach than his own conceptualization of the law of peoples. How to grapple ethically and politically with pluralism— legal pluralism as well as policulturalism—is crucial for the jurisgenerativity of constitutional ideals and principles in the new South Africa. I will contend that Benhabib's notion of *jurisgenerative* politics is rich enough to address policulturalism even when ontological diversity actually challenges the dominance of some of the most deeply held views of what the project of secular modernity demands of the structure of law, be it international or national. I will start with some of the salient points of Rawls's *The Law of Peoples* and then move to how some of his insights need to be deepened to grasp fully the challenges of the status of the customary law within the nation state of South Africa.

When John Rawls first published his essay "The Law of Peoples," many of his liberal admirers were confused by his argument that liberalism, no matter how broadly defined, cannot be the general and comprehensive worldview for the law of peoples and more sweeping proposals for global justice.

His commitment to the history of political philosophy always led Rawls to insist that there were many liberalisms, not just one that was the true way of liberalism. But both in the essay and the revised monograph with the same name that followed, he goes beyond the claim that there is a plurality of liberalisms, and insists that a law of peoples must not be based in liberal principles; otherwise it would be much too narrow and deny equal standing before such a law to many of the world's peoples who do not live in liberal societies.

Rawls thinks that any decent peoples, including liberal peoples, must find principles to confront the reality that there are many different religions in the world, some of which become politically dominant in certain states. His is a lone voice, within certain liberal circles, in seeking to defend as a matter of principle those societies that are not recognizably liberal because they do not institutionally and legally incorporate the separation of church and state. Nor do they rest on a liberal concept of personhood. Rawls defines decent hierarchical societies as having three necessary features. The first is that they do not seek to expand their own religious conception of life to other societies. If a certain religious creed does seek wider influence, it can only do so in ways that do not interfere with other peoples' civic orders and conceptions of liberties and rights. A creed, on Kant's account—and Rawls is following Kant here—is a religious point of view which, broadly defined, worships the order of things by having faith that our place in the universe is part of God's work and thus worthy of reverence and devotion. Of course, not all creeds deeply believe that they are the only true way to God. For Rawls, a creed that has such a belief institutionalizes itself hierarchically by conferring its members with privileges that followers of other creeds do not receive.

This assertion of the supremacy of a religious creed, however, is only permissible if it does not involve the persecution of other religions. This means that worshippers of other faiths cannot be denied citizenship and must be granted the space for their respective religious practices. Rawls recognized that even in 1999, there was a deep suspicion of the Muslim religion as being unable to provide the conditions for what he calls a "decent hierarchical society." He tried to counter that image of the Muslim religion by imagining an idealized Islamic people—Kazanistan. To quote Rawls:

> Kazanistan's system of law does not institute the separation of church
> and state. Islam is the favored religion, and only Muslims can hold the

upper positions of political authority and influence the government's main decisions and policies, including foreign affairs. Yet other religions are tolerated and may be practiced without fear or loss of most civic rights, except the right to hold the higher political or judicial offices. (This exclusion marks a fundamental difference between Kazanistan and a liberal democratic regime, where all offices and positions are, in principle, open to each citizen.) Other religions and associations are encouraged to have a flourishing cultural life of their own and to take part in the civic culture of the wider society.[5]

Rawls daringly describes this idealized people as interpreting *jihad* as a spiritually inspired ethical ideal rather than in military terms, making an important intervention into the reigning prejudice that *jihad* is necessarily a declaration of war. *Jihad*, interpreted as a spiritual ideal, is something akin to the kingdom of God that could actually promote inclusion of diverse religions in the Muslim state. As Rawls states:

> To try to strengthen their loyalty, the government allows that non-Muslims may belong to the armed forces and serve in the higher ranks of command. Unlike most Muslim rulers, the rulers of Kazanistan have not sought empire and territory. This is in part a result of its theologians' interpreting *jihad* in a spiritual and moral sense, and not in military terms. The Muslim rulers have long held the view that all members of society naturally want to be loyal members of the country into which they are born; and that, unless they are unfairly treated and discriminated against, they will remain so. Following this idea has proved highly successful. Kazanistan's non-Muslim members and its minorities have remained loyal and supported the government in times of danger.[6]

The idea that a particular creed can believe itself to be the only way to God and yet accept these limitations is not such a difficult notion to accept on Rawls's account. He thinks that one can believe wholeheartedly in one's own general and comprehensive worldview but nonetheless recognize that there are other people who believe deeply in their own. This even goes for certain academic liberals who believe that their general and comprehensive worldview is the one true way, if not to God, then to the best possible secular order. But just as political liberalism must temper itself by appealing to its own internal convictions and set of ideals, so must the great religions, including those obviously different from the Christianity espoused by a good many liberals.

The second feature of decent hierarchical societies is that they recognize certain basic human rights. The third feature of such societies is that they adopt what Rawls calls a common good conception of law. Rawls rejects the argument that any modern legal system must be founded upon principles of public and private rights rooted in individual autonomy—principles purportedly integral to a legal system's claim to validity.[7] Nonetheless, he does believe that, if law is to be accepted as such, it must publicly embody some degree of impartiality: that is, judges must take into account the interests of all members of society and their moral duties and obligations must be defined by some set of acknowledged standards that seem reasonable to the parties involved in conflict, religious or otherwise. Just as this kind of impartiality can only be hoped for if the hierarchical society possesses mechanisms for consulting with the different groups that comprise it, so there must be institutions such as corporate bodies and assemblies that can effectively represent divergent interests. Here Rawls follows Hegel:

> A first observation concerns why there are groups represented by bodies in the consultation hierarchy. (In the liberal scheme, separate citizens are so represented.) One answer is that a decent hierarchical society might hold a view similar to Hegel's, which goes as follows: in the well-ordered decent society, persons belong first to estates, corporations, and associations—that is, groups. Since these groups represent the rational interests of their members, some persons will take part in publicly representing these interests in the consultation process, but they do so as members of associations, corporations, and estates, and not as individuals. The justification for this arrangement is as follows: whereas, so the view goes, in a liberal society, where each citizen has one vote, citizens' interests tend to shrink and center on their private economic concerns to the detriment of the bonds of community, in a consultation hierarchy, when their group is so represented, the voting members of the various groups take into account the broader interests of political life. Of course, a decent hierarchical society has never had the concept of one person, one vote, which is associated with a liberal democratic tradition of thought that is foreign to it, and perhaps would think (as Hegel did) that such an idea mistakenly expresses an individualistic idea that each person, as

an atomistic unit, has the basic right to participate equally in political deliberation.[8]

For Rawls, it is plausible to presume that these minimum conditions can be met without imposing liberalism as the only basis for the law of peoples and that this plausibility is enough to allow for the extension of a veil of ignorance specifically tailored to hierarchical societies. If hierarchical societies endorsed the law of peoples, the endorsement would include human rights, given their commitment to consultation and to impartiality defined by a common good theory of law.

Still, we are left with several questions: how can we engage with peoples who do not endorse Anglo-American principles of a particular and limited view of the modern nation state and international law? How, more specifically, can we do so in countries like South Africa, where policulturalism has gone way beyond the demands of multiculturalism, as it has come to be understood in Anglo-American debates? Policulturalism, broadly construed, is the recognition that within South Africa, many ethnic, linguistic, and even "national" communities make political debates that challenge one very limited notion of national sovereignty, in which there is a national body that is unified in legal and political authority. How can we do so in the Rawlsian spirit of toleration and respect? Rawls invites us to answer such difficult questions by undertaking what, in his very late writing, he calls "conjectural reasoning." He associates reasoning by conjecture with the duty of civility in a politically liberal society. This duty starts with our respect for others as reasonable, rational, and equal in their ability to listen and reflect. Rawls suggests in his essay "The Idea of Public Reason Revisited" that

> we argue from what we believe, or conjecture, are other people's basic
> doctrines, religious or secular, and try to show them that, despite what
> they might think, they can still endorse a reasonable political conception
> that can provide a basis for public reasons. The ideal of public reason is
> thereby strengthened. However, it is important that conjecture be sin-
> cere and not manipulative. We must openly explain our intentions and
> state that we do not assert the premises from which we argue, but that
> we proceed as we do to clear up what we take to be a misunderstanding
> on others' part, and perhaps equally on ours.[9]

John Rawls wrote that he was not familiar with the Roman notion of the law of peoples, and that therefore his own work on what would be a possible overlapping consensus with a reasonable nonliberal people did not specifically turn on an interpretation of *ius gentium*. As I have already noted, the question of the status of a customary law, and what actually constitutes the living customary law, continues to be a hotly debated issue in South Africa, particularly when this "peoples' law" seemingly challenges some of the Eurocentric assumptions that have been incorporated into the new South African Constitution. This contest demands the expansion of the notion of the reasonable so as to give full respect to the various ontologies and spiritual realities which different peoples in South Africa deploy in their willingness to endorse the ideals and values that are embodied in the Constitution of the new South Africa and its developing jurisprudence. In other words, African worldviews[10] would become part of the explicit defense of those principles as crucial to the necessary process of "trans-cultural learning" (to use Tzvetan Todorov's phrase) so that no particular ontology, liberal or otherwise, would dominate the justifications of those principles.[11]

As has been noted time and time again, the South African Constitution has taken into account almost all of the proposed rights and policies advocated by strong multiculturalists in the North.[12] There is recognition of the right to religion, the right to language, the right to practice African spiritual rituals, and the recognition of a sphere of governance of "traditional leaders."[13] But what makes the South African Constitution exemplary is not only its explicit acknowledgment and incorporation of multicultural policies and rights, but also the actual practice of the courts, as they have developed a nuanced jurisprudence to grapple with the social and symbolic reality that South Africa is a nonsecularist society and that people do indeed live in completely different worlds. These divergent realities are often brought to bear in competing interpretations of what legal theorists and constitutional justices have defined as the *Grundnorm* of the entire constitution: dignity.[14] It is precisely in these struggles that we find the democratic iterations and *jurisgenerative* politics that are necessary for a constitution whose self-understanding is that it is transformative of the horrific, unjust relations of racial capitalism (that began long before the institution called apartheid). I will use the term *nonsecularist* to indicate several unique features of South African social life: First, there is not the sharp division between church and state in the South African Constitution that exists in the Constitution of the United States. Second, there is no rationalized or differentiated civil society in the sense described by Max Weber. Indeed, the Constitutional Court's interpretation of dignity mitigates against precisely the full rationalization of what many political scientists in the North call "civil society."[15] Third, there is no easy acceptance of the transcendence of a nation state as the ultimate body that mediates local identities. Fourth, the customary law of South Africa is action transcendent and thus not secular (in Charles Taylor's sense of the word), even as it evolves through its relationship with the new constitutional dispensation. To quote Taylor: "the traditional law is a pre-condition of any common action, at whatever time, because this common agency couldn't exist without it. It is in this sense transcendent."[16]

Indeed, as the case I am about to discuss will show, it is precisely this transcendence of the state, as well as the demand for respect for different ontologies, and perhaps even more significantly, the right to govern asserted by traditional leaders as part of their world view, that makes the clashes in South Africa not only multicultural, but what Jean and John L. Comaroff define as "policultural." The Comaroffs comment:

> In postcolonies, in which ethnic assertion plays on the simultaneity of primordial connectedness, natural right and corporate interest, the na-tion state is less multicultural than it is policultural. The prefix, spelled "poli-," marks two things at once: plurality and its politicization. It does not denote merely appreciation on the part of the national majority for the customs, costumes, and cuisine of one or another minority from one or another elsewhere. It is a strong statement, an argument grounded in a cultural ontology, about the very nature of the pluri-nation, about its constitution and the terms of citizenship within it; about the spirit of its laws, about its governance and its hyphenation. As we have already seen, in South Africa this takes the form of an ongoing confrontation between Euromodern liberalism and variously expressed, variously formulated notions of "traditional" authority.[17]

The following case, which the Comaroffs discuss at greater length in their essay, can help us understand why "policultural" is a better description than "multicultural" when it comes to clashes between peoples, or what the Co-maroffs refer to as vernacular law, and what I have referred to as the living customary law and the Constitution. The case involves a lawsuit brought by Mrs. Tumane, in a remote village of the North-West, and Chief Pilane un-der whose tribal authority the village fell. Mrs. Tumane refused to perform a burial right, called *mogaga*, after her husband's death. The ritual requires a newly bereaved spouse to sprinkle an herb on her path when she walks in a public space. Mrs. Tumane was a devout Jehovah's Witness and for religious reasons refused to practice the ritual. Her complaint was not only that her particular brand of Christian faith prevented her from participating in this particular ritual, but also that she could no longer leave her house because other members of her community had condemned her behavior as a disrespectful breach of a crucial ritual, and therefore she should be banished, because in a profound sense she had banished herself. Although *mogaga* is a ritual that is needed to protect against death pollution which can afflict men as well as women, it is more strictly enforced against women who are held to be more likely to be stricken by this contamination. As the Comaroffs point out, the *mogaga* ritual has been a contentious issue amongst Tswana since the early Christian missionaries sought to put an end to the practice.[18] It remains a contested issue: in a 2000 survey there were scores of cases brought against local people who were mainly immigrants from other regions for their refusal to perform proper mourning rites. Mrs. Tumane, herself part of that shared world, recognized that dire consequences for the entire community could ensue if the rites were not followed. These consequences could include a threat to the lives of cattle, a holding back of the rain, and indeed (in light of the anxiety regarding HIV/AIDS) could even promote a rise in the mortality rate. As the Comaroffs point out, "from this vantage, then, the performance of prescribed burial rites is not just a question of personal choice, nor even of respect for custom. It is a matter, literally, of life and death for the community at large—and, therefore, the responsibility of its traditional authorities."[19]

Prior to Mrs. Tumane's case, a group of concerned female members of the ANC and the Pan-African Congress presented a memorandum to another chief in the North West questioning whether such death rituals did not deny women their right to full citizenship. The Human Rights Commission intervened on Mrs. Tumane's side, and indeed certainly took notice of the gender tensions that were involved in the case.

As a result of the complaint brought about by the Human Rights Commission, Chief Pilane consented to call a gathering of the community at which he would announce the end of Mrs. Tumane's confinement, and at the same time permit the Human Rights Commission to inform the people of existing constitutional provisions relating to customary law and practice. The promised gathering was held, but the Human Rights Commission was not invited. And the purported outcome of the gathering was that Mrs. Tumane should be banished from her community because of the perils that were being imposed upon all due to her refusal to practice this rite. When the Human Rights Commission sought to remind the chief of his earlier agreement to hold a gathering, to let them attend, and to end Mrs. Tumane's confinement, Chief Pilane responded in a letter that he could not end her confinement, because this could only be ended if the tribe as a whole agreed to this, and they had not done so. He went on to appeal to the constitutionally protected dignity of "tradition," as well as the democratic practices of the community to which he was bound to adhere. Here, as in many cases, he appealed to section 36 of the Constitution, which covers the limitation of constitutional rights—a section of the Constitution that is frequently used when constitutional entitlement is in conflict with collectively endorsed custom. He also appealed to the fact that the dignity of the members of his tribe were at stake because they represented themselves through their democratically endorsed customs. Indeed, as Thandabantu Nhlapo has argued, a combination of S36 with a subtle, nuanced interpretation of dignity—both as a *Grundnorm* and as a right in the South African Constitution—can be used to address respectfully and mediate the claims of policulturalism.[20] This is done without simply imposing a modern liberal worldview that insists that the practices of civil society must be thoroughly rationalized. And as Thandabantu Nhlapo notes, "Article 10 in the Constitution provides: 'Everyone has inherent dignity and the right to have their dignity respected and protected.' This opens the way for the courts to incorporate this standard in practical ways when faced with competing systems of values."[21]

Mrs. Tumane responded that her dignity had been violated, and cited a number of constitutional provisions (including the rights to religion, culture, and language) to which the chief had also referred. The Human Rights Commission made an urgent application to the Mmabatho High Court, and the court ruled, as an interim measure, that it was in violation of her constitutional rights to compel the practice. According to the Human Rights Commission it had no effect on Mrs. Tumane's situation. The case became a major bone of contention across the North West and led to major debates amongst the traditional leaders, members of the Human Rights Commission, and members of the local government. Chief Pilane responded to the High Court's interim measure with a long affidavit. He claimed that he owed his position of chief to the democratic and collective approval of his tribe, and that rituals like *mogaga* were precisely what should remain under his governance and not the Constitution's mandates. He also argued that almost all of his people were Christians, and only a few Jehovah-Witnesses found something in the practice of *mogaga* to be in conflict with their religion. Indeed he claimed that there was nothing in the Bible, or in the constitutions of the local churches, that forbade such a custom. But in this affidavit he also stated that *mogaga* was not something that could be *externally* compelled, and that people who practice this ritual did so because they lived in a world in which they understood the dire consequences to everyone in their village if they did not practice it. As a result, however, of his statement that it was not compulsory, the interim decree of the High Court was dismissed. By that time, the requested period of mourning had ended.

As the Comaroffs point out, his contestation of the national authority of the Constitution was rooted in popularly mandated custom:

> While his disavowal of authority was somewhat disingenuous, the ruler's testimony rested on two broadly endorsed claims: first, that neglect of rites like *mogaga* is regarded by the majority of rural people as a clear and present danger to the physical and moral well-being; and, second, that the obligation to perform this particular rite had been legitimately affirmed by a *democratic* process, the Kgatla nation (*setshaba*) having voiced unanimous support for it in a public setting.[22]

The tension here is between members of the Kgatla nation, Chief Pilane as their governing authority, and the court system of the new South Africa. If we were to use the language of legal theorist Robert Cover, the Chief did not simply appeal to an *ethnos* but to a consistent *nomos*: a set of institutions structured around a coherent way of life, which includes *mogaga* as a central concept of who the group is. Cover strongly argued that claims of difference should be recognized only on two conditions: first, that the claim actually find itself in the normative aspirations of an ordered community, and second, that the difference be honored only when the participants in that community actually hold on to that principle as central to their way of life. Chief Pilane repeatedly points to the fact that most of the members of his tribe practice *mogaga* and see it as crucial to who they are as a tribe. In this sense then, what was being demanded was the recognition of this specific *nomos* as having the power to govern rituals like *mogaga*. This was indeed a competing *nomos* to the one voiced in the case brought by the Human Rights Commission, which focused on the rights of abstract citizens against the group, as opposed to the focus on the importance of democratic formation as necessary for the survival and respect of African traditions and customary law. But as the Comaroffs rightly point out, this case does not indicate a negation of belonging to the new South Africa, nor should it be considered a struggle between universalism and cultural relativism (as is often conceived in debates in political theory in the North). The struggle takes place within an effort to build a new South Africa in which African traditions and law, which were once fundamentally disrespected, should be given constitutional equality with other, competing worldviews. What makes South Africa exemplary in this instance is that it is opening up new possibilities of citizenship and democracy precisely through this tension between highly developed symbolic orders. It is in these political engagements that we see both democratic iterations and *jurisgenerative* politics at work, for it is the significance and the meaning of fundamental constitutional principles that are reinterpreted. Principles are reinterpreted without the imposition of ontological liberalism and its secularist presuppositions.

Charles Taylor has argued that modern secularism is fundamental to the imagined national community for two reasons: the horizontal direct access character of society, and its grounding in secular homogeneous space. The contest I have described challenged both of these concepts, because they are inadequate to the actual struggles between "tradition" and customary law, and to the construction of the new South Africa as a unique kind of imagined community, since it neither turns to homogeneity nor to horizontality, if it can be conceived as an imagined community at all. It is a "community" whose unitary projection of itself is fundamentally ethical and one that is constantly disrupted by the continuing reality and experience of profound tribal contest over spaces of governance. Homogeneous time is also challenged by practices such as ancestor worship—a ritual practice of the vast majority of the black population, which is, at least according to a recent study, not affected by education or entry into the First World capitalist aspects of the South African economy.[23] As we have already seen, customary law is action transcendent (in Taylor's meaning of the word). The tension between the new Constitution, the living customary law, and the democratic and ritualistic practices of specific communities and tribal affiliations disrupts the idea that the overlapping bonds and identities of South Africans can be ironed out into a field of homogeneous individuals.

Furthermore, Talal Asad's argument for a more complex notion of time and space in politics and ethics can help us understand, on the level of both theory and practice, the kind of contest that is continuously going on in South Africa through the claims of living customary law, traditional leaders, and the scope of their powers.[24] In addition to complex space, however, we need to think also of heterogeneous time: of embodied practices rooted in multiple traditions, of differences between horizons of expectation and spaces of experience—differences that continually dislocate the present from the past, the world experienced from the world anticipated—and call for their revision and reconnection that can only take place in a more complex process than one offered in most Anglo-American notions of secular time.

This goes to the heart of Thandabantu Nhlapo's argument that these contending *nomoi* in South Africa be postulated as equal to one another, a postulation of course that goes directly against the lingering ghost of apartheid with its structures of contempt for everything African. Often, as in the case I have discussed, there is an inherent appeal to the idea that certain privileged members of a tribe, who are mainly men, are seeking to protect their privilege against the constitutional rights of those whom they wish to continue to subordinate in the name of culture. Certainly there is reason to share the concern of some of the women of the ANC that "culture" can be used as a shield to protect privileged men against the rights of women.

There is, for Thandabantu Nhlapo, a more dangerous kind of privilege that often goes unnoticed and that is important to scrutinize against an overzealous human rights enthusiasm. This is the privilege of elites who have so deeply internalized values of modernization and Westernization that they are unwilling to share ethical space with alternative worldviews and ontologies, which may be perfectly consistent with the respect for the dignity of all the persons of South Africa. He argues, for example that African family law, including burial rights, is especially vulnerable because its institutions and practices tend to reflect a value system that challenges Western precepts head-on, not only in the structure of the kinship system but in the ceremonies and rituals considered important in the marriage process, reproduction, and death.[25] These practices provide fertile grounds for human-rights based critiques. I fully support Nhlapo's worry about the dangers of elitism, which often go unnoticed, particularly in a legal academic community (such as the one in South Africa) that remains overwhelmingly white and upper-middle class. Thus we should support in Nhlapo's conclusion that when there is no clear constitutional ground for ousting a particular practice or institution (as when it causes no demonstrable harm) the courts are urged should have regard to considerations that will protect the practice even where it is considered "unusual" by the still dominant "white" academic viewpoint on African practices. One of the considerations that should be taken into account is the notion of human dignity.

So far we have seen that for Nhlapo the ideal of dignity demands a careful practice of transcultural learning—one that is echoed in Rawls's idea of conjectural reasoning, which demands of us, at least, that we take seriously the other's viewpoint, stemming as it might, from a different ontology. Todorov's concept of transcultural learning is more demanding than Rawls's conjectural reasoning in that we must actually learn each other's ways, and grasp underlying competing values in order to even begin to make a judgment about the unconstitutionality of a ritual practice of customary law. Rawls's idea of conjectural reasoning is one of his most complex and remains suggestive. As we have seen, however, the notion of conjectural reasoning is that we at least have enough respect for other's points of views that we can appeal to them to share public reasons. Todorov is more demanding in that he is insisting that we actually *learn* about the others' ways and that this might be a very time-consuming and complicated process. Only then could we know what are the public reasons we might share. This process entails that transculturation cannot be limited to the ethical efforts of individual citizens that live in the "new" South Africa. Transculturation also lies at the heart of *jurisgenerative* politics in the specific sense that African ideals must themselves be incorporated into the development of a constitutional jurisprudence. One of the crucial South African ideals that was originally in the postamble to the Interim Constitution was uBuntu.

Briefly described, uBuntu is an activist virtue in which an ethical principle of humanness is brought into being and embodied in day-to-day relations of mutual support. It is not a contractual ethic in which self-interested individuals arrive at an agreement that is to their mutual advantage. Rather, the fundamental idea is that each one of us must initiate ethical action in the concrete situation before us, so as to bring about relations with other people that will underscore our common ethical commitments, thus providing support for networks of obligations, without which human beings cannot survive. The unsaid argument here is that uBuntu is not just an ethical ontology *of* a shared world, but is an ethical demand *to* bring about a shared world. uBuntu is a demand for the actual experience of building, enhancing, and at times repairing the moral fabric of any particular network of obligation. That is to say, cases like the one just reviewed are not just about legal arguments pitting notions of customary law against the constitution, but are actually about having a dialogue of the sort akin to the ancient, dialectical meaning of the word dialogue as it comes to us from *logos*.

Such a dialogue is about confronting the situation at-hand in its fullest sense. It is about questioning history to remind ourselves of the politics of missionaries in the northwest province in the first place. It is about deeply reflecting on what is at stake in defending living customary law and the real need for the ritual under question to ensure the well-being of the human beings whose lives are at stake if the ritual is not adhered to. uBuntu allows for a spatial and temporal unfolding of understanding across all symbolic forms—language, religion, politics, and social custom—whereby the goal is not necessarily jurisprudential victory, but mediation functioning as the crucial repair of the fabric of the larger community in its moment of strife, up to and including the new South Africa.[26] Justice Yvonne Mokgoro, of the Constitutional Court, explains uBuntu as follows:

> Generally, *uBuntu* translates as *humaneness*. In its most fundamental sense, it translates as *personhood* and *morality*. Metaphorically, it expresses itself in *umuntu ngumuntu ngabantu*, describing the significance of group solidarity on survival issues so central to the survival of communities. While it envelops the key values of group solidarity, compassion, respect, human dignity, conformity to basic norms and collective unity, in its fundamental sense it denotes humanity and morality. Its spirit emphasises respect for human dignity, marking a shift from confrontation to conciliation. (*State v. Makwanyane* 1995 (3) SA 391 (CC) para. 308, 101)

uBuntu was taken out of the 1996 Constitution, except as it was deployed to justify and demand the formation of the Truth and Reconciliation Commission. This limitation on uBuntu has been heavily criticized since uBuntu, for many, was seen as the grounding ideal of the black majority that made the Constitution possible in the first place. Debates over the language of law have raged ferociously in South African legal history—most notably those fought between the Afrikaners and the British. Still, given this history, the omission of uBuntu has led some critics to forcefully argue that the Constitution was de-Africanized in the redrafting process.[27] Yet Justice Mokgoro herself, whilst questioning the ethical and political wisdom of severely limiting the references to uBuntu in the 1996 Constitution, has also argued that, as the African principle of transcendence, uBuntu is the spirit that underlies the entire Constitution and should indeed direct the Constitutional Court when dealing with the complex issues raised by the reality of legal pluralism in South Africa, and that the customary law and the values and ideals it represents should be respected in accordance with dignity.[28] uBuntu clearly does not defend human dignity in the same manner as does Immanuel Kant, but what is important here is precisely that uBuntu can and does defend human dignity. Thereby it provides a powerful, if African, basis for the acceptance of the importance of dignity in the South African Constitution. By severely limiting the reference to uBuntu in the 1996 Constitution some would argue, and I would be amongst them, that uBuntu is relegated to a background justification for dignity, rather than foregrounded as both itself a core principle, and a powerful set of ethical arguments that are uniquely African, which demands respect for dignity of the person. If the Constitution is to survive the criticism that it has been de-Africanized, then the process of transculturation must take place at the level of constitutional jurisprudence itself, and indeed there seems to be great recognition on the Constitutional Court Bench of the importance of this process.

The struggle for the "new" South Africa is a demanding ethical task that can only take place through the transculturation of the white minority, beginning with the presumption that the long disparaged African modes of life and intellectual heritages are themselves recognized as being of equal value. This recognition of notational equality lies at the heart of a jurisgenerative politics that has allowed the basic principles of the South African Constitution to be resymbolized and reinterpreted through a constant struggle with the demands of policulturalism.

5

Living Customary Law and the Law:
Does Custom Allow for a Woman to Be Hosi?

We often hear it bandied about that customary law is premodern and inevitably patriarchal. The case I discuss in this chapter should show that this view of customary law is completely misguided. The *Shilubana* case addresses the decision of the Valoyi royal authorities to appoint a woman as a hosi or chief, and to do so because it was mandated not by the Constitution alone, but by their law.[1] This case provides an excellent opportunity to discuss the complexity of customary law in South Africa, and the debates of exactly what is the "living" customary law. The question is not just whether a woman can be a hosi under Valoyi law, but also what kind of challenge the living customary law poses to Anglo-American and European understandings of the meaning of law.

This deeper question explains the title of this chapter. Ultimately, the argument of the National Movement of Rural Women—an invited *amicus* for the case—that the living customary law does not develop in the sense that Anglo-American lawyers are used to understanding the word was not determinative of the outcome of the case. However, I defend the Rural

Women's notion of the customary law and the significance it has for the understanding of both the role of custom in law and the place of the past in living customary law. I am deliberately using the word *hosi* to address the specificity of the leadership that was at stake in this case. The word *chief* has understandably been criticized for its association with notions of leadership imposed by Western ideas of what constituted a tribe. Yet the words *tradition* or *traditional leadership* are also problematic, because they assume that somehow, these forms of leadership are artificially separated from modernity, when, as this case shows, they are clearly closely connected to it. I need to note that the argument of the National Movement of Rural Women was not available to the High Court or the Supreme Court of Appeals. Justice van der Westhuizen summarized their argument as follows:

> The Rural Women emphasize that customary law is a flexible, living system of law, which develops over time to meet the changing needs of the community. It is not rigidly rule-based, and courts must exercise caution in ascertaining the content of customary law from the written records of apartheid-era administrators, legislators and courts. Accordingly, the choice of Ms. Shilubana as Hosi should not be viewed as a "development" of the customary law, as customary law is necessarily flexible.[2]

Thus, in a certain sense the very question of development necessarily puts the customary law within the framework of the hegemonic notion of positive law as rule bound. This may seem a minor point in a carefully crafted case that justifies a decision made by Valoyi authorities to install a woman as their leader. But, indeed it is not, as I will discuss shortly. The living customary law has a different notion of living law and thus of custom than the one that dominates, certainly in English and American notions of the common law. Justice van der Westhuizen takes major steps in the direction of recognizing this difference and we will return to those shortly. But if true respect is to be given to the living customary law, it will ultimately be necessary to think deeply about the reigning notion of what law is and why we have it. That is the sweeping jurisprudential challenge of the living customary law. That said, the judgment is a huge step forward in the careful consideration it gives to the place of the customary law in the new dispensation, its analysis of who has authority within the specifics of a particular community and royal family, and the capacity of living customary law to grapple with the mandates of a new constitution that protects gender equality.

As Justice van der Westhuizen rightly notes, the issue in the case is not primarily about gender equality, but instead about the community's authority to promote gender equality in the succession of their leadership. In this particular case the promotion of gender equality also involved the question of whether or not "traditional" leadership had the authority to restore "chieftainship" to a house from which it had been removed because of gender discrimination, a discrimination that took place long before the passage of the 1994 Interim Constitution. In this case it was not the Constitution's protection of gender equality that went up against custom, because it was a certain part of the Valoyi leadership that had resolved to confer the position of hosi on Ms. Shilubana.

Let's briefly review the facts of the case. The dispute arose in the Valoyi community in Limpopo. Mr. Nwamitwa—the son of Hosi Malathini Richard Nwamitwa—challenged Ms. Shilubana's right to succeed Hosi Richard after his death. Ms. Shilubana was the daughter of Hosi Fofoza Nwamitwa, who died in 1968. The history of this dispute is as follows. Hosi Fofoza had no male heirs, and at the time of his death customary law was understood to confer succession to the eldest son. Since there was no son, Hosi Fofoza's younger brother Richard became chief or hosi of the Valoyi. In December of 1996, the Royal Family of the Valoyi met and unanimously decided to confer the position of hosi on Ms. Shilubana. Ms. Shilubana did not want to replace Hosi Richard at that time and indeed wanted him to remain the hosi for an unspecified period of time. In July 1997, Hosi Richard, in the presence of a chief magistrate and twenty-six witnesses, recognized Ms. Shilubana as the one to succeed him as chief. The Valoyi Tribal Authority sent a letter to the Commission for Traditional Leaders of the Northern Province of Limpopo stating that Ms. Shilubana would succeed Hosi Richard. In August 1997 the Royal Council confirmed that Hosi Richard would transfer his chieftainship to Ms. Shilubana. That same day, a "duly constituted meeting of the Valoyi tribe" under Hosi Richard resolved that "in accordance with usages and customs of the tribe," Ms. Shilubana would be appointed hosi. Hosi Richard wrote a letter two years later, that both the High Court and the Supreme Court of Appeals interpreted as withdrawing his support for Ms. Shilubana, even though the letter was not unequivocal. After Hosi Richard's death in November of 2001, the Royal Family, Tribal Council, representatives of local government, civic structures, and stakeholders in various organizations met and again agreed that Ms. Shilubana would succeed Hosi Richard. Some community members voiced support for Mr. Nwamitwa at about that same time. In July 2002, the Provincial Executive Council in a letter approved Ms. Shilubana's succession to hosi. The Department of Local Government and Housing scheduled an inauguration ceremony on November 29, 2002. This ceremony was interdicted by Mr. Nwamitwa. In September 2002, Mr. Nwamitwa instituted proceedings in the High Court of Pretoria seeking a declarator that he and not Ms. Shilubana was heir to the position of hosi. He also sought an order that letters of support for Ms. Shilubana be withdrawn. Both the High Court and the Supreme Court of Appeals held in Mr. Nwamitwa's favor.[3] They held that that even if the living customary law of the Valoyi now permitted women to be hosis, Mr. Nwamitwa as the eldest child of Hosi Richard still had the right of succession. Central to their holdings was a view as to what the customary law was and indeed, what it means to claim that some custom is law. Despite their nod to the living customary law's promotion of gender equality, at the end of the day and despite of some language to the contrary, these two courts questioned whether the change in "law" had truly become the law and replaced the much older custom of succession by the eldest son. We need to review a little more closely how the courts came to this decision. The High Court addressed four questions on which oral evidence was to have been presented. To quote the Constitutional Court's restatement of those questions:

> 1.1 Whether in terms. of the customs. and traditions of the Tsonga/ Shangaan tribe, more particularly the Valoyi tribe, a female can be appointed as Hosi of the Valoyi tribe?
> 1.2 Whether [Hosi Richard] was appointed as Hosi or acting Hosi since October 1968?
> 1.3 Whether when appointing [Ms. Shilubana] as a Hosi of the Valoyi tribe the royal family acted in terms of the customs and traditions of the Valoyi tribe i.e. of the Tsonga/Shangaan nation?
> 1.4 Whether decision No 32/2002 by the Executive Council of Limpopo Provincial Government dated 22 May 2002 appointing [Ms. Shilubana] as chief of the Valoyi tribe, is in accordance with the practices and customs. within the meaning of the Constitution of the Republic of South Africa Act 108 of 1996?[4]

All the relevant authorities recognized that the Interim Constitution could have changed the social reality of the Valoyi so that even if a woman could not have been appointed hosi prior to the new dispensation, the living customary law could possibly have changed as a result of the new constitutional regime. The nod to the possibility that a woman could be appointed chief after the Interim Constitution in a way affected the social reality that prior to that a woman could not be appointed hosi of the Valoyi. On the third issue, the court strongly argued that there was no precedent in the applicable customary law that allowed leadership to be transferred from one line of hosi to another, particularly when this transference took place because of the appointment of a woman. The court attributed the conferral of the position of hosi on Ms. Shilubana to a "bout of constitutional fervor."[5] The court also defended the proposition that proper customary proceeding for the appointment had not been followed, because the Royal Family can only recognize a hosi and not appoint one. The other bodies and their role in the appointment were ignored and instead the court held that without a "general poll" the customary law had not been changed.[6] According to the court, Hosi Richard had a successor. The reason why Hosi Richard had a successor was that he was appointed in 1968 and the customary law at that time held a right to succession as belonging to the eldest son. The problem was not one of gender but of lineage, since the appointment of Ms. Shilubana shifted the lineage of the chief to another line. Since gender discrimination was not the central issue, there was no constitutional question.[7]

The Supreme Court of Appeals actually suggested that the Valoyi might be confused about the own customary law.[8] It held that the Royal Family, Royal Council, and tribal authority decisions could alter the customary law so as to eliminate gender discrimination after 1994.[9] By so doing it implicitly disagreed with the High Court. Yet, the court also noted that difference noted that the gender discrimination took place before the Interim Constitution. Therefore, hosi custom in 1968 demanded that succession should proceed down Hosi Richard's family line. Although the authorities involved in the decision to appoint a woman could alter the customary line in accordance with the new constitutional dispensation, the Royal Family could not "elect" a hosi and therefore the appointment of Ms. Shilubana as hosi was against their custom.[10]

To the degree that this decision by the traditional authorities was inspired by "constitutional fervor" to eliminate gender bias, the decision of the Valoyi tribe was a dangerous fervor because it could never go far enough and would inevitably be ad hoc and thus in a basic sense undermine legal certainty and the customary law of succession, which provided that certainty. Ultimately the Court agreed with the High Court that there was no issue of gender discrimination.[11] The Supreme Court of Appeals also agreed with the High Court's response to the fourth question, namely that the official appointment of Ms. Shilubana was not in accordance with custom and since there was no constitutional issue that problematized custom, Ms. Shilubana should not be allowed to become hosi.[12] It declined to order that the relevant authorities issue letters of appointment for Mr. Nwamitwa or that the required ceremonial function should still be performed by the Royal Family. Instead, they simply ordered that Mr. Nwamitwa be appointed hosi.[13] Thus, the manner in which the order was articulated was itself disrespectful of the central importance of hosi customs of inauguration.

Ms. Shilubana applied to the Constitutional for leave to appeal. The chief justice issued an invitation to *amici* to supply further arguments on a case of this magnitude. In his argument before the Constitutional Court, Mr. Nwamitwa refined two of his earlier arguments. First, if the rule of primogeniture was discriminatory it was fair because if Ms. Shilubana would be appointed chief, a chief would not father the next hosi and this would cause chaos in the community. A second, colorful and rather bizarre argument was also added, namely that Ms. Shilubana actually accepted male lineage since she intended to appoint a male successor.

Before turning to the Constitutional Court's judgment two important observations are in order. The first is that both the High Court and the Supreme Court of Appeals failed to understand the meaning of the substantive revolution in South Africa and in a very specific sense. A substantive revolution is a term used by Hans Kelsen to describe a legal transfer of power where the reigning government gives up its sole hold on state authority.[14] This is precisely what the National Party did. But the word *substantive* is key here and has admittedly caused confusion in the judiciary and the South African academy. What was the substantive change? For purposes of this short comment, I am going to defend the proposition, which I have justified at length elsewhere, that the substantive revolution inverted the order of apartheid which denied the dignity of the black majority, by making the respect for the dignity of all others the *Grundnorm* of the entire Constitution.[15] Emeritus Justice Ackermann has most powerfully defended this proposition, relying heavily, at least at times, on Immanuel Kant. The *Rechtsstaat* established by the new Constitution did not create this demand for respect because it was always a moral demand, at least if one follows Kant. All human beings are of infinite worth because of an ideal attribution. We can lay down a law unto ourselves, the moral law, and do the next right thing. By following the moral law we act in accordance with our freedom. Morality is the realm of internal freedom. The realm of external freedom or *Recht* in Kant always turns on the recognition of the respect for all others. This respect is always a demand of any system of right. So in a sense then, the Constitution of the new South Africa did not create this respect when it made it law. It recognized a moral *Grundnorm* that is the basis of all right and that should have been respected all along. Thus, the Valoyi's bout of constitutional fervor—if that is what it was—was based on an understanding of how the substantive revolution of the New South Africa demanded the recognition and the correction of the past wrong of gender discrimination, which was wrong before the Constitution was passed. Admittedly, the idea of an objective normative order that is discovered by law goes against the grain of the dominant idea in Anglo-American law, which holds that a legal wrong is not a wrong until it is legally created as such. Hence the courts do not find it acceptable to correct discrimination before the 1994 Constitution because there was not discrimination before law announced it. The concern, of course, of the other way of thinking about law is that people's expectations will be violated because they will be held responsible for wrongs that were not illegal in the positive law. Of course the Valoyi were not following Kant. They were following their own understanding of the customary law. Whether or not the Royal Family and other authorities were following the view of the living customary law as always changing, as the National Movement of Rural Women suggests, may be an open question. To a certain extent, this is an empirical question, and there is now increasing ethnographic evidence that the living law proceeds as the Rural Women suggest. Therefore the Valoyi were following their own customary law.

To answer the concern that expectations must be taken into account, Justice van der Westhuizen gives three considerations for determining what the customary law is. He emphasizes, the customary law is the law of the majority, and millions of people live by and respect its dictates. Therefore, the question of how to define customary law is crucially important.[16] The first step is to consider the traditions of the community concerned. However, how to uncover this past is complicated by the distortion of the written customary law under apartheid and colonialism.[17] Secondly, the right of authorities to change and amend their law must be recognized. The stagnation of law, as Justice van der Westhuizen recognizes, was inevitable under apartheid. As he also recognizes, the very notion of a living law is precisely that it can adapt to the circumstances of the new South Africa. Thus, it is crucial for the courts to respect the free development of this law by the communities that know it best because it is "their law." Where there is a dispute over what is the living customary law, evidence must be produced not only about the past but also about the present development and the reasons for it.[18] Third, there must be the recognition that people do have expectations and that flexibility of the living customary law must be balanced against other factors such as legal certainty, vested rights and the protection of constitutional rights under the new dispensation. To quote Justice van der Westhuizen:

> The outcome of this balancing act will depend on the facts of each case. Relevant factors in this enquiry will include, but are not limited to, the nature of the law in question, in particular the implications of change for constitutional and other legal rights; the process by which the alleged change has occurred or is occurring; and the vulnerability of parties affected by the law.[19]

Even though the development of the customary law by the courts must remain distinct from the community's own practice and process, he continues, both must remain mindful of obligations under 39(2). The court held in *Carmichele*[20] that 39(2) imposes on all courts of law an obligation that law be developed so as to bring it in line with the substantive revolution and the objective normative order of the New South Africa. This obligation is imposed on the "traditional authorities" as well, even if their freedom to change the law in accordance with their own practice of custom must also be respected.[21]

The Rural Women challenged Mr. Nwamitwa's primary argument that the customary law upheld male primogeniture and even the idea that male primogeniture, an English law for the transference of property, was an adequate understanding of the practice of succession in which the position of hosi usually passed to the first-born son. This challenge was part of their larger challenge as to what kind of law customary law actually is, as a flexible set of practices and ethical principles. But for Justice van der Westhuizen it was necessary to address a prior question as to what role past practice can play in establishing customary law as law. To do so, he reviews the *Van Breda v. Jacobs* test, which has been used to determine when custom can be a source of law in the common law.[22] That test was that a set of practices must be "recognized as law, a practice must be certain, uniformly observed for a long period of time and reasonable."[23] But he discusses this test only to then argue that this test cannot and should not be used for the customary law.[24] Here Justice van der Westhuizen comes very close to the Rural Women's understanding of the customary law or at the very least, he recognizes, that the customary law incorporates a completely different understanding of law and custom than the one used in the common law. To quote Justice van der Westhuizen:

> Van Breda dealt with proving custom as a source of law. It envisaged custom as an immemorial practice that could be regarded as filling in normative gaps in the common law. In that sense, custom no longer serves as an original source of law capable of independent development, but survives merely as a useful accessory. Its continued validity is rooted in and depends on its unbroken antiquity. By contrast, customary law is an independent and original source of law. Like the common law it is adaptive by its very nature. By definition, then, while change annihilates custom as a source of law, change is intrinsic to and can be invigorating of customary law.[25]

Indeed the practice of the living customary law is flexible and context specific and thus always changing. This is the Rural Women's understanding of customary law, and it is obvious by now that I am in agreement with them and with the intellectual sources they rely on, primarily the outstanding work of John and Jean Comaroff. Although Justice van der Westhuizen does not go that far, he does understand that the legal status of the customary law cannot turn on whether it has been consistently practiced. The reason for Justice van der Westhuizen's recognition of a more nuanced practice in customary law is that a more rigid view would deny their right to develop their law. Since such development is amongst other things required by the Constitution, such an understanding of what makes custom law would be unconstitutional.[26]

As I have already noted, the Rural Women argued that women have, even if infrequently, been installed as leaders and that both the authorities who are in charge of such installation and the law of succession itself has been flexible because that is the nature of customary law. There is, in other words, no rule of recognition in H. L. A. Hart's sense of the phrase that tells us once and for all which body must do what when it comes to succession. Nor is there a rule of succession carved in stone. The Comaroffs have long since argued—and their work is cited by the Rural Women—that the process— and it is a process—of succession has always been adaptable to the needs of the community.[27] On the understanding of the Rural Women the installation of Ms. Shilubana as chief was the practice of the customary law and that should be the end of the story. Their alternative argument, however, was that this could be considered a development of the customary law and one that was mandated by the new Constitution. Justice van der Westhuizen ultimately does not think that enough evidence was offered by the Rural Women that this is how the customary law is practiced as law, although he obviously takes their submission very seriously, referring to it over and over again in his judgment.

Several of the most important commentaries on Shilubana have powerfully argued that the living customary law must be developed according to its own principles. J. C. Bekker and C. C. Boonzaaier agree with the Rural Women's submission that the customary law of succession does have the flexibility to allow a woman to be a chief.[28] But there is an irony in their argument. They are critical of the Constitutional Court's judgment because Justice van der Westhuizen did not recognize the flexibility of the customary law on the question of succession, and instead insisted that Ms. Shilubana's appointment was a development of the law. If it was a development of the law, it was a legislative function, and the Royal Family did not have such a legislative function. So on the one hand, they want to protect the customary law and its development on its own principles, and, on the other hand, they argue that the distinction between interpreting and making law—a Western distinction—should be applied to customary authorities. The reason for so doing is that it would be impracticable to allow such authorities to have such a legislative function:[29]

> In the present structures of government and administration, it would be
> impractical to accommodate lawmaking by traditional authorities. As
> has been pointed out above, there are some 800 traditional authorities.
> There will obviously be differences of opinion on what the law ought to
> be. The question also arises whether the laws are to be personal, or con-
> fined to the area of jurisdiction of the community concerned. If the laws
> are to be personal, should the law apply to the subjects wherever they
> are? If the laws are to be territorially restricted, would the laws have an
> impact on local government functional areas? Such permutations would
> clearly be untenable.

The significance of the Comaroffs' work and the Rural Women's submission is that there are no rigid rules for which body is appropriate for which kind of decision. Thus there is not the familiar distinction between interpreting law and making law, nor, as I have suggested, a rule of recognition that would tell us when a certain kind of law-making is legislative and when it is judicial. Thus, even though J. C. Bekker and C. C. Boonzaaier rightfully argue that the customary law would allow the succession of women, they still are imposing Western categories on what law is in their criticism of the constitutional decision, which they read as at least implicitly giving the Royal Family legislative capacity.

Nomthandazo Ntlama also argues that the living customary law should be allowed to develop in accordance with its own principles.[30] Here, however, we have another important misunderstanding of Justice van der Westhuizen's judgment. This does not concern his worry about bestowing legislative capacity on traditional authorities. Instead, the author is worried about Justice van der Westhuizen's argument that *Van Breda* did not apply to living customary law:

> According to the Court in *Shilubana*, the effect of such a treatment is that the proving of a custom no longer serves as an original source of law capable of independent development, but survives merely as a useful accessory. What is of greatest concern is the contention that the interpretation of the decision of the Valoyi community in the development of their own customs could also mean that, even if it had hitherto not been lawful under customary law, the authorities effected a development to the law to bring it in line with the Constitution.[31]

I have already argued that Justice van der Westhuizen does distinguish *Van Breda* as it deals with custom in the common law from the appropriate use of custom in the customary law. He does so precisely to recognize the living and flexible nature of the customary law. But he does not entirely disavow the past or past practice as one aspect of determining the customary law. Again, the question still stands: Are the Rural Women correct in their understanding of the customary law as a very different notion of doing law, and indeed doing justice, than the one we have developed in the West? Thus, my criticism of both commentators is that they don't go far enough in recognizing the difference in customary law from our Western notions of law, and that indeed Justice van der Westhuizen is beyond them in at least his attempt to see that which body decides is not engraved in legal stone, nor should custom and its use in law be interpreted through the lens of the common law.

This said, Justice van der Westhuizen still stops before the full recognition of the Rural Women's view of the customary law. Instead, he argues that the Valoyi authorities developed their laws and values in accordance with a very important aspect of the Constitution, which has as its very basis the assumption of the equal worth of all persons. Again, as we have already discussed, if this equality is understood to be premised on the ideal attribution of dignity to all persons, it can and should be understood as the *Grundnorm* of the entire dispensation. Thus, the Valoyi are promoting the spirit of the objective normative order that is the new South Africa and should be applauded for their "bout of constitutional fervor." As Justice van der Westhuizen concludes:

> In deciding as they did, the Valoyi authorities restored the chieftainship to a woman who would have been appointed Hosi in 1968, were it not for the fact that she is a woman. As far as lineage is relevant, the chieftainship was also restored to the line of Hosi Fofoza from which it was taken away on the basis that he only had a female and not a male heir.[32]

However, the issue of gender equality was not the primary issue of the case, and was not the only issue of the Valoyi authorities. The primary issue was the practice and flexibility of the living customary law, which in this case would allow a woman to become hosi.

Justice van der Westhuizen finally addresses the question of whether the Valoyi authorities and the Royal Family were the "right" bodies to make this decision. Again Justice van der Westhuizen strongly disagrees with the position of the High Court, which was that the Constitutional Court could not overturn the High Court's finding that in terms of existing customary law the role of the Royal Family was only formal and that there was not a legitimate appointment to hosi according to Valoyi custom:

> It must be noted that the traditional authorities' power is the high water mark of any power within the traditional community on matters of succession. If the authorities have only the narrow discretion the High Court found them to have had, it follows that no other body in the community has more power in this regard, since no other body has more power here than those authorities. This would mean that no body in the customary community would have the power to make constitutionally-driven changes in traditional leadership. The result can be seen if we consider what would have happened, on the narrow view,

if the traditional authorities in the present case had simply sought to install a woman as Hosi. Even if she were the eldest child of the previous Chief, it would follow on the narrow view that the traditional authorities would have no power to appoint her, unless there was no other heir or the male heir was unfit to rule. It would be necessary, on this view, to approach the courts before a woman could be installed as Chief.[33]

For Justice van der Westhuizen—and I applaud his decision—the narrow view is thus unconstitutional and in violation of section 211(2). Justice van der Westhuizen then applies his balancing test to this case arguing that this contemporary development should indeed be recognized as law.[34] Justice van der Westhuizen further notes what this case is not. It does not change the position of hosi to an elected position. Ms. Shilubana was born into her position as daughter of a hosi.[35] It is not just any woman who was selected. Since this altered position is now law, Mr. Nmamitwa does not have a vested right in the position of hosi. To the degree that the appointment of Ms. Shilubana leaves unanswered questions, these questions will be answered in the future by the living customary law. The future decisions of the living customary law were not before the Constitutional Court.[36] Justice van der Westhuizen does address the rather bizarre argument that there was no constitutional issue because Ms. Shilubana holds to the validity of gender discrimination and the argument that this kind of change will bring chaos with it. To this second argument Justice van der Westhuizen argues that, for now at least, discrimination is only being undone until 1968, although he notes that the Valoyi tribal authorities could take further steps as long as they were constitutional. Ms. Shilubana's decision as to who was to succeed her does not amount to gender discrimination, or her own investment in such discrimination.[37]

Shilubana is indeed a big step forward in the respect for the customary law and its powers to change laws. As such it should be applauded. Still, we will need to return to the Rural Women's argument that the correct understanding of the customary law is a flexible set of practices, processes, and ethical principles. This concept of the customary law needs to be studied more carefully. The challenge there is not just about this case, but about a much bigger set of issues. Philosophers like John Murungi have argued that African jurisprudence has an entirely different view of law as the doing of justice.[38] At least according to a powerful argument made by Roger Berkowitz this understanding of law as the doing of justice has died out in the West. To quote Berkowitz: "The divorce of law from justice informs our modern condition. Lawfulness in other words, has replaced justice as a measure of ethical actions."[39] Law is the positive law and exists precisely because we no longer believe in the doing of Justice. John Murungi, on the other hand, argues:

> Each path of jurisprudence represents an attempt by human beings to tell a story about being human. Unless one discounts the humanity of others, one must admit that one has something in common with all other human beings. To discount what one has in common with other human beings is to discount oneself as a human being. What is essential to law is what secures human beings in their being. The pursuit and the preservation of what is human and what is implicated by being human are what, in a particular understanding, is signified by African jurisprudence. Being African is a sign of being African, and being African is a sign of being human. African jurisprudence is a signature. In this signature lies not only what is essential about African jurisprudence, but also what is essential about the Africanness of African jurisprudence. To learn how to decipher it, which, in a sense, implies learning how to decipher oneself, paves the way to genuine understanding.[40]

We need such understanding of law and justice in South Africa if we are to overcome the disconnection of primarily white academics from the view of law and justice that may predominate in the black communities that comprise the majority of the population. The ultimate challenge of the Rural Women's submission is that it calls us to that process of carefully deciphering a view of law that is different than our own; perhaps even more importantly, that preserves the view of law as the doing of justice. Much more work needs to be done on what the living customary law is in the different black communities and nations in South Africa. The *Shilubana* case shows that the call for careful deciphering has at least been heard.

The Struggle over uBuntu

uBuntu, Pluralism, and the Responsibility
of Legal Academics

Pluralism is often reduced to a simple proposition. There are, in any given nation state, a number of competing social, cultural, and individual values, and these must be tolerated within an overarching sovereign order that both encompasses them all and allows them a degree of independence. Indeed, as John and Jean Comaroff have eloquently argued, there is a dialectic between neoliberal capitalism and the proliferation of values taken as facticity by our global society, because the hegemony of the Washington Consensus seemingly eclipses all the big ideals that once claimed to stand in for the ideal of humanity. Famously, one such ideal was an ethical, not simply an economic, version of socialism—from each according to her ability to each according to her need, to paraphrase Karl Marx's famous phrase. As the Comaroffs have also insightfully argued, the terrifying encroachment of neoliberalism, with its endless force of reverse transubstantiation, has left many peoples and cultures few options but to enter the legal arena and battle for some kind of barrier against this force. It is against this background that I will discuss the significance of legal pluralism in the new South Africa, which is clearly connected to a struggle against the hegemonic domination of modern European conceptions of sovereignty, and with them the supply-side economics that purportedly is simply the other side of liberal democracy. I want to begin, however, with a discussion of the philosophical basis of pluralism that directly challenges the neoliberal view of competing worldviews and value systems, all of which must ultimately be reconciled with the modern European notion of a thoroughly rationalized state and order of civil society.

Famously, one aspect of this push toward a thoroughly rationalized state was the movement of legal positivists who promised to turn law itself into a precise science. Historically, this effort begins in Germany with the philosopher Leibniz who devoted a lifetime to developing what he could defend as a fully scientific codified system of law. Leibniz, of course, is the first of many legal positivists who aspired to this idea of law as a science, both in codified systems of law and, more surprisingly, in Anglo-American systems of common law. From Hans Kelsen to H. L. A. Hart to the new positivists, such as Jules Coleman, the ambition is the same: to create a coherent set of rules that both identifies what law is and allows for the thorough rationalization of the rules of a legal system. Modern sociologists, such as Max Weber, were more cynical about what this process toward a rationalized legal system meant for human society, but still held that a rationalized system of law was inseparable from the inevitable disenchantment of the world and, with it, the end of the mytho-poetic thinking that had informed earlier customary notions of law.[1]

The great neo-Kantian philosopher Ernst Cassirer displaced the notion that man—and I use that word deliberately—has a unique place in the universe because of reason and rationality. It is impossible in this article to describe the intricacies of Cassirer's complex reworking of Immanuel Kant, and specifically, Kant's notion of the schema.[2] We need to focus, here, on how Cassirer argued that human beings are not primarily rational creatures but, instead, are symbolizing creatures, whose difference with the other animals with which we share the planet is in the range and diversity of symbols and, with that, the unique distinction we make between actuality and possibility. For Cassirer, all forms of knowledge, including science and myth, are symbolic processes with their own inherent logic—a logic which can only be known by an intricate study of the symbolic form in its actual workings.[3] According to Cassirer, all symbolic forms, including religion and myth, have an "I" standpoint, which allows for reflective judgment and a rational logic that is neither more nor less logical than any other symbolic form. Cassirer is important, then, because his entire work is a force against the assumption that modernity can be nothing else but the scientization of all reality, including social reality, and that this process of scientization would lead to the disenchantment of the world and toward a rationalized legal system. Mythical thinking on this Weberian understanding of modernity is necessarily relegated to the primitive and the superstitious—a way of thinking that will ultimately be overcome as more and more cultures concede to a modern European conception of human life. But, under Cassirer, pluralism is not a simple statement of the so-called social fact that there are competing value systems within any given society, but now becomes the recognition that the inevitable plurality of symbolic forms inheres in the very way human beings must approach their world, and that no one symbolic form, particularly that of science, will ever eclipse all the others in the great march of history towards European modernity. That said, the finite creature that we think of as a human being is marked both by ideality and universality in that all of human life and natural life only comes to us through a complex process of symbolization. Thus, the great philosopher of plurality is not a pluralist in the neoliberal sense. We may seem to have come a far distance from the question of legal pluralism, and particularly of legal pluralism within the new nation state of South Africa, but my hope here is to put the discussion of legal pluralism in a context that separates it from the value pluralism of neoliberal capitalism.

For this chapter, I accept Professor Chuma Himonga's succinct definition of legal pluralism:

> Legal pluralism in a deep sense . . . encompasses a situation in which non-State legal orders or normative orders, sometimes referred to as semi-autonomous social fields, co-exist with State law (including indigenous laws which have been recognized by the State as part of State law). The various legal orders existing in a State polity, that is, State law, indigenous law, and other normative orders are not completely independent of each other; they interact in various ways and at various levels. Presumably, their respective values also interact, or in some way rub against each other, so that they influence each other. In legally pluralistic States, therefore, one may find not only one but several, even mixed, legal cultures reflecting the interacting, diverse, legal systems.[4]

Throughout all of her work Himonga has argued that the living customary law of South Africa differs from both the English common law and the Roman Dutch law systems—the two systems that have historically made up the mixed legal system of the public criminal law and civil private law of South Africa. For Himonga this difference affects all aspects of law—the source of law, the ideas of law, the processes of law (such as rules of adjudication) and, indeed, how the very outcome of an actual legal conflict is envisioned. Thus, it affects the structure of the legal system, the institutions that make up such a system, and the form they take; the substance of the system, which is made up of rules, documents, principles, and statutes; and the culture of the system. First, the source of law is, to use Charles Taylor's phrase, "action transcendent" and thus not secular. More often than not, the source of living customary law is related to the ancestors. Thus, although the living customary law can evolve and change, and indeed certainly has been changing in accordance with the new constitutional dispensation, it does not change by a group of present living human beings gathering together and simply declaring the law changed. The change or evolution must take into account the roots of living customary law in the ancestors and the traditions associated with such a symbolic world. Secondly, the ideals of living customary law, such as uBuntu (to which I will return), have a profound effect on both the institutions of law and the actual rules and processes that guide legal conflict. As Himonga argues, in most living customary law institutions there is no formal lawyer present on either side; the rules of evidence are extremely flexible since the main purpose of the hearing is to let both sides tell their story; and what is sought is a solution and not a winner-take-all verdict. The solution entails the restoration of the breach of the social relationship, and therefore the remedies available go considerably beyond those of either the Roman Dutch private law or the English common law. Often the solution and restoration are evoked through a parable rather than through a conventional rule, and it is the parable that helps guide the remedy. In both Roman Dutch law and English common law the remedy of correction and restoration is usually funneled through much more conventional notions of repair and primarily through damages.

In the winter of 2004, I worked as a sangoma's assistant, and I will use an example of how she solved a particular conflict, leaving aside the question of whether a sangoma should be considered part of the law.[5] The sangoma had caught a young man who had stolen a television from an elderly neighbor. She and the young man returned the television to the neighbor. But the young man was further ordered to work for his neighbor for the next six months. The young man was an AIDS orphan, and therefore had not been taught the important ethical commitment and obligations that lie at the heart of the living customary law. For the sangoma, the only way for this young man to learn uBuntu was to do uBuntu. The young man accepted the order that he should work for his elderly neighbor and, indeed, the story has a happy ending in that they actually lived together until the young man graduated from Khayamandi High School. Roger Berkowitz has argued that "justice has fled our world" and that "lawfulness . . . has replaced justice as the measure of ethical action."[6] But as this example shows, both the sangoma's remedy and the acceptance of the young man to do uBuntu to the neighbor he had harmed, are close to what Berkowitz defines as a view of law doing justice. To quote Berkowitz: "Law is the experience of friendship and mutual reciprocity that, as Aristotle writes, inspires the acts of grace that unite a plurality into a unity."[7] Of course, before we even begin to elaborate on the living customary law as always developing, we need to have an extensive ethnography. As Francois Devilliers argues, to state what customary law is all too often leads us back to the customary law that was inscribed by the colonizers of South Africa and, therefore, even statements about what the law is must be met with caution, since if it is living it is changing. But if the story I have just told is to show us anything, it is that justice may not have fled from this world, and that the living customary law is much closer to law as just relatedness than its other contemporaries in South Africa. Emeritus Justice Mokgoro, for example, has daringly argued that the entire spirit of the South African Constitution should be interpreted to embody the spirit of uBuntu.

uBuntu has purportedly been difficult to define and its use in law has been sharply criticized. For now let me define uBuntu as the African principle of transcendence through which an individual is pulled out of himself or herself back toward the ancestors and forward toward the community and toward the potential each one of us has. The famous phrase *umuntu ngumuntu ngabantu* literally means: "a person is a person by or through other people." This phrase is often mistranslated with the addition of the word *only*; i.e., that a "person is a person only through other people." There are innumerable phrases and parables that are used in Xhosa and Zulu to teach us about uBuntu, and this is only one. Still, since it is so well known, we can begin with it in our examination of uBuntu.

Each one of us has the potential to embody humanity, or humanness, understood from an ethical perspective. Further, uBuntu requires us to come out of ourselves so as to realize the ethical quality of humanness. We are required to take that first ethical action without waiting for the other person to reciprocate. uBuntu then is not a contractual ethic. It is up to me. And, in a certain profound sense, humanity is at stake in my ethical action. Thus, if I relate to another person in a manner that lives up to uBuntu, then there is at least an ethical relationship that exists between us. Of course, if the two of us relate to others around us in a manner that lives up to an ethical understanding of humanness then we will have created an ethical community. The second half of that phrase means that people live through the help of others. But it is not simply sustenance that is implied here, although that is part of it. It is, more importantly, that an ethical world can only be brought about if each one of us takes it upon ourselves to live in conformity with the complex ethical demands put on each one of us living in a community that aspires to be just (in Berkowitz's sense of the word).

Thus, in a sense, uBuntu reconciles the longstanding Anglo-American feminist debate about whether justice or care should be given priority as the primary value. We can only act caringly toward an individual, in terms of uBuntu, if we also treat them with dignity and aspire to a just relationship with them. The relationship is not altruistic, but it is certainly one that denies that there is an ontologically based contradiction between selfishness and altruism. We are all served by living in an ethical community. So it is in our interest, understood in a particular way, to act ethically. The temporality of uBuntu is important here, for since we are "required to go first" it may not be in our immediate interest to act ethically. For example, if I give a bottle of water to someone who is brutally thirsty I may get nothing back from that person, besides, possibly, a "thank you." But twenty years down the line my daughter may find herself thirsty and without water, and someone will give her the water she so desperately needs because I have helped to build a community that lives by this demanding ethic which provides support for all the members of the community in the long run. A famous isiXhosa saying is: "what goes out the front door comes in the back window." The idea here is that we live in a force field in which ethical actions reverberate and encourage affirmative ethical environments. The closest we have in Anglo-American terms is "what you give out, you get back tenfold."

It is important to note that uBuntu is not just an ethical ontology of a purportedly shared world, but an ethical demand to bring about a shared world. Critics of uBuntu often implicitly identify uBuntu with a conservative ethical ontology—one that is both hierarchical and patriarchal. What is missed in this criticism is precisely the activism inherent in uBuntu. uBuntu is an ethical demand which promotes the actual experience of building, enhancing and, at times, repairing the moral fabric of an aspirational community inherent in the notion of the uBuntu as the African principle of transcendence. As we will see shortly in a discussion of Emeritus Justice Albie Sachs's judgment in *Port Elizabeth Municipality v. Various Occupiers*, what is at stake in uBuntu is the promotion of a dialogue in situations of conflict, of the sort akin to the ancient dialectical meaning of the term as it comes to us through logos. Such a dialogue is about confronting the situation at hand in its full sense. It is about questioning the history of colonialism to remind ourselves of the history, for example, of forced removals. It is about deeply reflecting on what is at stake in defending customary law, and what must be done to ensure the well-being of the larger community. The saying *a botho bag ago a nne botho seshabeng*, which literally means "let your welfare be the welfare of the nation," points us again to how uBuntu calls us to an aspirational community in which my well-being or welfare is built and enhanced by seeking to ensure the well-being of the larger community in which it is necessarily rooted.

In his work with the San people, Kabir Bavikatte has also found that the understanding of the San, of their interconnectedness with one another and to nature, focuses more on virtue than it does on rights and their vindication:

> A relational understanding of the self emphasizes less on rights in its engagement with the world and more on virtue—virtue being defined here as the sense that foregrounds one's connectedness rather than separateness. The practice of virtue on a number of occasions also resolves conflicting rights through the practice of connectedness by the manifesting of what we term here as "relational sentiments" such a graciousness, kindness, love, compassion, patience and generosity.[8]

Ethics of virtue are often taught by parables, and the teaching of uBuntu is no exception. There are an infinite number of such parables in the Zulu tradition. One such saying is "the visitor's stomach equals that of the size of a bird's kidney." The saying indicates that sharing your food with a visitor or stranger will not exhaust the host's food supply. Hylton White did path-breaking work on conceptions of inhumanity amongst the Zulus. His work shows us that the ethical meaning of humanness or humanity is often demonstrated through parables of what constitutes inhumanity and that colorfully describe how inhumane behavior takes over the individual who promotes it. Such parables are often used in Zulu customary law to draw out the meaning of how a community has been fractured by inhuman behavior.

So far I have described uBuntu philosophically, and it is crucial to recognize that uBuntu is a philosophical ethic. It is important to emphasize this point because uBuntu, like many other traditional African ideals, is trivialized as coming from an outmoded form of life or, alternatively, belittled as an ethic that black South Africans do not live up to. The uBuntu Project began its research with the examination of how and to what degree indigenous ideals, such as uBuntu, have survived the brutality of apartheid and the violence and dire poverty imposed by neoliberal capitalism. The ethnographic question is as separate from the justification of uBuntu as it would be in any ethic.

As Paget Henry has argued, colonization of Africans by Europeans made race the primary signifier of the difference between them. Race becomes integrally linked to other binaries such as primitive : civilized; rational : irrational; and prelogical : logical. To quote Henry:

> From this biological reduction was also a radical deculturization that shattered both self and world and also made the African's capacity to labor very visible to Europeans. However, this was no ordinary capital/labor relation. Faust, the capitalist developer, was here metamorphosed into Prospero, while his racialized worker was transformed into Caliban. The "Calibanization" of Africans could not but devour their rationality and hence their capacity for philosophical thinking. As a biological being, Caliban is not a philosopher. He or she does not think and in particular does not think rationally. In the European tradition, rationality was a white trait that, by their exclusionary racial logic, blacks could not possess. Hence, the inability to see the African now reinvented as Caliban, in the role of sage, philosopher, or thinker. In short, this new racialized identity was also the death of Caliban's reason.[9]

It is crucial then to the restoration of humanity of Africans to recognize that there is African philosophy, and more specifically, that Caliban does indeed have reason, even if it has been veiled by myopic imperial prejudice. The philosopher Lewis Gordon has suggested that African philosophy be identified as Caliban's reason. But this is not the only justification for engaging seriously with African philosophy and ethics. Henry has argued that African traditions—and he grapples primarily with the Yoruba spiritual tradition—offer a strong basis for a new African version of existentialism in which both psychic and communal disrepair, inevitable under colonialism, need not lead to tragic personal or communal collapse.[10] I want to argue that the philosophical recognition of uBuntu is necessary for the respect of Caliban's reason. Thus, crucial to the restoration of Caliban's reasoning is the recognition of uBuntu, not only in customary law, but in constitutional law.

One would expect uBuntu, if it were to be applied as a justiciable principle, to have an effect on all aspects of what I discussed as the parts of a legal system: the structure, substance, and culture. We can use Justice Sachs's judgment, which is an exemplary deployment of uBuntu, as I have described it earlier, to demonstrate that, in fact, it does affect all three aspects of a legal system. *Port Elizabeth Municipality v. Various Occupiers*[11] was a case brought by the Municipality against squatters who were unquestionably there "illegally" and did not want to leave their homes to be removed to the Walmer township, arguing that Walmer was a dangerous and crime-ridden area. In his judgment, Justice Sachs argues that the Prevention of Illegal Eviction from and Unlawful Occupation of Land Act (PIE) was adopted with the manifest objective of overcoming the brutal history of forced removals in the name of a future worthy of the values and ideals of the new constitutional dispensation. As I mentioned earlier, uBuntu demands this careful investigation of the sources and causes of moral and ethical breakdown. Once this history is fully taken into account it creates an ethical context that demands generous reading of the legal significance of PIE. To quote Justice Sachs: "In this context PIE cannot simply be looked at as a legislative mechanism designed to restore common law property rights by freeing them of racist and authoritarian provisions, though that is one of its aspects."[12] Justice Sachs argues that section 25 of the Bill of Rights, which protects property rights, and section 26, which ensures adequate housing, must be read together in the context of judging whether or not an eviction order is legitimate. But, for my purposes here—which is how Justice Sachs appeals to uBuntu—I need to stress first that the simple finding that squatters are illegally on the land does not solve the case. Again, to quote Justice Sachs: "The court is not resolving a civil dispute as to who has rights under land law; the existence of unlawfulness is the foundation for the enquiry, not its subject matter."[13]

For Justice Sachs there are a whole series of ethical criteria that need to be examined before any decision on an eviction order can be made. They involve such matters as how long the squatters have been living there, the reason or motivation for settling on the land (the squatters in the *Port Elizabeth* case believed they had been given permission by the owner), how serious an emergency it is for the people who have erected their shelters, what kind of housing plans the municipality has provided for (although information on this alone will not be determinative of the case), and whether or not there has either been formal mediation or at least some other attempt to give voice to all parties involved in the conflict. Thus, for Justice Sachs, the Constitutional Court is called to engage in active judicial management according to equitable principles, and these principles are best summarized in the value of uBuntu. Again to quote Justice Sachs:

> Thus, PIE expressly requires the Court to infuse elements of grace and compassion into the formal structures of the law. It is called upon to balance competing interests in a principled way and promote the Constitutional vision of a caring society based on good neighborliness and shared concern. The Constitution in PIE confirmed that we are not islands unto ourselves. The spirit of uBuntu, part of the deep cultural heritage of the majority of the population, suffuses the whole Constitutional order. It combines individual rights with a communitarian philosophy. It is a unifying motive of the Bill of Rights, which is nothing if not a structured, institutionalized and operational declaration in our evolving new society of the need for human interdependence, respect and concern.[14]

Here we see how even the institutional structure of the Constitutional Court was affected in that it was called to go beyond its normal operations. Certainly, the substance of law was affected, as indicated by Justice Sachs's argument, that the finding of unlawfulness was the beginning of the matter and not the end. Both the importance and promotion of mediation reaches to both the legal system's institutions and its culture. Since mediation is not justified simply as a cost-saving device, but as crucial to the respect that must be given to both sides of the conflict (particularly such that formally disempowered and silenced people would be given equality of voice), then it must be rooted in an ethical justification. And that ethical justification is, for Justice Sachs, uBuntu. Indeed, Justice Sachs, in a recent interview with the uBuntu Project argued that without uBuntu he would not have been able to resolve adequately the complex legal and institutional aspects involved in the case so as to justify overturning the eviction order.[15]

It is clear that indigenous ideals affect the way in which property and property ownership are viewed and understood. Bavikatte's current work, which has developed within the framework of the Convention on Biological Diversity, has strongly advocated that law in itself must be open to the spiritual understandings of the San who do not understand indigenous knowledge through the Western intellectual property rights models. Indeed, indigenous knowledge is not a thing, or even an information set, that can be reduced to a product. In other words, the very idea of a patent implies a way of knowing that runs against the ethos of San indigenous knowledge. To quote Bavikatte:

> The 1997 Heart of the People Declaration states that "We uphold the sacredness of life and oppose ideas, systems, world views and practices, including global finance and patent laws; which define the natural world, its life forms and the knowledge of indigenous peoples as property or commodities."[16]

Thus, again, the philosophical notions of the person and the ideals that are integrally connected to them affect the way in which legal principles are understood. For example, Bavikatte and others working with him have argued that Article 8J of the Convention on Biological Diversity, which seeks to protect indigenous knowledge from misappropriation, must redefine misappropriation. The focus has primarily been on conventional definitions of misappropriation—such as theft, or accessing another's property without permission. The struggle here has been to define misappropriation on the basis of an interpretation of the San's ethical framework, which would not focus on theft or other abuses of property but would, instead, define misappropriation as disrespect for the relationality and process of knowledge. This redefinition of misappropriation would also change the way in which protection is understood beyond the receipt of monetary rewards for the sale or lease of their knowledge. I use the word "struggle" here because, as John and Jean Comaroff have insightfully argued, many ethnic groups have, indeed, successfully incorporated their ethnicity—i.e., they have made a bundle.

What is at stake then is the way in which neoliberal capitalism becomes integral to interpretations of indigenous knowledge, both in its definition and in its struggle for an understanding of indigenous knowledge that resists the commodification of neoliberal capitalism. For the Comaroffs, and I agree with them, culture should not be understood as a functional adaptation to neoliberal capitalism. Instead, it must be grasped through an internal dialectic of both alienation and resistance. For example, Hylton White has argued that we can only understand how rural homes for the dead are constructed and understood in Zululand against the tragic history of migrant labor. The division between work in the city and a home in the rural area takes on a special meaning that continues in the postapartheid era. Workers could only truly return "home" after their death. During their lifetime, if they were faithful family men, they would continue their migration, sending wages to their families. I have argued that uBuntu is an African principle of transcendence that turns us back to the ancestors. But what White shows in his careful study of the dwelling of culture is that this past is also a future for the individual migrant, in which he can finally dwell in the "Time before Whiteness." To quote White:

> The cultural space in which the dead dwelt was at once a space of the
> past and of the future. . . . Past in a sense familiar from culturalist dis-
> courses everywhere: the home imagined the space of a powerful heritage
> passed down from a time before "whiteness" had entered and dominated
> the social world. The living could come to know about and participate
> in the qualities of that heritage, but whatever they invented in the pres-
> ent did not share its fully authentic status as culture. On the other hand,
> the space infused with that pastness was a space that lay *ahead* in time
> for individual migrants. It was in their personal futures that they would
> come to dwell in culture as ancestral spirits themselves. So the dead who
> while alive had been so intimately familiar with the forms and ways of
> life under "whiteness"—those very same dead could hope to turn after
> death into subjects of culture. They could hope to become apparitions of
> a powerful difference unsullied by the forms of subjection to power that
> made difference what it was.[17]

Thus, even the way houses are constructed is part of a complex dialectic, first with the brutal realities of colonialism, and now with conditions of "liberation within neoliberalism" (to quote the Comaroffs' telling phrase).[18]

What is written here is in no way meant to deny the importance of the development of indigenous ideals as resistance, but simply to grasp the dialectic by which indigenous groups define that resistance and indeed live out custom. It is almost by definition that the living customary law, as it is involved in this dialectic, must be studied from the ground up. But there is another reason why customary law must be studied from the ground up: the source of customary law is more often than not defined as action transcendent. Thus, the process by which African customary law changes should not be expected to come in abrupt shifts in direction. In their work in Limpopo, Professors Chuma Himonga and Rashida Manjoo have begun a dialogue with 120 traditional leaders, including men and women, from 108 villages in the tribal authority area, including the royal spokesperson, to ensure a dialogic relationship that would allow for the possibility of bottom-up engagement. A meeting of the researchers and tribal leaders was held prior to the beginning of the fieldwork to discuss the broad terms of the proposed research and the logistics of it so as to establish consensus on the part of the leaders regarding their participation in the research. Focus group discussions and debriefing plenary sessions were facilitated by both the researchers and preselected interpreters from the local community. The interpreters were afforded an intensive time for discussion on the theoretical underpinnings of the research itself so that community members would be involved in all levels of the research program. Himonga and Manjoo's research seeks to identify both the connections and the tensions between the South African Constitution and customary law, as well as the ways in which local communities resolve such tensions. The key issues to be addressed in the dialogue are domestic violence, succession and inheritance, and traditional leadership. But the method of study implies a critical understanding of what it means to examine living customary law in a postcolonial setting: a method deeply respectful of the subjects of the study as holders of knowledge and agents of change.

Given that the customary law is often represented as action transcendent, its evolution (by the people themselves) will take a different shape to that associated with a predominant version of modern positive law. Thandabantu Nhlapo has warned against a dangerous kind of snobbery that is often mobilized by human rights enthusiasts against the alleged elitism and hierarchies of purportedly traditional tribes. To be sure, Himonga and Manjoo's work is concerned with gender equity. But the question of what gender equity means in the course of the living customary law is complex indeed, and its own process of change must be respected. Nhlapo argues that all too often, legal elites have deeply internalized values of modernization and westernization to the point that they are unwilling to share ethical space with alternative world views and ontologies which may be perfectly consistent with the respect for the dignity of all persons in South Africa. As Nhlapo explains:

The discussion suggests that the era of African family law is especially vulnerable because its institutions and practices tend to reflect a value system that challenges Western precepts head-on, not only in the structure of the kinship system but in the ceremonies and rituals considered important in the marriage process. . . . Such a system provides fertile grounds for human rights-based critiques. This essay questions whether these [critiques] are always legitimate. Where there is no clear constitutional ground for ousting a particular practice or institution (as when, objectively, it causes no demonstrable harm) the courts are urged to have regard to considerations that will protect the practice even where it is considered "unusual" by the dominant culture. One of the considerations may well be the notion of human dignity.[19]

Thus, law reform itself, important as it is, must take care to respect the competing systems of values and ideals that exist within South Africa, including the values and ideals embodied in the customary law. Certainly there must be respect for the plurality of the customary laws within South Africa. But that said, justifications (often ethical) for respecting legal pluralism do not easily apply in a postcolonial nation state. Robert Cover argued that claims of cultural and legal difference should be legally recognized by the overarching nation states only on two conditions: first, that the claim actually is rooted in the normative aspirations of an ordered community; second, that the difference be honored only when the participants in that community actually hold onto that way of life.[20] There are at least two difficulties with Cover's two criteria for the acceptance of legal pluralism. The first is that it underestimates the colonial shattering of coherent ways of life. The second point is not that the shattering is complete, and that traditional ways of life are wiped out, but that instead the complex dialectic of alienation and resistance described by the Comaroffs is the result. Thus, their term "policulturalism" seems the more apt, both to grasp and to respect legal plurality in the post colony.[21]

We need to note here that neither uBuntu nor dignity claims the status of relative values, but they both claim to represent the idea of humanity. And it is precisely the contest over ideals of humanity, as well as their relationship with each other, that demands transculturation. This is my second reason for claiming that legal pluralism does not adequately grasp uBuntu and dignity: both claim to be universal ideals. But to advocate that we understand legal plurality and cultural plurality through the term *policulturalism* in no way undermines Nhlapo's claim that dignity, and certainly uBuntu, demand something like Todorov's concept of transculturation.[22] Transculturation demands that we must actually learn each other's ways and grasp underlying competing values in order even to begin to make a judgment about the unconstitutionality of a ritual practice of customary law. Transculturation, in a deep sense, lies at the heart of a constitutionalism that would be truly transformative of the former institutionalized racism of the legal system. There is good reason, as we have seen in the discussion of Justice Sachs's judgment, that the process of transculturation has been incorporated into constitutional decision making.

uBuntu was limited to a justification for the Truth and Reconciliation Commission in the 1996 Constitution. This has been heavily criticized since uBuntu was, by many, seen as the grounding ideal of the black majority that made the Constitution possible in the first place. Debates over the language of law have raged ferociously in South African legal history—most notably those fought between the Afrikaners and the British. I will return shortly to the significance of the omission of uBuntu from the 1996 Constitution. For now I need to look at another aspect of the relationship between linguistic plurality, clearly recognized in South Africa since there are eleven official languages, as this in turn relates not only to uBuntu and the Constitution, but also what it means to respect the actual plurality of languages.

Section 35(3)(k) of the Constitution provides that an accused person has a right to be tried in a language of her choice and, where this is not possible because of practical constraints, there must be an interpretation or interpreter in the chosen language. However, there has been a difficulty in realizing the mandate of the Constitution, at least in the stronger demand that the defendant be able to choose, because so few magistrates and High Court justices speak African languages. This problem does not stop in actual litigation: many black students speak English only as a second language. The fact that most, if not all materials are English takes a great toll on their ability to take exams and make sense of the very words spoken in class. Language always points to a whole set of cultural practices that could well be unrecognizable to someone not fluent in that language. It would seem, therefore, that serious language reform needs to be undertaken by all universities in South Africa—reform that would at the very least provide translations of the fundamental coursework into isiXhosa and other African languages. We certainly should not take the inability of magistrates and justices to speak African languages as a reason to reduce the meaning of section 35(3)(k), but rather read it as a mandate for those that are in the legal community of South Africa to take upon themselves the responsibility of learning at least one African language as a crucial part of the process of transculturation.

South Africa is clearly facing a constitutional crisis. Yet Justice Mokgoro, while questioning the ethical and political wisdom of limiting the use of uBuntu in the 1996 Constitution, has also argued that, as the African principle of transcendence, uBuntu is the spirit that underlies the entire Constitution and should indeed direct the Constitutional Court when dealing with the complex issues raised by the reality of legal plurality in South Africa. uBuntu clearly does not defend human dignity in the same manner as does Immanuel Kant, but what is important here is precisely that uBuntu can and does defend human dignity. Thereby it provides a powerful African basis for the acceptance of dignity as the *Grundnorm* of the Constitution. By limiting the use of uBuntu in the Constitution, uBuntu is relegated to a background justification for dignity, rather than foregrounded as a core principle. If the Constitution is to survive the criticism that it has been de-Africanized, then the process of transculturation must take place at the level of constitutional jurisprudence itself, and indeed there seems to be great recognition by the Constitutional Court of the importance of this process.

I have just argued that the "good news" is that there can clearly be an "overlapping consensus," to use the expression of John Rawls, between uBuntu and dignity.[23] This is the case even if uBuntu is rooted in Afro-modernity and carries with it a different notion of the person from that of European modernity, and other views of dignity, including that defended by Kant (a view that has made its way into the Constitution through the judgments of Justice Ackermann). But what needs to be noted here is that both uBuntu and the Kantian view of dignity ground law in an ethical justification, even if the Kantian view does so through an imagined social contract. Section 10 holds that everyone has dignity, and on one interpretation of the Constitution that I strongly support, dignity is a moral ground of the entire Constitution.[24]

In Kant, there is no distinction between law and morality, at least not in the sense that law is not moral. Law is the realm of external freedom, and as such is a realm of morality. For the purposes of this chapter, I want to emphasize that the Kantian social contract is thus explicitly moral and ethical turning on a hypothetical experiment of the imagination in which we seek to actualize the Kingdom of Ends in a legal system, and that only such a contract could ever hold people together under the law. In his essay, "On the Common Saying: 'This May be True in Theory, but it Does Not Apply in Practice,'" Kant argues that a Hobbesian social contract of any sort, which imagines that human beings "contract" so as to yield to the power of the sovereign and of the positive law because of the drive for security, will always falter because of its absence of a moral ground.[25] Simply put, there are too many ways to find security or manage risk that allow individuals to opt out of the social contract. And, indeed, many of the problems of rational choice theory are about what to do when so many are finding ways to opt out of the social contract. If the only basis for abiding by a legal system is fear and security, and there is no moral reason to do so, then there will always be acceptable reasons to opt out of the social contract. Indeed, in its most cynical version, we are to expect that everyone is trying to opt out at every moment. Kant's point that the Hobbesian social contract will fail is prophetic in that it anticipates a profound tension between the very idea of a social contract, if it is based only on the social coordinating of risk-managing, utility-maximizing subjects, and the cohesion and togetherness that law, and certainly justice, demand.

The Kantian social contract, on the other hand, imagines human beings joined for moral and ethical purpose in order to regulate themselves in the name of the Kingdom of Ends. The cohesion is rooted in Kant's own connection between freedom (understood as autonomy) and the possibility that as such beings we can harmonize our interests and aspire to live together in the Kingdom of Ends. Thus, if Kant is right about Hobbes, and I believe that he is, then the Kantian ideal of a free people regulating themselves and their laws through the Kingdom of Ends is one moral image of the world that allows us to begin to defend the Constitution. Such a moral view may well be, and I would argue that it is, incompatible with the brutal realities of neoliberal capitalism. Karl Marx would certainly have agreed with me. Thus, an ultimate defense of the Constitution must take seriously the dire poverty in which half of the people in South Africa live as integral to the demand for social and economic reorganization of society. If this is the case, there must be a serious consideration, not only of socio-economic rights, but of socio-economic organization of society as a whole. Both dignity and uBuntu demand nothing less than that we examine the reasons for the failure of the Constitution to deliver on its promise for a better life for everyone.

7

Rethinking Ethical Feminism through uBuntu

Transnational feminism, as both an ethical ideal and an actual struggle to form political alliances, raises some of the most difficult and burning issues of what it means to challenge profound Eurocentric biases that have often stood in the way of such a coalition. In this chapter, I will address how and why such a transnational alliance actually demands of us that we open ourselves to rethinking some of our most cherished feminist ideas, such as freedom and equality, without giving up on those ideals. That is, in a profound sense, the challenge of how we rethink the feminist project, without in any way conceding anything to the horrific oppression women suffer under global apartheid.[1] The complexities of this challenge have led me to rethink what I have long ago called "ethical feminism," and indeed to deepen my understanding of ethical feminism through an engagement with the works of Judith Butler and Gayatri Spivak. Sometimes, when the issues are so big, they can best be examined by looking at a specific case, and in this case an alternative non-Western (South African) ethic: uBuntu. The ethic of uBuntu, as we will see, raises questions about some Anglo-American assumptions about freedom and equality, specifically freedom and obligation. Part of the reason I turn to uBuntu is somewhat autobiographical, because I have been working in South Africa for twelve years. But I turn to uBuntu more generally to try to address what it might mean for us to respect a non-Western ethic that does not justify itself through an appeal to its indigenous roots, but instead through a claim to universality.

RETHINKING ETHICAL FEMINISM

In the mid-1990s, I argued that feminism must involve an apotropaic gesture against the incessant fading of the diversification and differentiation of the feminine within sexual and within cultural representations.[2] This gesture not only operates against simplistic notions of what women supposedly are, but also brings to light how reigning definitions of the feminine undergird notions of civilization and a philosophically bloated conception of Man. Thus, feminism was for me then and is now ethical in three senses. First, it challenges the close connection between morality and conceptions of Man as these are rooted not only in a narrow Eurocentric view of "men," but also in a conception of civilization that in its very premises has become both genderized and whitened. Gayatri Spivak has emphasized over and over again how so-called ideals of civilization have been used to prop up notions of the human that not only exclude certain women from the field of meaning and representability, but are also used as justifications for the worst kinds of violence.[3] Thus, feminist struggles are not only against the subordination of women—although, of course, feminism must fight against that subordination; more broadly construed, feminism is both a political and an ethical struggle against hegemonic meanings and institutions that deny the being of anyone as fully human. This expands the reach of feminism to fight alongside all others who are dropped below the bar of humanity by this pumped-up notion of "Man" as the civilized as well as the civilizer. This is the second sense in which feminism is ethical, in that it fights against a process of othering that drops human beings below the bar of what purportedly constitutes "our" humanity. In this second sense of what I am now defining as ethical feminism, there is no feminist struggle without the battle against racism, neocolonialism, and continuing forms of imperial domination. We need to remember this integral connection because even the most sophisticated psychoanalytic justifications for why civilization demands that woman be barred from full humanity are inseparable from the idea that "Man" must reign.[4] Here, "Man" is the very definition of what it means to be human and thus civilized. As Frantz Fanon and so many others have reminded us, that "Man" is always imagined as white.[5] So-called "civilization" then sets up a bar against others, who make Man what he purportedly stands for, precisely by marking his difference from these others. Thus, feminism is always against this othering, which takes some beyond the reach of humanity and registers them as less than human. As Gayatri Spivak writes:

> Why have I written largely of women to launch the question of the recognition of ceaselessly shifting collectivities in our disciplinary practice? Because women are not a special case, but can represent the human, with the asymmetries attendant upon any such representation. As simple as that.[6]

Thus ethical feminism expands the reach of feminist politics, and integrally connects it to antiracist struggles, as well as the worldwide politics against global apartheid.

The second aspect of ethical feminism was based in a defense of an aspiration to a nonviolent relationship to the other and to otherness in the widest possible sense of the word. I deliberately used a broad brush in defining the ethical relationship, although I also clearly meant to evoke the spirit of Emmanuel Levinas. Crucial to this aspiration is the responsibility to struggle against the appropriation of the other into any preconceived meaning of her difference and her singularity, a precarious undertaking indeed, as Spivak reminds us in her rightfully renowned essay, "Can the Subaltern Speak?"[7] I am using the word *precarious* deliberately, because in a profound sense the struggle for a nonviolent relationship to the other—and it is a struggle—has to come to terms with what Judith Butler has recently called "precarious life."[8] For Butler, this precariousness involves at least two aspects. The first is a fearless confrontation with our shared corporal vulnerability that demands nothing less than that we put our defenses down that keep us from facing that it is we, too, who can be violated, harmed, and indeed killed:

> Negotiating a sudden and unprecedented vulnerability—what are the options? What are the long-term strategies? Women know this question well, have known it in nearly all times, and nothing about the triumph of colonial powers has made our exposure to this kind of violence any less clear. There is the possibility of appearing impermeable, of repudiating vulnerability itself. Nothing about being socially constituted as

women restrains us from simply becoming violent ourselves. And then there is the other age-old option, the possibility of wishing for death or becoming dead, as a vain effort to preempt or deflect the next blow. But perhaps there is some other way to live such that one becomes neither affectively dead nor mimetically violent, a way out of the circle of violence altogether. This possibility has to do with demanding a world in which bodily vulnerability is protected without therefore being eradicated and with insisting on the line that must be walked between the two.[9]

The second aspect, related to the first, deepens and extends the Levinasian mandate with its biblical roots, "Thou shalt not kill." For Butler—and I am in agreement with her—human beings can be violated by a force so great, whether through indeterminate detention, poverty, or other sources of cruelty and oppression, such that they are "derealized," to use her phrase, as a human being long before they actually die: "What is real? Whose lives are real? How might reality be remade? Those who are unreal have, in a sense, already suffered the violence of derealization. What, then, is the relation between violence and those lives considered as 'unreal'? Does violence effect that unreality? Does violence take place on the condition of that unreality?"[10] Thus I think we need to deepen our understanding of what is required to even aspire to a nonviolent relationship to the other through the evocation of precarious life.

And this leads me to a third aspect of ethical feminism. For many years now, Butler has powerfully argued that the incompleteness of any appeal to the universal, which must necessarily be caught in the particularity of language and culture, is that this appeal always demands that we engage in the ethical task of mutual translation.[11] So has Spivak in her careful suturing of any human rights discourse to an ethics of responsibility.[12] Both authors emphasize that the appeal to universality *must* include the demand for translation, in order to push against both the silencing that pushes women in the Global South below the bar of representability, and against what Butler has called the violence of the "derealization" of a human life. Spivak and Butler's work has never been more important, in that both continue to advocate for a nonviolent ethic, and in Spivak's case explicitly, for a complex Marxist project of global transformation. The aspiration to a nonviolent ethic, and with it, the struggle for global transformation, has itself become controversial, in that some thinkers have argued that it is a form of bad utopianism, that either runs up against some ontology of the human and social relations as inevitably violent, or worse yet, refuses the fundamental violence which inevitably defines the political.[13] Sometimes, the insistence on the connection between politics as necessarily violent and the ethical rupture or relationship as madness allies itself with the Left, and even the project of global transformation.[14] Nothing, however, in the aspiration to a non-violent relationship to the other necessarily implies pacifism or the complete abdication of the use of violence in all circumstances. If we are to take the struggle against global apartheid seriously, then it may well be necessary at times to turn to certain kinds of violence.[15] But what kinds? And must they involve violation in any of the senses defined by Butler and Spivak? These are two questions that must be raised if we are to aspire to a nonviolent ethic. So while I stand behind the three aspects of ethical feminism I defended long ago, we also need to deepen the understanding of ethical feminism through the recent work of Butler and Spivak.

Further—and this is the central issue I will address in this chapter—the call for translation must not only be made, it must be heeded. What follows is, in a very real sense, such an effort at translation through an engagement with the South African notion of uBuntu, and an attempt to understand what this ethic might teach us about different notions of freedom and obligation that inspire feminists to action. There are again two aspects to the call to comprehend universality as carrying within it an ethical demand for translation. The first is to take seriously the idea that other intellectual heritages do offer us competing notions of freedom and obligation. The second is that these heritages do not—or at least frequently do not—base their advocacy of an ethic on the particularity (i.e., indigeneity) of a language and culture, although those particularities may well be why an ethic is compelling to those who live in this heritage. Such counter-viewpoints, values, or ideals are often defended as universal in their reach, which in turn means that we should not only take them seriously: we should seriously consider them as a possibly more integrative way of thinking about freedom and obligation, equality, and freedom than those offered to us in even the best philosophical traditions of European and Anglo-American constructions of those ideals. It is the second step that is too rarely taken. Thus the call for translation is also a call to judgment, including a call to judgment about the value of Anglo-American traditions of freedom and equality. But this call to judgment should not be mistaken with either a simple-minded moralism or the romanticism of going native ("they have it right, we have it wrong").

Rather, the call to judgment recognizes that there is a complex terrain of competing universals; that if we actually engage in that terrain, assuming the notational equality of other intellectual heritages, then we may be called to change and revise our own ideals, as we engage with the universals of others and with other universals. Only then are we taking seriously the idea that other cultures, or what I am calling *intellectual heritages*, offer universal justifications that put a demand on us to both translate them and to engage them in such a way that we are open to a shift and a challenge to the hegemony of Eurocentric philosophy.

More specifically, in this chapter I will examine how uBuntu offers us a notion of freedom that is certainly different from the main definitions of freedom that feminists in the West have often taken for granted, and yet still is an ethic of freedom. Saba Mahmood raises the following question for us:

> How does one rethink the question of individual freedom in a context where the distinction between the subject's own desires and socially prescribed performances cannot be so easily presumed, and where submission to certain forms of (external) authority is a condition for the self to achieve its potentiality? What kind of politics would be deemed desirable and viable in discursive traditions that regard conventions (socially prescribed performances) as necessary to the self's realization?[16]

uBuntu does indeed take certain socially prescribed performances as necessary to self-realization. To draw out the relationship between uBuntu, freedom, and obligation, I will first discuss an important constitutional judgment on succession, and then give an interpretation of the autobiography of a lesbian activist who is also a practicing sangoma. A sangoma is a spiritual leader of the highest order, and accepted as such by most of the tribal affiliations in South Africa. To begin to address the complex ethic of uBuntu, I will examine an actual and controversial case that came before the South African Constitutional Court—the *Bhe* case.[17]

UBUNTU, OBLIGATION, AND SUCCESSION: THE *BHE* CASE

Bhe actually involves three cases: Bhe, Shibi, and an application for direct access to the court by the South African Human Rights Commission and the Women's Legal Center Trust. I now offer a short summary of these cases and will start with *Bhe*. Ms. Bhe and the deceased had lived together as husband and wife for twelve years. They had two girl-children; both of whom were minors at the time of their father's death. The deceased died without a will, and during their life together as husband and wife, they had acquired immovable property in Khayelitsha (a township of Cape Town), in which they lived together, and in which Ms. Bhe and her daughters continued to live after her husband's death. After his son's death, the father of Ms. Bhe's partner claimed that he was the administrator and sole heir of the estate in terms of African Customary Law because there were no sons born in the marriage. Further, he wanted to sell the property in order to cover the funeral expenses for his son's funeral, even though Ms. Bhe and the daughters were still in residence. The magistrate of Khayelitsha appointed the father as administrator and sole heir of the property. The magistrate arrived at this judgment through an appeal to the Black Administration Act (BAA)—a notorious piece of legislation that was passed during the apartheid era—which gave recognition to the principle of male primogeniture.

In the *Shibi* case, the applicant's brother had also died without a will, had no children, and was not survived by parents or grandparents. Because she was a female, she was excluded from inheriting under the same notorious Act, and her brother's estate passed to the closest male cousin. Both the South African Human Rights Commission and the Women's Legal Center Trust applied for direct access to the Constitutional Court, acting in their own and in the public interest. They sought to strike down the whole of section 23 of the BAA—which deals with succession and inheritance of deceased African people—as unconstitutional because of its inconsistency with section 9 (the equality clause), section 10 (the dignity clause), and section 28 (that guarantees the rights of children). The two issues before the Constitutional Court were then the validity of section 23 of the BAA, as well as whether the rule of primogeniture was constitutional as it was codified not only in the BAA but in other sources of the written customary law.

The High Court declared section 23 of the BAA to be fundamentally unconstitutional and against the spirit of uBuntu because the rule of primogeniture denied women their full humanity. The High Court also found section 23 of the BAA to be racist and fundamentally against the Constitution. The judge struck down section 23 of the BAA not only because it was unconstitutional but because it was against the spirit of uBuntu. But he also found that not only was the BAA against the spirit of uBuntu, but the rule of primogeniture in the written customary law which would replace section 23 once it was struck down, was against uBuntu as well. The Constitutional Court also held that section 3 of the BAA was fundamentally unconstitutional and in violation of a number of sections of the Constitution. The Constitutional Court further held that the exclusion of women and extra-marital children from the status of heir under the principle of primogeniture in the written customary law violated the equality clause (section 9), as well as the dignity clause (section 10). It ruled further that the Intestate Succession Act as altered to make provision for polygamous unions should replace the impugned section 23 of the BAA until Parliament had a chance to act.

In his dissenting judgment, Justice Ngcobo firmly agreed that section 23 of the BAA was one of the pillars of the apartheid legal order, and that it must be struck down. His disagreement with the majority judgment might seem to be a small one at first. Justice Ngcobo argued that until Parliament could act, the rule of primogeniture should be developed and not simply struck down. Under section 39 of the Constitution, the courts have a mandate to develop both the customary and the common law in accordance with the purpose and the spirit of the Constitution. Thus Justice Ngcobo argued strongly that the Constitutional Court should develop customary law, not simply strike it down, as this is crucial to giving recognition to the customary law. Furthermore, it places customary law as being on par in the new Constitutional dispensation to the English common law and the Roman Dutch private law. He also held, against the majority, that minor children could be justifiably refused the status of heir under the limitations clause (section 36). In the South African Constitution, no right remains supreme. To quote section 36:

> 1) The rights in the Bill of Rights may be limited only in terms of law of general application to the extent that the limitation is reasonable and justifiable in an open and democratic society based on human dignity, equality and freedom, taking into account all relevant factors, including: a) the nature of the right; b) the importance of the purpose of the limitation; c) the nature and extent of the limitation; d) the relation between the limitation and its purpose; and e) less restrictive means to achieve the purpose. 2) Except as provided in subsection 1) or in any other provision of the Constitution, no law may limit any right entrenched in the Bill of Rights.

We will return shortly to Justice Ngcobo's limitations analysis in more detail. For now, let me just stress that for Ngcobo, the limitations of the rights of children could be justified in this way, precisely because the family's successor had to be old enough to fulfill the obligations, including caring for his or her entire family. But what lies at the heart of the seeming small legal issue—whether or not the Intestate Succession Act should be the law until parliament could act—actually implies a huge ethical question. To quote Justice Ngcobo's dissent:

> A sense of community prevailed from which developed an elaborate system of reciprocal duties and obligations among the family members. This is manifest in the concept of *uBuntu—umuntu ngumuntu ngabantu*—a dominant value in African traditional culture. This concept encapsulates communality and the interdependence of the members of a community. As Langa DCJ put it, it is a culture which "regulates the exercise of rights by the emphasis that it lays on sharing and co-responsibility and the mutual enjoyment of rights." It is this system of reciprocal duties and obligations that ensured that every family member had access to basic necessities of life such as food, clothing, shelter, and healthcare.[18]

As Justice Ngcobo argues, inheritance and succession under African customary law are completely different rationalities in terms of the division of estates. In African customary law, as Justice Ngcobo points out, the main matter is not the division of the property of the deceased. In agricultural societies, succession had as its primary goal the maintenance of the family, and the one who succeeded the deceased did not inherit *property*, which was often owned in common; he inherited the responsibility to take care of all of his family and to make sure that their wellbeing was maintained. To quote Ngcobo:

> The concept of succession in indigenous law must be understood in the context of indigenous law itself. When dealing with indigenous law every attempt should be made to avoid the tendency of construing indigenous law concepts in the light of common law concepts or concepts foreign to indigenous law. There are obvious dangers in such an approach. These two systems of law developed in two different situations, under different cultures and in response to different conditions.[19]

Formerly, in an agricultural society, the demand that the head of the household remain in the family homestead led to the exclusion of women from taking the status as successors, as women were thought to marry and leave the family homestead. Whatever the reasons for justifying primogeniture in agricultural societies, those reasons are no longer applicable to "modern" rural or urban societies. This inapplicability is due both to the fact that under apartheid, women were forced into the workplace, and to the struggle for the rights of women. Thus, Ngcobo powerfully argues that the living customary law should be developed so as to remove the defect of male primogeniture. To quote Ngcobo again:

> The defect in the rule of male primogeniture is that it excludes women from being considered for succession to the deceased family head. In this regard it deviates from section 9(3) of the Constitution. It needs to be developed so as to bring it in line with our Bill of Rights. This can be achieved by removing the reference to a male so as to allow an eldest daughter to succeed to the deceased estate.[20]

The ethical significance of Justice Ngcobo's dissent is twofold: first, he insists that indigenous law has a very different notion of community than that represented in the Intestate Succession Act. That notion of community in the living customary law must be respected and therefore developed, rather than simply struck down and replaced by a system of inheritance that is completely foreign to indigenous law. Secondly, the living customary law (as opposed to the law written down by foreign officials) is dynamic and indeed, has been transforming itself in accordance with the constitutional demand for the respect of dignity and equality of women. Thus, it needs to be developed to respect its very dynamism. Some feminists received the majority judgment as a great victory, but many black women on the ground powerfully argued that it was a violent imposition on the dynamic system of living customary law; that it completely failed to grapple with the difference between inheritance and succession; and that with its different understanding of the relation between succession and inheritance the court failed to grasp the relationship between freedom and obligation in the living customary law.[21] Indeed, the conflation of the indigenous practice which upheld that the eldest male son would be the one to step into his father's shoes with all of his obligations, as the rule of primogeniture, was itself criticized as a misunderstanding of this practice. Primogeniture was a narrow English rule, which was about inheritance, not obligation, and had as its main goal the maintenance of as much land as possible in the hands of the main heir. But it was not a system of obligation, and therefore, to even identify these two practices is mistaken. More importantly, for the feminist critical of the decision, there are significant signs on the ground that changes are being made in the practice of succession, so that women can indeed become the ones to succeed to all of the obligations of their family. In like manner, women can now receive lobola, which is a wealth exchange upon marriage, while in preconstitutional times only the father or senior male relative could receive lobola for the woman. Justice Ngcobo's plea was to respect indigenous law and let indigenous law correct the defect of gender inequality, or have the Constitutional Court itself develop that law. That there were resources within the law to do so is demonstrated by the High Court decision in which the law of primogeniture was challenged as against uBuntu, because it violated the full humanity of women and of extra-marital children.

Both Justice Ngcobo in his dissent and Justice Langa in his majority judgment refer to uBuntu as one of the most important values underlying the idea of familial obligations, inseparable from the idea of succession. But we need to turn now to the meaning of uBuntu as it was appealed to as an important resource for correcting the defect of gender inequality in the indigenous law. In uBuntu, to paraphrase Justice Ngcobo, human beings are intertwined in a world of ethical relations and obligations from the time they are born. This inscription is part of our finitude. We are born into a language, a kinship group, a tribe, a nation, a family. But this inscription cannot simply be reduced to a social fact. We come into a world obligated to others and these others are obligated to us, to support us in finding our way to becoming a unique and singular person. Thus, it is a profound misunderstanding of uBuntu to confuse it with Anglo-American concepts of communitarianism. It is only through the engagement and support of others that we are able to realize a true individuality, and rise above our mere biological distinctiveness.

HOW TO THINK ABOUT THE ETHIC OF UBUNTU

Famously, at birth in the Xhosa and Zulu traditions, the baby's umbilical cord is buried and the place of burial marks the beginning of one's journey to become a person. This achievement of singularity is always a project that is inseparable from the ethical obligations to which one is tethered in one form or another from the beginning of life. We could say that the person is ethically intertwined by others from the beginning. But this intertwinement does not constitute who we are or who we might become. Instead, we must find a way in which to realize our singularity as a unique person. In that singularity, we become someone who will define our own ethical responsibilities as we grow into our personhood. If a community then is committed to individuation and the achievement of a unique destiny for each person, often reflected in the individual's name, but not determined by the name, then the person in turn is obligated to enhance the community that supports him or her; not simply as an abstract duty correlated with a right, but as a form of participation that allows the community to strive for fidelity to difference and singularity; what D. A. Masolo has called "participatory difference."[22] For Masolo, this participatory difference recognizes that each one of us is indeed different from all others. Part of this difference is that we are also called to make a difference, by contributing to the creation and sustenance of a humane and ethical community.

For the great African philosopher Kwasi Wiredu, participatory difference includes the principle of sympathetic impartiality as we seek to imagine ourselves and others as uniquely singular beings. Sympathetic impartiality in this unique meaning calls us not to seek likeness, but to imagine others in their difference from us and in their singularity. For Kwasi Wiredu, this principle is one that could only develop in association with others and as part of our ethical and moral training in our journey to become a person. The problem then of how we can develop such a connection to otherness is explained in part because we are always already ethically entwined with others, and they are in a profound sense a part of ourselves. Critics of uBuntu—including critics who conflate uBuntu with outdated modes of social cohesion and hierarchy—make the mistake of reducing uBuntu to an ethical ontology of a purportedly shared world. What is missed in this criticism is precisely the activism that is inherent in participatory difference. uBuntu clearly has an aspirational and an ideal edge. There is no end to the struggle to bring about a humane world, and to become a person in that humane world who makes a difference in it.

Professor Mabogo P. More brings together different aspects of uBuntu in his own profound yet succinct definition:

In one sense, uBuntu is a philosophical concept forming the basis of relationships, especially ethical behaviour. In another sense, it is a traditional politico-ideological concept referring to socio-political action. As a moral or ethical concept, it is a point of view according to which moral practices are founded exclusively on consideration and enhancement of human well-being; a preoccupation with "human." It enjoins that what is morally good is what brings dignity, respect, contentment, and prosperity to others, self, and the community at large. uBuntu is a demand for respect for persons no matter what their circumstances may be . . . In its politico-ideological sense it is a principle for all forms of social or political relationships. It enjoins and peace and social harmony by encouraging the practice of sharing in all forms of communal existence.[23]

As an ethical as well as politico-ideological concept, then, uBuntu always entails a social bond, but one that is always in the course of being reshaped by the ethical demands it puts on its participants. uBuntu in a profound sense encapsulates the moral obligations for human beings who must live together. It implies a fundamental moralization of social relationships, and this moralization of social relationships is the one unchanging aspect of uBuntu, instructing us that we can never escape from this ethical world that we share together. But the actual demands of uBuntu must change, since uBuntu is inseparable from a relationship between human beings, yet it is also connected to how we are always changing in those relations and our need of changing with them. The aspirational aspect of uBuntu is that we must strive together to achieve the public good in a shared world so that we can both survive and flourish, each one of us in his or her singularity. It is uBuntu's embeddedness in our relationships that makes it a transformative concept at its core, but this transformation can never be taken away from the moralization of social relationships. It would have been absurd five hundred years ago if uBuntu demanded access to electricity, since there was no access to electricity at all. Now, however, it is not at all absurd to make such an argument because electricity is integral to securing a human life in modern society.

Thus it is not surprising that uBuntu is often hailed in the new counter-hegemonic movements that are challenging the neoliberal policies of the African National Congress in their demand for an ethical politics. It has been commonplace since the pathbreaking work of V. Y. Mudimbe that Africa has been invented, but invented through actual and philosophical struggles of what Africa can or should be in modernity.[24] It would be a mistake under Mudimbe's idea of invention to argue that there is no such thing as Africa, or African social thought, and I have been suggesting that uBuntu is certainly part of South African social and political philosophy as well as part of its law.

Although it is beyond the scope of this chapter to address Achille Mbembe's argument, I do want to stress here that uBuntu is a principle of Afro-modernity and can best be understood as the African principle of transcendence for the individual and for the law of the social bond. Thus it would be a serious mistake to reduce uBuntu to the crypto-radicalism or naïve nativism that Mbembe characterizes as a primary mode of African self-writing that is unable to ascend to the status of universality:

> The emphasis on establishing and "African interpretation" of things, on creating one's own schemata of self-mastery, of understanding oneself and the universe, of producing endogenous knowledge have all led to demands for an "African science," and "African democracy," and "African language." This urge to make Africa unique is presented as a moral and political problem, the re-conquest of the power to narrate one's own story—and therefore identity—seeming to be necessarily constitutive of any subjectivity. Ultimately, it is no longer a matter of claiming the status of alter ego for Africans in the world, but rather of asserting loudly and forcefully their alterity.[25]

There are two important general points to make in relation to dominant Western notions of the social contract as these differ from uBuntu. Feminists have criticized neoliberal notions of freedom as well as Kant's notion of equality, and yet, as Saba Mahmood points out, we remain dangerously ensnared in these notions. The notion of freedom as lack of restraint can only accept the social bond, and a legal system, because without law we would exist in a world of horrific violence and brutality. Thus for Thomas Hobbes, for example, we can yield authority to the Leviathan, so long as it protects our basic rights and provides us with basic security and a world of stability, so we can know what to expect.[26]

In Kant, of course, because it is at least a practical possibility that human beings can postulate themselves as autonomous in that they can lay down a law unto themselves, we might be able to represent ourselves as free from the pull of our day-to-day desires that drive us and indeed knock us about like bits of flotsam and jetsam. The relationship of the realm of internal freedom, of morality, and the realm of external freedom of right has long been debated in Kantian scholarship.[27] But clearly, there must be a connection between the two realms. If there were no connection, then there would be no ground for the realm of external freedom in which we can imagine how we can coordinate our ends with one another in a way that is consistent with each other's freedom. Kant's hypothetical experiment in the imagination, in which we can configure the conditions in which human beings aspire to the great ideal of the Kingdom of Ends, turns on the possibility that as creatures of practical reason, we can harmonize our interests and do so in accordance with our freedom.[28]

The dignity of human beings, for Kant, is precisely to be found in the possibility offered to us by our practical reason: to aspire to live together, guided by the great ideal of the Kingdom of Ends. However, even the great Kantian hypothetical experiment of the imagination in which we can configure the ideal conditions of a social contract rooted in the respect for the freedom of other human beings still begins with imagined individuals, even if moral individuals. It is still individuals that agree to accept some degree of coercion, even if rooted in the basic understanding of Kant's notion of right, which is that individuals are allowed the greatest possible space for their freedom as long as it allows for the freedom of others within the social contract. As Mahmood points out, as different as these European conceptions are, they both root freedom in the individual. Thus he or she succumbs to the greater interest of security, or alternatively, transcends her day-to-day desires. In uBuntu, the social bond is not one that proceeds from our personal life through an imaginary social contract. Nor is our freedom separable from the ethical relationships in which we are interpellated, yet which at the same time support us in the ethical journey to become a person.

As Mabogo P. More emphasizes, uBuntu is not only an ethical concept, but also an ideological and a political one, which insists that democracy should not be understood primarily as an engagement with the representational apparatus of the state, but is instead found in face-to-face participation.[29] Therefore uBuntu underwrites a political ethic, which for example has been echoed in the word adopted by the Shack Dwellers—"Abahlalism," which means: "the people together."[30] There is clearly no split in uBuntu between the phenomenal and the noumenal as there is in Kant, and thus uBuntu is not in the strict Kantian sense a regulative ideal, even if it has an aspirational edge.

uBuntu is materialized in ethical actions, which has often led to the charge that it is vague. More specifically, it is materialized in the struggles of individuals in conflict. This enactment of uBuntu materializes a more humane world. There are several philosophical points important to the debates in Anglo-American and Western-European feminism here, in that care and dignity or care and justice are not separable. Some Western feminists have contrasted the two conceptions, while others have argued that they are not incompatible.[31] In uBuntu, they are integral to one another. First, to respect the dignity of a person is to respect her in her singularity, and in her material existence, not to respect her in her abstract equality. And this respect will change its demands in regard to the circumstances. Second, feminists have criticized the notion of the independent individual whose freedom is an individual attribute, either ideal or otherwise.[32] As Mahmood reminds us, we need to ask the question how we can think about freedom as other than these two conceptions (and I would also add, as she does, the Foucauldian notion of freedom as resistance). Then it would no longer be a matter of thinking freedom either as the basis of an abstract morality, as lack of restraint, or as resistance to hegemonic norms, but instead as an activist ethic that can only be realized in and through ethical relations to other people. Thus it is freedom through obligation, even if it includes the freedom to be oneself, through the support of others, rather than against that support. Freedom through other people is underscored by uBuntu, which is undoubtedly why uBuntu, as mentioned earlier, has become one basis of constitutional justifications by the South African Constitutional Court of socio-economic rights in the name of freedom for all.

It is precisely this idea of freedom through others that Justice Ngcobo underscores in his dissenting argument in *Bhe*. In living African customary law, no one has the freedom to take the money and run. Instead, the successor is in a profound sense the guarantor of the wellbeing and in that sense of the freedom to flourish of all those in his or her family. Let me stress here that it is a serious error to designate the living customary law as premodern. It is as modern as the other sources of law in South Africa, such as the British common law and the Roman-Dutch law. Anthropologists John and Jean Comaroff have argued that the living customary law is best understood as vernacular law, in order to avoid the mistake of contrasting it as a premodern form of law to other forms of law.[33] What is significant in South Africa is that all other sources of law have to be rendered consistent with the Constitution, including the living customary law. At stake in this debate is the question how the customary law should be developed, and not whether or not it is modern and a valid source of law.

INTERPRETING THE AUTOBIOGRAPHY
OF AN ACTIVIST LESBIAN SANGOMA

I stress the modernity of the living customary law to make a further point, which, as I state in the opening of this chapter, is underscored by Judith

Butler in her call for translating universals. In his powerful, hard-hitting book, *First as Tragedy, Then as Farce*,[34] Slavoj Žižek reminds us that we must be thoroughly modern. He uses the example of how the slaves in Haiti sang the Marseillaise, and by so doing enacted universality as a political category, and also profoundly shook the soldiers who were fighting against them, making them wonder if they were on the wrong side. Žižek rightly warns us against any kind of facile notion of "multiversality" or even multiple modernities. He suggests that colonial powers often engage with delight in singing the fight songs of the colonized. Of course, to do so would mean that the colonizers had actually mastered the languages of the colonized, and at least in South Africa a minuscule number of whites speak any language other than English and Afrikaans, while the black majority frequently speaks both English and Afrikaans in addition to other languages. Žižek's point is well-taken, however, that at crucial moments in an emancipatory struggle, the taking up of what is best in the European tradition does indeed shift that tradition. My only point is that it can also go the other way, in which the mobilization of non-European intellectual heritages, and even the battle over language, can also enact a political universality. Think for example of the Soweto uprising, which is commemorated on "Youth Day," where hundreds of thousands of children refused to be educated in Afrikaans, the language of the group that they saw as the primary oppressor. This uprising did indeed enact a political universality, in which the particularity claiming to be the language of education was challenged, not simply by arguing that Xhosa should be the name of education for Xhosa speakers, but in the name of freedom of education, and of the struggle against the institutions of apartheid more generally. So although we need to worry about simplistic language of tolerance and facile notions of diversity, we also have to follow Butler in recognizing that the incompleteness of universality means that political universality can be enacted in different struggles through appeals to non-European values and ideals as much as to European ones. Both will have the effect of changing the intellectual heritages toward political universality.

So my argument for uBuntu—and I have made this argument extensively elsewhere[35]—is not simply that it is African, but that it claims a universality that should be taken seriously in the development of any nonviolent ethic and the political alliances of transnational feminism.

So far, I have been talking about uBuntu from a philosophical and legal perspective. But is the idea of freedom underwritten by uBuntu actually a resource for women's freedom in on-the-ground struggles? To answer that question I will turn to the autobiography of a lesbian sangoma whose political practice was rooted in uBuntu and who became one of the leaders in the South African struggle for gay and lesbian marriage. Sangomas are spiritual healers, who undergo a rigorous, often life-threatening training period, and are regarded as major resources for recovery from both psychic and physical illnesses; they also play a major role in day-to-day conflict resolution in both the townships and countryside. If they are not part of the written customary law of South Africa, or even officially part of the living customary law because they have no enforcement power by the state, they are certainly part of the people's informal law both in townships and rural areas. But how does the role of the sangoma relate to the idea that freedom can be found in an endless reworking of ethical obligations, into which one is born and yet is constantly empowered to shape and reconfigure, given one's own unique difference, where each person is called to "participate differently" given her or his own singularity?

Sangomas often see themselves as the upholders of uBuntu under the very difficult conditions of liberation under neoliberal capitalism.[36] A sangoma may seem to be someone whose life is as far away as possible from the idea of freedom of choice, since her rigorous training obligates her to devote her life to her ancestors and to her community. There are at least four stages in the training of a sangoma after one is called, which is a very confusing time, and often brings a person to the point of nervous breakdown. The first stage is when your primary ancestor or ancestress possesses you and you know who he or she is. Depending on the specificity of different trainings, these may or may not be bloodline ancestors. The second stage is a stage of dancing, in which one learns how to welcome ancestors. The third stage is one of the most difficult, in which one not only learns how to welcome ancestors and ancestresses, but to cleanse them of the weaknesses they had when they were alive. For example, if your primary ancestor was an abuser of women, you must cleanse him of that abuse, as part of learning both to live with the ancestor, to negotiate with him, and to change him. This part of the practice can at times take years. The last trial involves a series of ordeals in which all areas of the training are tested. A sangoma is not allowed to take money for her services, although she is allowed to be paid for the materials she needs for her work.

Black Bull, Ancestors and Me: My Life as a Lesbian Sangoma, the autobiography of Nkunzi Zandile Nkabinde—a sangoma who is an out lesbian and an organizer of same-sex sangoma associations—demonstrates the complex play between roots in an intellectual heritage and identity and the struggle for the political universality she evoked in her defense of gay and lesbian marriage.[37] Zandile is a strong supporter of the new constitutional dispensation, and she is a tour guide at Constitutional Hill. Zandile was born as a twin, which in Zulu culture comes with dire consequences, sometimes even death. Her twin brother died at birth and Zandile was raised without any knowledge of him, only having access to his spirit when she became a sangoma. Zandile was taken to KwaZulu Natal to live with her mother's ancestors so that she could be kept safe from what might have been an early death, given that she was a twin. Her mother worked primarily as a domestic worker and her father was a long-distance truck driver who was often away from home. Her mother took her to live with her when she was eight in an overcrowded shack in the Meadowlands, and Zandile remembers being raped by her uncle at the age of eight. Her parents' marriage was difficult, and ultimately the father deserted the family. Zandile's description of her early years tracks the brutality of apartheid. From an early age, Zandile knew she was different and came out as an open lesbian in high school. It was coming out to her mother, however, that truly freed her to become herself sexually. To quote Zandile: "After telling my mother, I felt completely free to be myself. I accepted that I was a lesbian and I was not afraid of anyone. I shaved my head and became a tomboy. At weddings and other ceremonies where boys and girls were separated, I would stand on the side of the boys."[38] As she explains, her sexuality was not something given to her by the ancestors, it was something that she took as crucial to who she was: "I feel my sexuality was with me from birth. It is not from my ancestors, but my ancestors supported me. When I was a child I didn't have a choice."[39]

Zandile's big dream was to become a journalist, but as it turned out, she felt that the ancestors had other plans for her. Like many sangomas who are called, her first experience with the ancestors was one that led her to feel she was losing her sanity, and she actually ended up in a mental hospital. After her sisters took her to a sangoma, the sangoma told her that she was not crazy but was simply called to follow the arduous journey to become a sangoma. As I have already discussed, the first step in training is when your primary ancestor reveals himself or herself to you. Zandile's primary ancestor was a Zulu man named Nkunzi, which means "black bull." After he presented himself to her as her primary ancestor, she took his name, following Zulu ritual, and from now on I will refer to her as Nkunzi.

> There were many sides to Nkunzi. He was a Zulu man, a dictator who made the rules and expected people to obey; he liked to drink traditional beer and expected his wives to serve him; he was a fighter who could be abusive and even violent at times; and he liked the company of women. He was also a dreamer who would withdraw from human company and spend hours, sometimes days, in silence.[40]

Nkunzi describes how her ancestor was extremely difficult at times, and how it was a huge effort for her to struggle with him. Nkunzi the ancestor was not only a stubborn Zulu man, he was the sort that was unused to listening to women. So part of the difficult process for the living Nkunzi was learning how to take the abuse out of her ancestor and indeed to cure him of his sexism so she could get a word in. This is perhaps one of the least understood aspects of being a sangoma in a relationship to the ancestors, for they are not only supposed to control the ancestors but also to help them get rid of the negative characteristics which they may possess, such as abuse towards women. Here we find a profound complexity between certain ideals like freedom and equality for women and the practice of ancestor worship. Thus in a sense, the struggle to become a full human being, one capable of uBuntu, does not end with death, but becomes a joint undertaking with the one whose body the primary ancestor possesses.

Although Nkunzi is the living Nkunzi's primary ancestor, she has successfully struggled for him to let other ancestors in, including female ancestresses. This stage of learning to engage with the ancestors is indeed one of the most trying and difficult stages of becoming a sangoma. Due to Nkunzi having a primary male ancestor who is more often with her than not, her body actually changes in accordance with her possession. So for example, when Nkunzi is with her she stops menstruating and grows a beard, and her voice changes. It is now commonplace to argue that the sex-gender is symbolically and socially constructed, but here we are talking about a very different concept of the limits of the body, for Nkunzi's body is not drawn simply by the outlines of her flesh. When the ancestor Nkunzi is with her, she takes on the male characteristics of her ancestor and indeed, since Nkunzi was sexually active, the two of them often argue over who the living Nkunzi is to have sex with—who gets to pick the partner. Both Nkunzi's prefer women. Other African feminists have noted that this is a very different conception of bodily limitation and bodily boundaries than ones associated with Anglo-American notions that "this body is mine" and is separated from others by the surfaces of the skin.[41]

Nkunzi does have female ancestresses, and when they are with her, her period begins again and she takes on a different voice and a more feminine manner of being. However, as she jokes, she is always a lesbian. A number of African feminists have pointed to how masculine and feminine do not have the contained—even if socially constructed—meanings of one sexed body, precisely because of the complexities of spiritual possession, so that one can be primarily a man one week and primarily a woman the next week.[42] We have already seen, for example, that Nkunzi's body actually changes in its physicality when she is possessed by a different ancestor or ancestress. In a profound sense, then, Nkunzi lives her life as a transgendered person. But the basis of that transgendering is rooted in her ancestor engagement. That said, she is also a militant supporter of the rights of the transgendered, as well as of those of gays and lesbians, whether or not the transgendered share in her own life process of becoming "trans."

Through her work with GALA, Gay And Lesbian Archives, Nkunzi interviewed a number of same-sex sangomas in order to create an archive of how common it was for there to be gay and lesbian sangomas in Zulu life. But in her own life, her trainer as a sangoma deeply resisted Nkunzi's celebration of her life as a lesbian. In fact, when she took her on as a trainee she promised her family that in the process of becoming a sangoma, Nkunzi would be cured of her lesbianism. Through her work with GALA, Nkunzi had become so "out" that her training sangoma felt it necessary to call her to account in front of the elders, and insist that she change her sexuality or at the very least hide it. But Nkunzi stood up to her trainer: "I told her being a lesbian was as African as being a straight person,"[43] and even the elders could not convince her to closet her sexuality, as she told them her mother had accepted her and gave her the freedom to be who she was and she had no intention of ever hiding her sexuality. Finally, her training sangoma gave in, and accepted, in part in the name of uBuntu, that Nkunzi should be allowed to live out her sexuality. But the encounter led Nkunzi to organize groups of same-sex sangomas so that they would have a chance to support each other. Indeed, for Nkunzi this work of bringing people together is part and parcel of her work as a sangoma that embodies the ethic of uBuntu.

I realise that our organization must continue because there will always be this tension in the Sangomas community. Today there are 40 same-sex Sangomas aged between 18–34 in my organization. When we get together we talk about the herbs we are using and what we are using them for and when we go to ceremonies we don't feel isolated. I wanted people to feel connected, not rejected. In this we have been successful.[44]

Part of the work of the same-sex sangomas organization has been to take a clear stand that the constitutional right for gays, lesbians, and the transgendered to be allowed to legally marry is consistent with the living customary law. Nkunzi had an arranged marriage set up by the ancestor Nkunzi, with a much older woman. At first she balked at this marriage, feeling no desire for this woman whatsoever, but her ancestor insisted that she go through with the marriage because this woman was not going to live much longer and would transfer her powers to her. In her interviews with other same-sex sangomas it became clear that some did not even identify or think of themselves as lesbians. In her case the ancestral wife was not a lover, but in other cases the ancestral wife *is* a lover and therefore, for a woman to openly live with another woman as her wife is a part of Zulu living customary law. This flexibility then when it comes to same-sex marriage is built into the complex relationship of one's "sex" to one's ancestors. Thus the space was open for same-sex sangomas to make an argument that the living customary law of the Zulus had always accepted same-sex marriage, and therefore it should be an easy step to accept the constitutional right of all gays, lesbians, and the transgendered to marry. Thus they openly fought with CONTRALESA, the established association of traditional leaders, who were opposed to same-sex marriage, and who referred to the customary law to support their anti–gay and lesbian marriage position. It is important to note that Nkunzi takes being Zulu very seriously and yet is able to question certain Zulu rituals such as virginity testing. As she writes:

> For example, there is a part of me that believes in virginity testing. My ancestor, Nkunzi, also influences my beliefs. For Nkunzi, virginity testing is a way of keeping Zulu culture alive. Nkunzi believes in keeping power in the hands of the elders because they are the ones who know what is best for the community. When I look around at the young girls of these days who are getting pregnant by different fathers at the age of 14 or 16 or 18, and when I see the way that AIDS is spreading like a fire in the youth, I understand what Nkunzi is seeing and I think that

> virginity testing could also be a good thing. Then on the other side I un-
> derstand that because of our Constitution, girls have certain rights and
> virginity testing stands in the way of those rights. Because I have these
> different sides in me I can see the traditional way and the modern way;
> I can see the way of a Zulu man and I can see why some women—
> especially gender activists—have a problem with virginity testing.[45]

The struggle then is to see the complexity, and to recognize how "tradition"
is always in the process of changing and developing, not only in accordance
with the new constitutional dispensation, but also within the changing circumstances in which sangomas must interact.

We need to stop for a moment to underscore two points. The first is that,
as we have seen, ancestor worship—as it is at times often referred to by those
who do not practice it—is much better understood as *engagement* with the
ancestors. Famously, writers who are suspicious of ancestor worship and advocate a liberal cosmopolitanism as the preferred identity for a sophisticated
modern person, find that this kind of "worship" is a form of a straitjacket
that ties the individual to the past and to a narrow sense of identity. But as
we have seen, Nkunzi the sangoma has actually helped Nkunzi the ancestor
rid himself of his abusive sexist ways so that even as dead he can respect the
rights provided by the new constitution. Here again we see the complex play
between modern ideals and Zulu ritual practices, in that the new Constitution is a thoroughly modern document, and one that Nkunzi advocates
must be brought to her ancestors. Further, the ancestors support Nkunzi in
her sexuality. Of course, her open life as a lesbian sangoma further opens
spaces for different ways of being human that must be recognized and accepted by the community: "My ancestors helped me to become who I was.
They guided me knowing that I was going to grow up being the way I am.
My sexuality is from childhood."[46]

Second, nothing in this complex engagement with the ancestors who
themselves must be modernized necessarily ties you to the past or straitjack-
ets you in a static identity. Remember that Nkunzi works as a tour guide
in Constitutional Hill. In this work she always makes it clear to those she
guides through some of the worst remains of the brutal past of apartheid
that it is a mistake to dwell on the past in the sense of victimization, but
that instead the journey through Constitutional Hill is precisely a reminder
of the past so that we can build a better future together. Nkunzi's ancestor

engagement, then, is one of struggle and support, but perhaps most importantly, one that allows her to be free to be who she is as a Zulu, a lesbian, and a sangoma. This is not identity as a straitjacket but as a journey to realize your own personhood and singularity. Yet as I argued at the outset, if freedom is understood primarily as choice, Nkunzi's life would seem to have little to do with freedom. One cannot *not* choose to be a sangoma: if one is called one cannot refuse the call. Nor is Nkunzi's life, as she herself puts it, lived primarily for herself: "My life is not only for me, it is also for my ancestor, Nkunzi. When I am about to dance before a ceremony, when I am in my spiritual way, I praise Nkunzi. It is him who is talking, he is praising himself using my body. It is him talking, expressing love for himself."[47] The reigning liberal notions of freedom seem incompatible with Nkunzi's life. But Nkunzi clearly writes that with her mother's acceptance she was free to be herself and that this freedom includes her acceptance of the calling to be a sangoma. Even the term *self-realization* does not quite reach this other notion of freedom, because it still turns on something that is rooted in the self. Freedom in this sense is the freedom to become who you are, and as we have seen in the discussion of uBuntu, it involves a highly ethical journey to become your own person as you are supported by others and support others. So in a profound sense, Nkunzi was free to become herself with the support of her mother and with the support of her ancestors. Without such support she would have been thwarted in her journey to become a modern African woman, a Zulu, a lesbian, and a sangoma.

Obviously, uBuntu implies a very different way of thinking about freedom and obligation—different even from that offered by Kant—in which freedom and obligation are integrally tied together. Am I advocating that we entirely replace notions of Kantian freedom, or indeed the project of freedom more widely defended in German idealism, and later, in the writing of Karl Marx? Obviously not, since I myself remain a socialist and take very seriously the idea of rethinking communism. But what I *am* advocating, in accordance with some of the most searing insights of Butler and Spivak, is that we allow ourselves to engage with competing ideals of freedom, and indeed open ourselves to their significance, so that we may actually be able to form transnational alliances that can accept that there are competing universals, concerning the most important ideals. uBuntu is one such ethic, and as we have seen, it is often integrally tied to struggles for social and economic transformation.[48] We have to risk this openness that demands that we drop our defenses, so as to allow for a truly contested terrain of different meanings of such great ideals as freedom. Only by dropping our defenses can we hope to enter a transnational feminist coalition that does not fall into the kind of violence Gayatri Spivak constantly warns us, in which poor women of the Global South are reduced to objects of our imposed meanings.

8

Is There a Difference That Makes a Difference between Dignity and uBuntu?

In South Africa, legal and philosophical scholarship frequently draws sharp contrasts between dignity and uBuntu. In this chapter I want to challenge some of the assumptions that underlie these sharp contrasts. I will also argue, however, that there is a *difference that makes a difference* between uBuntu and dignity, and that this difference is important in the continuing struggle for a truly *new* South Africa, particularly in efforts to challenge the neoliberal policies of the African National Congress (ANC) undertaken on a daily basis by on-the-ground movements. Legally, uBuntu is important, as would be expected, in the arena of socio-economic rights—but not just there. Both uBuntu and dignity have been deployed in the battle to maintain an "outside" to the capitalization of all human relationships. I will argue that uBuntu, rather than dignity, may well serve as the more adequate opposition to the drive to turn all human relationships into commodities and cash them out for their value in the marketplace.

Think for example of the *Dikoko* decision.[1] There, Justices Sachs and Mokgoro both rely on uBuntu to argue that what was at stake in the violation of reputation was not money but rather the reconciliation of the individuals involved—and indeed, that the long accepted idea that money is the appropriate award for personal injury actually exacerbated the damage to the relationships between the parties to the lawsuit.

But I am getting ahead of myself. First, let me contrast dignity and uBuntu with a broad brush, as they have often been painted in the literature. Dignity is usually associated with individual human rights, with a strong emphasis on autonomy and personhood, while uBuntu is associated with communalism and such virtues as loyalty and generosity. When it comes to constitutional law in South Africa, however, what they have in common is that neither seems easily reconcilable with reigning notions of legal positivism. That said, uBuntu has been more persistently attacked as supposedly untranslatable into a justiciable principle of constitutional law. For modern legal systems such as the German one, dignity is a foundational principle. Article 1 of Germany's 1948 Basic Law makes human dignity an inviolable right and one that is to inform the spirit of the legal system as a whole. In international law, meanwhile, the 1948 Universal Declaration of Human Rights establishes the dignity of all persons as the basis for freedom and justice in the world.

Dignity then, at least since World War II, has a rich legal history—one that has certainly played a role in the development of the dignity jurisprudence in South Africa, and many have argued that the depth and breadth of the dignity jurisprudence is one of the most significant contributions of South African constitutionalism. Can the same be said of uBuntu? The answer is yes and no. Certainly one does not find uBuntu in the Universal Declaration of Human Rights. On the other hand, if one puts uBuntu in the rich tradition of African Humanism and Socialism—and I think it should be connected to this intellectual heritage—then uBuntu (and similar African ethical principles such as *Ujamaa* in Tanzania) has a very rich history indeed, and one that places such principles at the heart of the creation of a post-colonial Africa.

Given the troubled history of constitutionalism in Africa, the legalization of such principles has been mixed, yet they clearly play a major role in defining the *Grundnorm* of an ethic for a new society. A *Grundnorm* is Hans Kelsen's word for the grounding moral or ethical principle that undergirds not only the legal system but the society as a whole.[2] Such a *Grundnorm* was explicitly defended by many of the African leaders after the revolutionary struggles for independence through principles of African Humanism such as *Ujamaa* and uBuntu.

If one were to interpret uBuntu as the ethical law of the new South Africa, then it would be uBuntu that would ground the constitutional *Grundnorm* of dignity, and not dignity that calls for the recognition of African humanist principles such as uBuntu. Note that I have used the word *African* because uBuntu or uBuntu/botho, even as they are words in South African languages, should be understood as part of the rich intellectual heritage of African Humanism.

KANTIAN DIGNITY

First, I will turn to the most sophisticated European defender of dignity, Immanuel Kant, to contrast the Kantian justification of dignity with a re-thinking of uBuntu, remembering also that in South Africa, Kant has been explicitly incorporated into constitutional jurisprudence. Former Constitutional Justice Ackermann has defended Kantianism as one important secular justification for the understanding of dignity as an ideal attribution of persons such that all persons have intrinsic worth. His constitutional judgments boldly suggest that the new South Africa should be understood to aspire to the great Kantian ideal of the Kingdom of Ends.

For Kant, a human being is of incalculable worth and has dignity precisely because through our practical reason we can potentially exercise our autonomy and lay down a law unto ourselves, which for Kant is the moral law or the categorical imperative. Kant is not arguing that we actually do exercise our autonomy most of the time in our daily lives. Nor is he defending autonomy as some kind of truth about how we actually are—a common misreading of his argument. Kant argues instead that we are creatures who live our desires and our needs as do all other animals, and yet we are creatures who have the *possibility*—because it can neither be theoretically demonstrated nor theoretically refuted as a fact about ourselves—to act other to the mechanics of those desires and needs.

Kant is often accused of being a prude because Kantian negative freedom is mistakenly identified with not doing what you want to do. But that is not the case. For Kant, a human life is purposive, and when we take ourselves seriously as creatures who can set ends for themselves as long-term directions in life, we should also find ourselves capable of coordinating our purposes and ends with the ends of others. Indeed, the idea of humanity, famously presented as a formulation of the categorical imperative, is inseparable from the possibility that each of us can project our ends as a reasonable creature, who can promote a community in which *mine* harmonizes with *yours* in the Kingdom of Ends.[3]

Negative freedom can entail limiting our own immediate desires through our attempt to live a purposive life, but it is not simply antagonistic to needs or desires. As finite beings we must make choices. We cannot be everywhere at once, and if we did not make choices we would not be able to represent them as part of our own life project. In this specific sense we have to exercise our prudence. Positive freedom for a creature that must live in a finite body, bound by the laws of nature, must proceed through a notion of autonomy that reconciles law and freedom. Indeed, positive freedom for Kant is causality through moral action, in which each of us potentially creates a new beginning as a moral person and with other persons, and aspires to create a new social and political order guided by the Kingdom of Ends.

For Kant, autonomy is not at all reducible to being left alone by others— not even in a more affirmative sense of aloneness as self-determination. This is precisely because for Kant freedom must be law-like, which means we exercise our autonomy not when we are strictly self-determining—true self-determination is beyond the reach of a finite creature for Kant—but rather when we represent our ends as our own and not merely determined by the pulls and tugs of the day-to-day world. In the strongest sense, we can only hope to attain freedom by imposing a law upon ourselves which allows us to represent ourselves as the source of a different ethical causality, a new moral beginning. Negative and positive freedom together, as Kant understands them, should be taken to mean that it is human beings who set value on ends; we make them *ours* in that we project an "I" as a necessary postulate of the very practical reason to which we must return to justify our ends.

To understand freedom and autonomy in this way is extremely significant for the law of the new South Africa, as the judgments of Emeritus Justice Ackermann demonstrate. First, as I have already suggested, the Kantian notion of positive freedom or autonomy gives us a defense of equality that does not depend on human persons being materially alike—a problem that has plagued some theorists in the Anglo-American academy. Human beings have equal worth because we all have the possibility of guiding our actions through practical reason. We should, as a moral mandate—and in the case of Justice Ackermann's "new South Africa" also as a constitutional mandate—regard all other human beings through the representation of that possibility. Thus, Kant introduces the idea of horizontal thinking, by which I mean the recognition that all creatures defined by this possibility have equal worth. Therefore, any return to hierarchies that deny to any human being that he or she partakes in this possibility must be rejected.

As an ideal attribution, dignity can be violated even as it remains the basis of our moral worth, because as creatures that have at least the possibility of moral action we might be able to bring about a new beginning. That is, dignity as an ideal attribution of our sameness before this possibility can be violated, but not lost. Here we see the difference between sameness and likeness for Kant. We are the same before this possibility even if many, if not all of us, often give ourselves long (sometimes endless) moral holidays. Nor does it matter for a defense of our intrinsic equal worth that we are actually different in our physical selves. Kant defends a view of autonomy rooted in how we *might* be: in this sense he does not offer a moral or ethical ontology of who we are rooted in any theory of human nature. Indeed, to the degree that Kant speculated in the anthropology of his time, he had a rather sour view of human nature.

For Emeritus Justice Ackermann, the moral categorical imperative for the new South Africa is precisely the recognition of this sameness, which, of course, is a complete moral inversion of the dreadful history of apartheid. For Ackermann, the constitutional imperative demands that never again will dignity be violated, and that its respect requires that dignity not only be treated as a right (as it must be under section 10 of the Constitution) but also as an ideal that informs how the other rights in the Bill of Rights are to be interpreted. On this understanding, when a justice uses dignity as a constitutional imperative, that justice is not locked into a kind of formalistic reasoning that says we respect the Constitution because it is the Constitution—as some critics of the dignity jurisprudence have suggested. For Ackermann, it is dignity that is the *Grundnorm* of the entire Constitution.

Again, a *Grundnorm* is the moral or ethical principle or ideal that undergirds the moral as well as the legal order of society. We need to note that the distinction between moral and legal rights is only made in Anglo-American jurisprudence, while for Kant legal rights *are* moral rights. The meaningful distinction in Kant is between the realm of internal freedom, morality, and the realm of external freedom, law. More on that distinction shortly.

In the case of South Africa this understanding of dignity can yield an interpretation of section 10 of the South African Constitution that separates the two clauses of section 10.[4] If everyone has dignity as an ideal attribution, then it is that ideal attribution that is recognized as a right. Dignity is what Justice Ackermann establishes as the *Grundnorm*, following Kelsen's definition, and he thus places dignity at the heart of the substantive revolution of South Africa. For Kelsen, two kinds of revolution are possible.[5] The first is the more familiar kind of revolution, a full revolution. A full revolution in South Africa would have obliterated the entire preceding legal system, which would have included firing all the judges and declaring all former law invalid. A substantive revolution, on the other hand, is when the new order proceeds legally even as the old order validates the creation of a new government—and yet it still turns the world upside down by creating a new objective, normative legal order that is based on an ethical principle that negates the ethical acceptability of the old order. Hence, the word *revolution* applies. Under Justice Ackermann's dignity jurisprudence, the South African Constitution is the law of a substantive revolution. The newness of this process is that it is one of the very few substantive revolutions to take place in world history (depending on how one reads some of the new dispensations in South America). Thus, if the Constitution ceased striving to embody the ideals of an objective normative order worthy of a substantive revolution, it would no longer be worthy of respect as the supreme law of the land of the new South Africa. This is not what the letter of the Constitution says, but it is the very spirit of the constitutional mandate that Justice Ackermann seeks to express in his judgments concerning the moral and constitutional significance of dignity.

But how is the social bond that undergirds Kant's notion of law as the realm of external freedom represented? The relationship between the realm of internal freedom (of morality) and the realm of external freedom (of right or *Recht*) has long been debated in Kantian scholarship. As Allen Wood explains:

> It is unclear whether Kant holds that the two moral legislations of right and ethics are derived from a common principle such as the supreme principles of morality that receives a three-fold formulation in the *Groundwork*. It speaks in favor of a common or unified basis that Kant regards duties of right as categorical imperatives and also that he grounds the single innate right possessed by persons (the right to freedom) on the humanity of persons (hence apparently on the second main formula of the principle of morality, the formula of humanity as an end in itself). . . . But it speaks against a unified basis of right and ethics that

the principle of right is described as analytic, whereas the principle of morality is synthetic, and also that the principle of right itself does not actually command us to do anything, but merely tells us what it takes for an action to have the status of a "right" action within the system of right.[6]

Clearly, and despite Kant's waffling, there must be a connection between the two. If there were no connection, there would be no moral ground for the realm of external freedom in which we coordinate our ends with one another. Kant's hypothetical experiment in the imagination, in which we configure the conditions in which human beings could aspire to the great ideal of the Kingdom of Ends, turns on the possibility that as creatures of practical reason we can harmonize our interests. For Kant, we represent the realm of external freedom through a hypothetical experiment of the imagination in which we configure the conditions of a social contract rooted in the respect for all other human beings. Under this experiment in the imagination, we imagine the conditions in which individuals are given the greatest possible space for freedom, as long as it can be harmonized with the freedom of all others. The social contract imagines us as moral beings that can exercise their practical reason and potentially guide their actions in accordance with its mandates. In his essay, "On the Common Saying: 'This May be True in Theory, but it Does Not Apply in Practice,'" Kant argues that the Hobbesian social contract will always falter precisely because the basis for that contract is not rooted in our potential to act morally.[7] Hobbes's social contract imagines human beings as forsaking their natural liberty and yielding to the coercive power of the sovereign and of the positive law only out of the drive for security and the protection of expectation. Thus, simply put, if the only basis for abiding by a legal system is fear and security with no moral reason for obligation, there will always be a reason for opting out of the social contract.

CRITICISMS OF THE KANTIAN DEFENSE OF DIGNITY

It is impossible to rehearse the rich critical literature on Kant in this chapter. Paraphrasing some of the most well-known critiques of Kantian dignity, I will focus particularly on those criticisms that will help bring into focus the similarities and differences between uBuntu and the Kantian notion of dignity.

The first criticism is that since our dignity lies in our potential to abide by the dictates of pure practical reason, and since most of us do not do this most of the time, dignity so defended is out of touch with the reality of human nature. Secondly—and many feminists have passionately asserted this criticism—what of human beings who for some reason cannot act rationally, even as a potential? Do they not have dignity? Even if dignity is an ideal attribution it turns on a potential or possibility that some people do not have because they lost it at birth or have yielded to the physical realities of old age or illness that undermine rational capacity. Dignity so conceived, then, is too narrow in its reach. It fails to assert the dignity of all human beings.[8]

Next, the Kantian notion of autonomy is sometimes critiqued as too individualistic. Yet this criticism argues that Kantianism fails to grasp how human beings belong together in primordial ways. Critics claim that even the hypothetical imagined social contract which imagines us as capable of acting morally and building a new world together, still begins with individuals. A version of this criticism is that human beings are never truly self-determining and thus autonomy is not a possible representation of ourselves as moral creatures: it is a fantasy, a dangerous one that can end up justifying self-righteous moralism. Feminists have emphasized another aspect of this criticism, which is that autonomy denies human fragility and our need for care and support.[9] This feminist emphasis on human fragility argues that Kantian autonomy is a male myth that bolsters a sexist view of the human. Another related criticism is that Kant grounds our dignity in a mystical noumenal otherness outside our actual phenomenal lives. Thus, our dignity seems to pit itself against both individual happiness and a collective promise of the common good.

To be fair to Kant, some of these criticisms are based on misreadings of Kant's critical idealism. As I have already suggested, autonomy is not self-determination for Kant but rather our determination by a law, albeit a law that we lay down to ourselves. Thus, Kant is not an individualist, at least not in the common English understanding of the word. To the degree that we are creatures of intrinsic worth, we have autonomy because of a sameness that we share. Dignity does not turn on individual characteristics or even some essential idea of our singularity. Autonomy is not a fact of our individuality. Nor does Kant argue that we can know for sure that we are acting rightly. As phenomenal creatures we can always get it wrong even as we try to abide by the moral law. In the *Critique of Practical Reason* Kant himself argues against the dangers of self-righteousness. This said, Kant does argue that our dignity is inextricably associated with our capacity for reason. The social bond, even if it aspires to our acting together under the guidance of the great ideal of the Kingdom of Ends, still begins with imagined individuals.

THE ALLIANCE BETWEEN AFRICAN HUMANISM AND KANTIAN ETHICS

As we will see, uBuntu does not defend dignity through our capacity for reason and does not think that the social bond is an experiment that begins with imagined moral individuals. And yet, there is an alliance of a Kantian notion of dignity with the intellectual heritage of African Humanism. The connection I am drawing with African Humanism should not be taken to mean that there is nothing unique about uBuntu or that African Humanism is not a complex tradition differentiated both by time and space. But since this intellectual heritage is often ignored or disparaged, it is important to remind ourselves of the important role it has played in Afro-modernity, including its role in the struggles for national independence and the reemergence of an ethical view of socialism that was deployed in economic development. Africa has a complex history of attempts to realize an ethical ideal of socialism, and I in no way want to ignore that history, nor do I want to simplify it. Fortunately, much deeper work is now being undertaken to study what was and what was not achieved, for example, in Tanzania under the leadership of Julius Nyerere. My emphasis in this chapter is on the intellectual heritage to the degree that there are important links with uBuntu.

To come back to the alliance of Kantianism with African Humanism, to some degree this alliance should not be surprising because Kant—and in particular Kant's notion of dignity—has played a major role in the work of European thinkers, who also argue that socialism is an ethical ideal and not a stage in a Marxist science of development and progress. Kwame Nkrumah, for example, argues that his philosophy of consciencism was an attempt to find an alternative justification for Kantian ethics, and particularly dignity, consistent with the African conscience. To quote Nkrumah:

> If ethical principles are founded on egalitarianism, they must be objective. If ethical principles arise from an egalitarian idea of the nature of man, they must be generalisable, for according to such an idea man is basically one in the sense defined. It is to this non-differential generalisation that the expression is given in the command to treat each man as an end in himself, and not merely as a means. That is, philosophical consciencism, though it has the same ethics as Kant, differs from Kant

in founding ethics on a philosophical idea of the nature of man. This is what Kant describes as an ethics based on anthropology. By anthropology Kant means any study of the nature of man, and he forbids ethics to be based in such a study.[10]

More commonly, the dignity of human beings is connected to a phenomenology of African social life, including the struggle against colonialism. This grounding in other African thinkers—if it is in the phenomenological sense African—is still ethically justified as universal, even without Nkrumah's attempt to develop a unique African notion of materialism that is to serve as the basis for an egalitarian ethic that would re-ground Kantian dignity.

Kenneth Kaunda, the first president of Zambia, also argues that African Humanism is a different approach to Kantian ethics, and yet one that also insists on dignity. Let me quote Kaunda's phenomenology of the African extended family as it helps us to think differently about the basis for ethics:

> The extended family system constitutes a social security scheme, which has the advantage of following the natural pattern of personal relationships rather than being the responsibility of an institution. It also provides for richness in knowledge and experiences for those fortunate enough to be part of it. Granted, I have been describing the character of small-scale societies and it could be argued that such a system would not work where hundreds of thousands of people are gathered together in cities or towns. But the attitudes to human beings, which I have set out, are not solely a function of social organization. They are now part of the African psychology. I am deeply concerned with this high valuation of Man and respect for human dignity, which is our legacy. Our tradition should not be lost in the new Africa, however "modern" and "advanced" in a Western sense the new nations of Africa will become. We are fiercely determined that this humanism will not be obscured. African humanism has always been Man centered. We intend that it remain so.[11]

Julius Nyerere echoes Kaunda in his summation of the Arusha Declaration, which is also a commitment to a particular quality of life. It is based on the assumption of human equality, on the belief that it is wrong for one man to dominate or exploit another and on the knowledge that every individual hopes to live in a society as a free man to lead a decent life in conditions of peace with those around him. The Declaration, in other words, is "Man centered." Inherent in the Arusha Declaration, therefore, is a rejection of the concept of national grandeur, as distinct from the well-being of the nation's citizens, and a rejection too of material wealth for its own sake. It is a commitment to the belief that there are more important things in life than amassing riches, and that if the pursuit of wealth clashes with human dignity and social equality, then the latter will be given priority.[12]

Kaunda further argues that there are three key social virtues that are crucial to African Humanism: mutuality, acceptance, and inclusiveness. The intrinsic worth of a human being, which justifies an egalitarian ethic, is not based, as it is in Kant, in that being's potential to act in accordance with the dictates of reason. Nor is the worth of a human being derived from his or her actual achievements. As Kaunda emphasizes:

> The success-failure complex seems to be a disease of the age of individualism—the result of a society conditioned by the diploma, the examination, and the selection procedure. In the best tribal society people were valued not for what they could achieve but because they were *there*. Their contribution, however limited to the material welfare of the village, was acceptable, but it was their *presence*, not their *achievement* which was appreciated.[13]

A human being has dignity because she is a unique being born into the human community, raised and supported there. For Kaunda the keystone for judging any society is whether the older people are respected: "The fact that old people can no longer work, or are not as alert as they used to be, or even have developed the handicaps of senility in no way affects our regard for them. We cannot do enough to repay them for all they have done for us. They are embodied wisdom; living symbols of our continuity with the past."[14]

UBUNTU AND AFRICAN HUMANISM

We may seem to be far away from uBuntu, but we are not, precisely because uBuntu also emphasizes the virtues of mutuality, inclusiveness, and acceptance. In like manner, respect for dignity is rooted in singularity and not in our capacity for rationality. Emeritus Justice Yvonne Mokgoro has defended uBuntu as the law of law of the entire new dispensation. uBuntu is a principle of transcendence for the individual as each one of us transcends our biological distinctiveness that marks us as unique from the beginning of life as we struggle to become a person. The burying of the umbilical cord marks the biological distinctiveness of each person. We are distinct from that moment of the cutting of the umbilical cord, with an origin shared by no other. But we only become a unique person through a struggle to define who we are, and we only do this with the support of others who help us in our effort at self-definition. Thus the law of transcendence for the individual, uBuntu, is also the law of the social bond. And why is this the case?

In uBuntu individuals are intertwined in a world of ethical relations and obligations from the time they are born. This inscription by the other is not simply reduced to a social fact. We come into the world obligated to others, and in turn these others are obligated to us, to the individual. Symbolically this is demonstrated in the burying of the umbilical cord. Others do that for us and create the origin from which we began our unique journey. What is marked in this ritual is our uniqueness. Thus, it is a profound misunderstanding of uBuntu to confuse it with simple-minded communitarianism. It is only through the support of others that we are to realize true individuality and rise above and beyond our biological distinctiveness into a person whose singularity is inseparable from the journey to moral and ethical development. Individuation is an achievement that involves struggle and the acceptance of rites of passage. Ifeanyi Menkiti captures this relationship between biological distinctiveness and personhood in the following passage:

> In the stated journey of the individual toward personhood, let it therefore be noted that the community plays a vital role both as catalyst and as prescriber of norms. The idea is that in order to transform what is initially a biological given into full personhood, the community of necessity has to step in, since the individual himself or herself cannot carry through the transformation unassisted. But what are the implications of this idea of a biologically given organism having first to go through a process of social and ritual transformation, so as to attain the full complement of excellences seen as definitive of the person?[15]

One conclusion appears inevitable, and it is to the effect that personhood has to be achieved, and that it is possible to fail at this achievement. Another way of putting the matter is to say that the approach to persons in African Humanism is generally speaking more exacting, insofar as it reaches for something beyond such requirements as the presence of consciousness, memory, will, soul, rationality, or mental function. Being or becoming a person is truly a serious project that stretches beyond the raw capacities of the isolated individual, and it is a project laden with the possibility of triumph, but also of failure.

If the community is committed to individuation and the achievement of a unique destiny for each person, the person in turn is obligated to enhance the community that supports him or her, not simply as an abstract duty that is correlated with a right, but as a form of participation that allows the community to strive for fidelity to what D. A. Masolo has called "participatory difference."[16] For Masolo, this participatory difference recognizes that each one of us is different, but also that each one of us is called upon to make a difference by contributing to the creation and sustenance of a humane ethical community. We can understand, then, that our ethical relationship to others is inseparable from how we are both embedded in and supported by a community that is not outside of us, something "over there," but is inscribed in us. The inscription of the other also calls the individual out of himself or herself. uBuntu is in this sense a call for transcendence. The individual is called back toward the ancestors, forward toward the community, and further toward relations of mutual support for the potential of each one of us.

We have seen, however, that this does not imply any simple notion of communitarianism or social cohesion. Each one of us is called to become her own person and make a difference so as to realize the ethical quality of humanness, and to support such a quality of humanness in others. Although others support me, and an ethical action is by definition ethical because it is an action in relationship to another human being, it is still up to me to realize my own personal destiny and to become a person in the ethical and moral sense of the word. Thus, it is humanness, as Justice Mokgoro emphasizes in her own definition of uBuntu, and not just my community that is at stake in my actions. If I relate to another person in a manner that lives up to uBuntu, then there is at least an ethical relationship between the two of us. The concept of a person in uBuntu is an ethical concept. A self-regarding or self-interested human being is one that has not only fallen away from her sociality with others; she has lost touch with her humanity. One crucial aspect of doing justice to such a person is that we who are participating in an ethical community help that individual get back in touch with him- or herself. Thus, cohesion and harmony are not the ultimate good because they must always be submitted to the doing of justice. As John Murungi argues:

> Certainly in Africa, but not only in Africa, personhood is social. African jurisprudence is part of African social anthropology. Social cohesion is

an essential element of African jurisprudence. Areas such as criminology and penology, law of inheritance and land law, for example focus on the preservation and promotion of cohesion. This cohesion is a cohesion tempered by justice. Justice defines a human being as a human being. Thus, injustice in Africa is not simply a matter of an individual breaking a law that is imposed on him or her by other individuals, or by a collection of individuals who act in the name of the state.[17]

It is a violation of the individual's duty to himself or herself, a violation of the individual to be himself or herself—the duty to be a social human being.

Thus, this specifically ethical manner in which personhood is conceived has important implications for how the social bond that underlies any notion of law is defined. This means of course that this idea of personhood, as Murungi points out, underlies the central concepts of African jurisprudence, as these in turn set the meaning of law. Again to quote Murungi:

> Each path of jurisprudence represents an attempt by human beings to tell a story about being human. Unless one discounts the humanity of others, one must admit that one has something in common with all other human beings. To discount what one has in common with other human beings is to discount oneself as a human being. What is essential in law is what secures human beings in their being. The pursuit and the preservation of what is human and what is implicated by being human are what, in a particular understanding, is signified by African jurisprudence. Being African is a sign of being African and a sign of being human. In this signature lies not only what is essential about African jurisprudence, but also what is essential about the Africanness of African jurisprudence. To learn how to decipher it, which in a sense implies learning how to decipher oneself, paves the way to a genuine understanding.[18]

In a profound sense then, African jurisprudence articulates the principles of African Humanism. uBuntu can and should be grasped as part of this other jurisprudence and view of law. It is indeed a different story of law and justice than the one imagined and told in Anglo-American and European law. I will return to that difference when I discuss the contrasts and similarities between Kantian dignity and uBuntu.

For now I want to discuss Justice Mokgoro's judgment in the *Xhosa* case, a judgment in which she does not actually use the word *uBuntu*, but one that is infused with uBuntu thinking.[21] The case raised the issue of whether noncitizens who were permanent residents would be eligible for certain social welfare grants as long-standing members of the community. Justice Mokgoro's judgment granted such eligibility, but her justification for so doing is what is important to my argument. Remember that Kaunda emphasizes three main virtues of African Humanism: mutuality, acceptance, and inclusion. All three entered into Justice Mokgoro's reasoning in the *Xhosa* case. First, the overriding idea of African jurisprudence is reflected in the judgment. What would it mean to deny noncitizens social welfare grants if "what is essential to law is what secures human beings in their being?" Further, Justice Mokgoro emphasizes mutuality. The people who are seeking grants are members of a community, and mutuality here means that we must respect their contributions to the community, but, more profoundly, that they are part of us and we are part of them.

This turns us back to an earlier point in this chapter in which I emphasized that the community is not something out there, but instead signals how we are inscribed in each other. Just as noncitizens have obligations to the community, so the community, including the state, has obligations to them. Secondly, a humane community is both accepting and inclusive. To refuse to grant them eligibility would render them outsiders to whom we do not owe relations of mutuality. In a sense then, to deny them social grants would violate their dignity precisely because the mark of outsider is not only to push another out of the community, but also outside what is owed to another human being as a human being. They would be pushed outside of the human world of mutual relations. Throughout, Justice Mokgoro emphasizes actual belonging and interconnectedness, which underscores how mutuality, acceptance and inclusiveness reinforce one another. If we ignore the needs of those who have become part of us, then we are at risk of losing our own humanity. The emphasis, then, is not so much on dignity as an individual right—although Justice Mokgoro does appeal to dignity—but on dignity understood as the ethical core of relations of mutuality.

CRITICISMS OF UBUNTU

I will summarize the criticisms of uBuntu in broad outline. First, there is the criticism that uBuntu is a communal ethic that denies the importance of individual autonomy. It emphasizes obligations to the group at the expense of individual rights. Some critics read *umuntu ngumuntu ngabantu* to mean only that a person is only a person through other people. This reading promotes the criticism that there is no place for individuality and creativity in an uBuntu ethic. Secondly, there is a criticism that uBuntu is inherently conservative. Worse yet, its appeal to cohesion privileges dangerous hierarchies, corrupt tribal authorities over the people they supposedly lead, men over women, etc. Thus, uBuntu is both authoritarian and patriarchal and should be mistrusted as such. Thirdly, even if uBuntu was once an important value in the struggle for liberation and indeed, for survival in horrific circumstances, it is dying out under the force of advanced capitalism. Thus, what remains of uBuntu is a shadow of what it used to be, and as a result, it easily falls prey to manipulation, not just by corrupt traditional authorities but also by the ANC leaders who want to maintain a compliant workforce in the face of the demands of neoliberal capitalism. Given these three criticisms, uBuntu is rejected for being backward-looking and not forward-looking. Thus it is denied that uBuntu has the same aspirational edge as dignity as an ideal.

Before turning to the contrast with Kantian dignity, it should be noted that some of these criticisms involve a fundamental misunderstanding of uBuntu. Often, critics of uBuntu make the mistake of reducing uBuntu to an ethical ontology of a purportedly shared world. What is missed in this criticism is precisely the activism in participatory difference. This activism is inherent in the ethical demand to bring about a humane world. uBuntu clearly has an aspirational and ideal edge—there is no end to a struggle to bring about a humane world, and who makes a difference in it.

As an ethical concept, uBuntu is always integral to a social bond. In a profound sense, uBuntu encapsulates the moral relations demanded by human beings who must live together. As we have seen, it implies a fundamental moralization of social relations, and what never changes is that society is inherently moral. The actual relationships uBuntu calls us to must change since uBuntu is inseparable from a relationship between human beings that is always present, yet it is also connected to how we are always changing in those relationships, and our needs are changing with them. The aspirational aspect of uBuntu is that we must strive together to achieve the public good and a shared world. It is uBuntu's embeddedness in our social reality that makes it a transformative ethic at its core. It is the moralization of social relationships that inevitably demands the continuous transformation of any society.

In like manner uBuntu has no given position on the equality of women. Certainly there is sexism in African thinking as there is in African social and political life. uBuntu has been used to justify sexism in the name of tradition, and it has been deployed on the other side to fight it. That it can be used on different sides of a struggle over what is right does not mean that uBuntu can mean anything. It does mean that it is embedded in a complex and changing world, so that what was believed to be right for women hundreds of years ago has been profoundly challenged by women on the ground. Again, to turn to Murungi's definition that "law secures human beings in their being," law in the sense of doing justice does not separate between civil and socio-economic rights. Both are necessary to secure and protect our humanity in the moral sense that is echoed in Emeritus Justice Mokgoro's *Xhosa* judgment and in the writings of the African philosophers—all of whom represent different aspects of African Humanism.

Some of the criticisms represent a misunderstanding of uBuntu, as I have discussed. uBuntu does not undermine the concept of personhood; indeed, it demands the thinking of the ethical conditions of individuation. Yet it does not embrace individualism and rejects the notion of self-determination. I will return to the significance of this misreading of Kant shortly for the history and the future of the ideal of dignity. As I have already argued, Kant also does not reduce autonomy to self-determination. Whether or not uBuntu has been undermined by modernity, apartheid, and capitalism is an empirical question and must be addressed as such. At least in the townships of the Western Cape, the uBuntu Township Project has undertaken to investigate whether an uBuntu ethic is alive, as well as the forces that either support it or undermine it. Such empirical work can also help us grapple with the undoubted reality that some leaders in South Africa have manipulated uBuntu for their own purposes. I will return to these important criticisms of uBuntu shortly.

SIMILARITIES WITH KANT

As I have discussed above, there is an alliance between Kant and African Humanism. I want to emphasize two crucial aspects of that alliance.

First, both draw a close connection between freedom and morality, freedom and obligation, and freedom and necessity. One is not free outside of the ethical, but through it. A human being cannot be free by doing whatever he or she wants. We are constrained by the laws of nature. Our freedom is expressed in our laying down a particular kind of law unto ourselves. It is a particular kind of law, but it is a law. When we live up to the obligations of the moral law we are also representing ourselves as free. What has come to be known as the reciprocity thesis, that freedom and the obligations imposed upon us by the moral law are two sides of the same coin, should show us how far we are, in Kant, from the identification of freedom with self-determination. In his later writing, Kant also argues that it is not only as a moral personality that we have dignity but also through our humanity.[19] Kant underscores that even when we act in our self-interest we do so through reason, by making a desire a maxim that we choose to follow. In *Religion Within the Boundaries of Mere Reason*, Kant holds that reason guides us in our humanity as well as in our moral personality, a distinction he did not make in his earlier work.

But that said, it is through our capacity for practical reason and our potential to be dictated by the demands of the moral law that humanity itself becomes a moral ideal. And here we find the second basis for the alliance with African Humanism. Humanity matters because it is an ethical ideal. Surely there are different notions of the meaning of the ethical ideal of humanity, but broadly construed they share the insistence that personhood and morality are inseparable. Hence, both Kantianism and African Humanism strongly promote human dignity. It is important to note here that the misreading of Kantian autonomy that identifies it with self-determination has had serious consequences for the Western discourse on autonomy. As Roger Berkowitz has accurately argued:

> The problem that plagues all of these modern invocations of dignity from Dworkin to Habermas is that they understand dignity as self-determination and then stumble upon the contradiction in self-determination. Self-determination—the right to personal autonomy that underlies human and civil rights—is frequently at odds with self-determination—the democratic right of citizens to collectively govern themselves. Indeed, the tension between individual and collective self-determination is at the root of many of the great human rights tragedies of the modern era.[20]

For Hannah Arendt, this dilemma, which has haunted human rights discourse, cannot easily be theoretically or practically overcome since it lies at the heart of modern liberalism. And so she calls for a new political principle, a new law on earth.[21]

As we have seen, Kant himself did not identify autonomy with self-determination. Yet there is little doubt that most of his modern interpreters have done so. Can we still rely on Kant as the basis for dignity? Or do we need another discourse? Even under the most sophisticated interpretation of Kant, our dignity lies in our capacity for reason. For a thinker like Arendt that capacity has carried little force against the horrors of the twentieth century. Kant of course did not base his idea of dignity in how we actually act but in how we should act, and it is always a possibility for us that we might act rightly if we abide by the moral law. But is that enough for a new law on earth?

DIFFERENCES BETWEEN KANTIANISM AND UBUNTU

There are several important differences that need to be emphasized between Kantianism and uBuntu. First, dignity in uBuntu thinking is not rooted in reason because of an ethical concern shared with many feminists that this would deny dignity to too many human beings. Thus, such a ground for dignity runs afoul of the virtues of inclusiveness and acceptance. Instead, dignity is rooted first and foremost in our singularity and uniqueness, and at the same time in our embeddedness as part of a human community. Furthermore, the social bond is conceived differently, and thus, although both traditions moralize law—and would find it equally incomprehensible to separate law and morality in the Anglo-American sense—they rely on different conceptions of moral personhood to do so. Even the great Kantian hypothetical experiment in the imagination, in which we configure the conditions of the social contract rooted in the respect for all other human beings, still begins with imagined moral individuals. It is still individuals who agree to accept some form of coercion, even if rooted in Kant's basic understanding of right, which is that individuals are allowed the greatest possible space for their freedom as long as it can be harmonized with the freedom of all others in the social contract. If freedom is inseparable from morality then at least as a possibility, we can represent ourselves as free human beings who can harmonize their interests in the Kingdom of Ends.

uBuntu, alternatively, does not conceive of the social bond through an imagined social contract undertaken by imagined moral individuals. We are born into a social bond but it is not as if the social is something outside the individual. It is the network of relationships in and through which we are formed and whose formation is ultimately our responsibility. There is a flow, back and forth, between the individual and others as he or she undertakes the struggle to become a person, always conceived ethically, which is difficult to think of even in the best of European philosophy. It is certainly not impossible to think of such a back and forth, but it is difficult because the social is sedimented as something outside the individual. Of course, if we add Kant to Hegel and Marx we begin to see possibilities for such a dialectic. Am I suggesting that uBuntu thinking and African Humanism are better resources on which to ground the new law on earth, the new political principle to which Arendt calls us? I am certainly arguing that a reinvigorated defense of dignity, whether as the *Grundnorm* of the South African Constitution or as a new universal political and ethical principle must bring this intellectual heritage into the debate as an equal partner. Such a dialogue is long overdue, and necessary for the continuing defense of human dignity in South Africa and the rest of the world.

9

Where Dignity Ends and uBuntu Begins:
A Response by Yvonne Mokgoro and Stu Woolman

If I am not for myself, then who will be for me? If I am not for others, then who am I?
If not now, when?
    —HILLEL

Haeba ke sa itlhokomele, ke mang ea tla ntlhokomela? Haeba ke sa hlokomele ba bang ba
heso, na ke botho? Haeba re sa hlokomelane ha joale, re tla hlokomelana neng?
    —ANONYMOUS

History doesn't repeat itself, but it often rhymes.
    —MARK TWAIN

In the decade or so in which Professor Cornell has engaged South Africa's
jurisprudence, her name has become synonymous with academic discourse
about and around the values of dignity and uBuntu. As colleagues and col-
laborators, it is often hard to know where Drucilla Cornell's thoughts on
these subjects end and one's own ruminations begin.[1] What follows is an
amplification of, or a riff upon, Professor Cornell's "Is There a Difference
That Makes a Difference between Dignity and uBuntu?" Contestation is
not in the cards. But emotion is. Adjudication and academic scholarship
in the social sciences—as much as any other form of judgment—requires
"emotional intelligence"[2] and a kind of connected spectatorship based upon
mutual respect, care, trust, and loyalty.[3] As Professor Cornell insists throughout her immense and influential body of work,[4] law cannot be reduced to
a benighted Hartian set of first-order rules of recognition and the second

order rules that flow from them.[5] Cornell's persistent emphasis on law as far more than a body of rules functions as a regular reminder that our "formal" training (at institutions as geographically far apart as the University of Bophuthatswana or Columbia Law School, but ontologically proximate with respect to the Hartian indoctrination into legal doctrine that we received) was missing something critical to the creation of a just legal order. No matter how much law strives to have a formal existence, messy human beings living out different ways of being in the world must learn to accommodate one another when it comes to determining the meaning of the basic law and honoring the constraints that the text invariably imposes.[6] Following Henk Botha and Larry Tribe, we write neither "for those who feel confident that canons of appropriate constitutional construction may be derived from some neutral source" nor "for those who have convinced themselves that anything goes as long as it helps end what they see as injustice."[7] When we write about the relationship between uBuntu and the Constitution, we provide substantive grounds (expressly present in the Interim Constitution and implicit in the Final Constitution) for how we believe judges on a South African bench ought to read the text. Put slightly differently, though uBuntu may shadow Western notions of dignity (drawn from the work of Kant) or communitarianism (drawn from the work of Rousseau or Marx), it provides a distinctly Southern African lens through which judges, advocates, attorneys, and academics ought to determine the extension of the actual provisions of the basic law. It hardly seems controversial to ground the South African Constitution in the lived experience of South Africans so long as an uBuntu-based reading does no violence to the text.

That's not an opinion. It's the law.

When the Constitutional Court handed down *Makwanyane* in 1995, it clearly decided the matter in the spirit of uBuntu. The enabling environment at the Constitutional Court—of equals serving amongst equals with a deep sense of consideration and respect for each other's views, and of a commitment to the ideal of a new constitutional democracy in which every contribution counts—allowed members of the court to plant the seed of uBuntu jurisprudence. The textual source of the seed can be found in the postscript of the Interim Constitution. While most of the Justices emphasized the violation of the right to human dignity or the right to freedom and security of the person as a basis for finding the death penalty infirm, several others based their findings upon accepted axioms of uBuntu:

Generally uBuntu translates as humanness. In its most fundamental sense it translates as personhood and morality. Metaphorically it expresses itself in *umuntu, ngabantu ngabantu,* describing the significance of group solidarity on survival issues so central to the survival of communities. While it envelops the key values of group solidarity, compassion, respect, human dignity, conformity to norms and collective unity, in its fundamental sense it denotes humanity and morality. Its spirit emphasises respect for human dignity making a shift from confrontation to conciliation.[8]

Members of the *Makwanyane* court found the death penalty repugnant because retribution and group catharsis as the bases for punishment are inconsistent with an uBuntu-based jurisprudence of reconciliation, restorative justice, and democratic solidarity. As importantly, their findings should be understood as broadly representative of South African views regarding the moral underpinnings of the basic law. The presence of uBuntu as a guiding norm in the interpretation of our basic law is essential for the legitimation of our legal system.[9]

We ignore uBuntu at our own peril. Indeed, without saying much more on this subject, a growing sense of disjunction between the ideals of the Constitution and the lived experience of most South Africans warrants a reappraisal of the place of uBuntu in South African law. It is this difference between dignity—as espoused by Kant and other Western philosophers—and uBuntu as practiced by the majority of South Africans that animates Professor Cornell's essay on the subject. We need to do more than infuse our dignity jurisprudence with a soupçon of uBuntu. The legitimation of the South African legal order depends upon our ability to synchronize these two closely related, but distinct terms. In *Khosa,* the court offered the following South African gloss on the demands of dignity—one framed in a decidedly South African lingua franca—in finding that the state's refusal to provide permanent residents with social welfare benefits constitutes a violation of the right to social security and the right to equality:

> Sharing responsibility for the problems and consequences of poverty equally as a community represents the extent to which wealthier members of the community view the minimal well-being of the poor as connected with their personal well-being and the well-being of the community as a whole. In other words, decisions about the allocation of

public benefits represent the extent to which poor people are treated as equal members of society.[10]

If dignity and uBuntu can be squared in such a fashion, and in the context of such a difficult case as the right to adequate access to social security, then one might ask, as Professor Cornell does—why has uBuntu been met by the academy and by the courts with such resistance?

We can identify two sources for this resistance: the problem of translatability; and the tension between radical reconstructions of uBuntu (such as those understandings proffered by Professor Cornell and others)[11] and conservative manifestations of this indigenous philosophy often used to block egalitarian (and especially feminist) reform of highly stratified patriarchal structures in traditional communities and South Africa's capitalist economy.

Rosalind English deserves credit for engaging uBuntu long before it was fashionable to do so. However, she remains skeptical of its uses all the same: "In relying on uBuntu as a form of community consensus, the Court has tried to appear to be reaching out for some external order of values and, at the same time, to be resurrecting indigenous values that have been allowed to fall into destitution. Neither of these efforts has quite come off."[12] In sum, neither the court nor other participants in this conversation about the place of uBuntu in our constitutional order could quite make it do the work that its proponents wanted it to do. But did those efforts not come off because uBuntu was dropped from the text of the Final Constitution or because its expositors could not convey with precision in the dominant language (English) and political culture (liberal capitalism) a term that was well understood in indigenous cultures throughout South Africa? We think that the failure of engagement reflects (in part) a general malaise on the part of academics and jurists. For some, this lassitude takes the form of a rather thin and potted poststructuralist or postmodernist account of other cultures—as in "it's a black thing, we couldn't possibly understand."[13] But as Professor Cornell's writing and her uBuntu Project make clear, no good reason exists to countenance such relativism. Our point here is decidedly Davidsonian.[14] What all relativists have in common is a notion of "incommensurable conceptual schemes." Davidson writes:

> Philosophers of many persuasions are prone to talk of conceptual schemes. Conceptual schemes, we are told, are ways of organizing experience: they are systems of categories that give form to the data of

sensation; they are points of view from which individuals, cultures, or periods survey the passing scene. There may be no translating from one scheme to another, in which case the beliefs, desires, hopes, and bits of knowledge that characterize one person have no true counterparts to the subscriber to another scheme. Reality is relative to a scheme: what counts as real in one system may not in another. . . . Conceptual relativism is a heady and exotic doctrine, or would be if we could make sense of it. The trouble is, as so often in philosophy, that it is hard to improve intelligibility while retaining the excitement.[15]

That is about as charitable as Davidson can be in dismissing epistemological claims made by philosophers working within postmodern or poststructuralist frameworks. About the confusion associated with conceptual schemes, he argues:

Since knowledge of beliefs comes only with the ability to interpret words, the only possibility at the start is to assume general agreement on beliefs. . . . The guiding policy is to do this as far as possible. . . . The method is not designed to eliminate disagreement, nor can it; its purpose is to make meaningful disagreement possible, and this depends entirely on a foundation—*some* foundation—in agreement. . . . We make maximum sense of the words and thoughts of others when we interpret them in a way that optimizes agreement.

. . . Where does that leave the case for conceptual relativism? The answer is, I think, that we must say much the same thing about differences in conceptual schemes as we say about differences in belief: we improve the clarity and bite of declarations of difference, whether of scheme or opinion, by enlarging the basis of shared (translatable) language or of shared opinion.[16]

The apposite conclusions to be drawn from Davidson's analysis are (a) that no good reason exists to think that the large majority of beliefs held by members of another culture are somehow beyond our ken, and (b) that it is our intellectual job as academics and jurists, and our ethical responsibility as members of the same South African polity, to try to get our heads and hearts around words and concepts that undoubtedly feel (at first instance) foreign and uncomfortable.

The greater challenge, we believe, lies not in whether we can understand or determine the exact contours of uBuntu, but in describing and defending a certain conception of uBuntu. Here we think that Professor Cornell would be well served not only to defend uBuntu against its usurpation by the constitutional *Grundnorm* of dignity, but to tackle head-on conservative variants of uBuntu that would block her social democratic vision of a future South Africa. *Bhe v. Magistrate, Khayalitscha*[17]—in striking down traditional rules of male primogeniture—or *Shilubana v. Nwamitwa*[18]—in upholding changes to traditional norms that had previously permitted only male ascension to tribal authority—may seem like easy cases when analyzed in terms of the existing jurisprudence of rights to equality of sex and gender and the right to dignity. But they are most assuredly not. Why?

Two reasons. First, a significant proportion of our country's denizens view the Constitution "as read" in cases such as *Shilubana* and *Bhe* as dramatically out of step with their "lived experiences."[19] Indeed, a growing contingent of scholars and members of social movements contend that our Western-style constitutional democracy is viewed as an imposition, as an extension of colonial rule and white power through law (as opposed to violent, fascist, and expressly racist oppression).[20] Second, the process of "recollective imagination" and "transformative legal interpretation" of uBuntu into a set of beliefs and practices that will bring about a representative or democratic socialist South African polity cannot be assumed. The critique of uBuntu as a potentially conservative brake on this country's emancipatory project cannot be cavalierly dismissed. If uBuntu is connected—however unreflectively—with practices such as male primogeniture, male ascension to leadership positions, male circumcision rites, or compensation for teacher-student, male-on-female sexual violence, then such practices must be rooted out before uBuntu can lay claim to the mantle of revolutionary constitutional doctrine. We can agree with Professor Cornell's desire to place uBuntu at the core of South African constitutionalism even as we insist that her efforts must convert those members of South African society who, when they speak of uBuntu, imagine a very different set of (conservative) political institutions and legal doctrines.

Professor Cornell's reflections on uBuntu and dignity are neither inventions in the German Idealist tradition nor fantasies about the underlying philosophy of many South African communities. What Professional Cornell's writings exhibit is a two-fold effort to excavate the profound and unique communitarian thought embedded in uBuntu and a rolling-up-of-the-sleeves exercise in determining the content of uBuntu-based forms of life throughout South Africa. They are also an exercise in speculative, philosophical anthropology. But they are more than that. By tying her un-abashedly political project to classically anthropological work in the field, Professor Cornell promises the possibility of a fully worked-out African ethics and politics. If there is a tension in Professor Cornell's work, then it is a most natural tension between academic pursuits and practical politics. As a Kantian scholar of the first order, a long-standing student of uBuntu, and a savvy analyst of politics in South Africa, the challenge before Professor Cornell is to get individuals and communities within this radically hetero-geneous country singing off the same hymn sheet. No easy task.

As her chapter reflects, Professor Cornell struggles mightily to close the gap between uBuntu and dignity—at the same time as she recognizes the differences between both constitutional norms. Need we try so hard to rec-oncile the two? No one has suggested that we need to square uBuntu with equality or freedom, or reduce it entirely to community rights. We might do well to consider allowing these values to occupy their own separate spaces—closely aligned, but with different roles to play when we apply our minds to constitutional conflicts. Perhaps a Twainian twist is in order: uBuntu and dignity do not map directly onto one another, but they do rhyme.

Given this added layer of complexity, we might ask whether Professor Cornell can make good on the promise of *both* her uBuntu and dignity projects. She has already more than started. Yet a sense of urgency in South African politics (yes, an incipient violence) lingers over her poignant mani-festos. We can ask of the uBuntu Project, as Hillel did of his brethren over two millennia ago, "If not now, when?"

Conclusion:

uBuntu and Subaltern Legality

The value of uBuntu is disputed in South Africa. In all the burning debates, uBuntu is often deployed on both sides of the question. Part of the reason that uBuntu is used in the streets as well as the courts—and I have argued this elsewhere—is that it remains an ethical force in the day-to-day life of South Africans. uBuntu has an odd history, in that it is a Zulu word that has often been combined with the Tswana word *botho* to yield uBuntu/botho. But then uBuntu/botho is picked up in just that form, and not further translated. So it is already a "South African" expression in the complexity of its meaning, and as I have repeatedly argued, uBuntu/botho defends itself as an appeal to our ethical humanness, which should be universally vindicated, not justified because of its roots in indigeneity.[1]

There has been a flurry of recent articles about the extremely troubling attacks on gays and lesbians, including "corrective rapes" of lesbian women. Many of these articles point to the disconnect between the constitutional values and this seemingly aggressive rejection of those values by at least part of the population that uses violence against those who have sought and gained recognition of their dignity at the level of the Constitutional Court. Jean and John L. Comaroff have powerfully argued that this kind of disconnect is not some mysterious force, but a basic trend of neoliberal capitalism, which has so profoundly fractured the modern sense of the ideological mission of the nation state, and replaced it with what they call "ID-ology," which is an expression that has been used in the South African press.[2] To quote the Comaroffs:

> In postcolonies, which are endemically heterogeneous, citizenship always exists in an immanent tension with policulturalism; note the term, we shall explain it below. As a result, it is a terrain on which increasingly irreconcilable, fractal forms of subjectivity, embodied in self-defined aggregates of persons, may seek to open up possibilities for social action, possibilities in pursuit of interests, ideals, passions, principles. It is on this terrain that the modernist sense of ideology gives way to ID-ology, the quest for a collective good, and often goods, authorized by a shared identity. And, in the process, both the liberal modernist polity and the kingdom of custom are transformed.[3]

I refer to the Comaroffs for two reasons. The first is that we need to keep in mind the demand for a careful analysis of this kind of disconnect. For there is a profound danger that we fall into diverse forms of "Afro-pessimism," which have haunted the history of the struggle in Africa for decolonization and liberation. But the second reason lies at the heart of this paper: a defense of the reasons that the uBuntu Project has insisted on the importance of the legalization, including at the level of the Constitution, of the value of uBuntu. The Comaroffs argue that one form of ID-ology is new forms of what they call "lawfare" and the use of the courts by many of the counterhegemonic movements in Southern Africa. They do not, like some thinkers, argue that we can know in advance whether this turn to lawfare will have a liberating potential for the subaltern. Their focus is on a detailed analysis of why lawfare is a part of ID-ology, and perhaps unavoidably so. To thoroughly understand this point, we have to return to why the Comaroffs associate ID-ology with what they call "policulturalism." As I have discussed earlier, policulturalism, for the Comaroffs, implies a combination of plurality and politicization, which often challenges the nation state as the sole body in charge of both violence and law.[4] When we combine the Comaroffs' insights into the relationship between ID-ology and policulturalism, we can

deep our understanding of why the uBuntu Project has engaged in both
descriptive and prescriptive work on the importance of uBuntu as an ethical
and legal value in the new South Africa. Again, all one has to do is pick up a
newspaper in South Africa to see how uBuntu and other indigenous values
have been thoroughly politicized.

Why is the defense of uBuntu, and particularly the struggle over its legalization, so important in the new dispensation? The defense is important for
postcolonial societies of African ideals and values, and more comprehensively,
for African or Africana philosophy. This defense is important for at least two
reasons. The first is, as the Comaroffs have repeatedly reminded us, amongst
others, that African modernity is as *sui generis* as European modernity, and has
made its own contribution to the world view of the modern, as does any of
the other so-called "geographies of reason" that currently exist on our planet.
In other words, Afro-modernity is not an alternative modernity, if one means
by "alternative" an alternative to Europe and the United States, as if Europe
and the United States and Africa could be neatly separated.

Second, this recognition of African modernity is part and parcel not only
of the struggle against Eurocentrism as a bias and a particularity that pre-
tends to be universal, but is also part of a struggle to combat what Paget
Henry has so elegantly described as Caliban's purported lack of reason.[5] For
many of the Afro-Caribbean philosophers—including Paget Henry, Sylvia
Wynter, Eduard Glissant, Lewis Gordon, and many others—the struggle
against antiblack racism is not only a political matter, but also a philosophical one, in that it challenges how philosophical conceptions of everything
from reason and morality to humanity have been tainted by thoroughgoing
racialization that "whitens" the very philosophical notion of "man." Therefore, if there was to be a new humanism, as called for in the struggle against
antiblack racism, a humanism advocated from a wide range of thinkers in
Africa from Fanon to Biko, there must be a challenge—- politically, ethically, and philosophically—to racism, and a defense of the human beyond
the thoroughly racialized categories of philosophy.

Hence the first defense of uBuntu. uBuntu, for all the struggle over its
political and ethical meaning, points us to a new humanism, to a new ethical notion of being human that implies a thoroughgoing philosophical, political, and ethical critique of racism. Let us throw the gauntlet down. To
even take uBuntu seriously, or more precisely, to demand that uBuntu be
taken seriously, is to challenge the racism that somehow this African value,
because it is so contested in its meaning, is too vague to have any moral,

let alone legal purchase. The uBuntu Project has been in a deep sense both descriptive and prescriptive, because the project advocated that an African ideal might be one that could and should universally inform us. To even hypothesize the reach of an African ideal in this manner implies an antiracist stance and is therefore not neutral, as if such neutrality could exist in research, but is prescriptive as well.

So the first aspect of the defense of uBuntu was that it is indeed an important ideal and value in the day-to-day life of South Africa, which is precisely why it is so contested. And secondly, because it defends itself as a new ethical way of being human together, we need to judge it then, not simply because it is African or South African, but because of the philosophical project it offers of solidarity, and indeed, if one takes "revolutionary uBuntu" seriously, a project of radical transformation. The phrase "revolutionary uBuntu" has been coined by the Shack Dwellers movement, as well as other movements of the poor in South Africa, to argue that uBuntu is itself an anticapitalist ideal, and that capitalism cannot be rendered consistent with it.[6] As I have written elsewhere, the economist Sampie Terreblanche describes 350 years of patterns of "unfree black labor," to underscore that the transformation of South Africa could not be complete unless it completely undid that history.[7] For Terreblanche, amongst other South African economists, the transformation of South Africa could only take place if the destructive aspects of this long history of unfree black labor, which clearly began long before the institutionalization of apartheid, were completely undone, and this could only be done by some form of social democracy or socialism. My addition was that the expression that Terreblanche uses, unfree black labor, should also be read as a telos that points toward a different history of free human beings. It is important to underscore that the very term unites race and class, and points to how the so-called modern project of neoliberal capitalism turns on forms of indentured servitude that continue to allow for the superexploitation of a large majority of humanity. Within South Africa, Terreblanche's powerful argument is that the failure to combat in all its forms the residues of unfree black labor in the name of a new humanity has completely undermined the transformation of South Africa into a "new" South Africa. I will not repeat his arguments here, but underscore two points: that revolutionary uBuntu points toward the free human being that is finally unchained from unfree black labor, and second, that there can be no serious transformation of South Africa without a thoroughgoing economic transformation.

In his earlier pathbreaking work, *A History of Inequality in South Africa: 1652–2002*, Terreblanche painstakingly described the devastating economic effects in all forms of life of unfree black labor. There he argued that the shift in political and ideological power represented by the electoral victory of the African Nation Congress was incomplete. In his latest book, *Lost in Transformation*, he poignantly argues that the transformation may have faltered or indeed failed before its refusal to take seriously what revolutionary uBuntu demands: free human beings living together in an ethical community.[8]

So far, we have been discussing revolutionary uBuntu as it has been explicitly associated with social ideals and anticapitalist struggle on the ground in South Africa. Yes, uBuntu can be used for conservative or even reactionary purposes. So can dignity. So the question becomes: How and why can one advocate for revolutionary uBuntu as a possible "ideal" for transformative counterhegemonic struggles that are breaking out in South Africa as I write, and further, as a possible justiciable constitutional principle that might work as a form of subaltern legality to overcome the disconnect that is being described in the press right now, between the Constitution and people on the ground. I should be clear that the uBuntu Project did not start out as a project to reconstitutionalize uBuntu as a justiciable principle in the new constitutional dispensation. In part because, like many on-the-ground, collectively run research projects, the project developed over time in a number of different directions, and still does. But the question of uBuntu's legal status became pressing in the project early on, because of the political furor over the removal of the epilogue of the interim constitution, in which the word *uBuntu* was used broadly, to a much more watered down use of uBuntu in the 1996 Constitution. In that document, uBuntu was only used to justify the formation, indeed the mandated formation, of a Truth and Reconciliation Commission. In the interim constitution, uBuntu was explicitly mentioned in the epilogue, and the epilogue was seen as having constitutional force. Indeed, in the foundational antideath penalty decision, *Makwanyane*, numerous justices referred to the epilogue and the use of uBuntu to underscore their own judgments as to why the death penalty could not be allowed in the new South Africa.[9]

At first I thought perhaps it was a biographical coincidence that I was a lawyer and a founder of the uBuntu Project that made law come to the fore. But I am now convinced that the Comaroffs are right about politics in South Africa, and that lawfare is very much at the heart of it on all sides.

But note that lawfare is a kind of politics and is therefore not based on the distinction between law and politics that is so familiar to us in the European or Anglo-American academy. This point is also underscored by Steven L. Robins, who argues that both rights and liberalism are challenged by the complex discourse of movements on the ground in South Africa. Robins is a South African ethnographer who has carefully documented that the use of rights talk in South Africa, as well as appeals to ethnic identity, do not necessarily appeal to any discourse of "injury," but rather are part of new mobilizations that are extraordinary in their creativity, given the ANC's attempt to render the subaltern governable. To quote Robins:

> The case studies in this book have drawn attention to the ambiguous and contradictory character of rights-based approaches to political mobilisation in post-apartheid South Africa. They question assumptions about the individualising and depoliticising nature of rights discourses (Brown 1995). The cases also draw attention to the diverse political rationalities and identities that NGOs and social movements encounter in their daily work. These include hybrid political discourses that defy the enduring binary categories of citizens and subjects, liberals and communitarians, modernists and traditionalist and so on. The NGO and social movement activists discussed in this book appear to have recognised the profoundly hybrid, provisional and situational character of politics in post-apartheid South Africa.[10]

My argument is, then, that the struggle over uBuntu is part of this rich political discourse, which sometimes involves the appeal to law very broadly construed. As I will show shortly, this connects the uBuntu Project with a larger project of subaltern legality, which by its very combination of terms, challenges the conventional definition of legality in Anglo-American jurisprudence, as a set of institutionalized state structures that legitimize both coercive power and a recognizable system of rules and principles that can be known as law (as opposed to law and ethics).

Therefore, the battle over uBuntu and its constitutionalization became an important site for whether or not African values and ideals could be seen as thoroughly modern, and therefore defensible within a modern legal system that would seem to foreclose them as outmoded forms of the "kingdom of custom."[11] So the defense of uBuntu as a constitutional principle was and continues to be fraught with all the sweeping implications of the battle against antiblack racism, the struggle for the recognition of Afro-modernity, and the engagement with Africana philosophy as one of the most important philosophical contributions to what we think of as modernity. This battle is of course about the constitutionalization of uBuntu, which has indeed become a frequently used constitutional principle through the recent judgments of the court. There is little doubt that Emeritus Justices Albie Sachs and Yvonne Mokgoro played a crucial role in the struggle for the recognition of uBuntu as a justiciable principle, but they have not been alone.

The question of whether the constitutionalization of uBuntu undermines its "subversive" value as a form of counterhegemonic politics and legality remains with us. There can be no grand-sweeping answer to this question, other than in the day-to-day politics, ethics, and reinterpretation of uBuntu at the level of legality and politics within South Africa. And that, to some degree, is the Comaroffs' central point in that pathbreaking book, *Theory from the South*. I would like to underscore, with them, that the recognition of Afro-modernity, as well as a serious engagement with Africana philosophy, does not lead in any sense to a disavowal—and it would be that in the Freudian sense of the word—of European philosophy. Obviously, uBuntu changes when it is brought into the context of constitutional jurisprudence, and it in turn changes constitutional jurisprudence. It is this untidy dialectic, to paraphrase Frantz Fanon's famous expression, that still opens up the space for new forms of both politics and ethics, and yes, of subaltern legality. As the Comaroffs remind us, this way of thinking about the relationship of lawfare and ID-ology, rejects the out-of-hand dismissal of battles for a subaltern counterhegemonic legality, to use Boaventura de Sousa Santos's telling phrase, because such a legality would necessarily inscribe "bad traditionalism," conservative identity politics, and the like. These questions cannot be answered apart from the struggle itself, including the struggle over the interpretation of uBuntu at the level of law. But it is important to note, here, that the struggle over the legalization of uBuntu actually also challenges the notion of legality as earlier defined in this conclusion and throughout this book. As Hylton White, amongst others, has emphasized, law is often brought to on-the-ground struggles by those, like sangomas, who have no institutionalized relationship to the state, and indeed forsake it.[12] De Sousa Santos has argued, and I agree with him, that there is a profound difference between subaltern legality and conventional Anglo-American and European definitions of law, because it challenges the difference between politics and law, and even the difference between legality and illegality. Much subaltern legality is illegal under the institutions of the state, and that is part of the reason it is counterhegemonic. To quote De Sousa Santos:

> A strong politics of law and rights is one that does not rely solely on law or on rights. Paradoxically, one way of showing defiance for law and rights is to struggle for increasingly inclusive laws and rights. Manipulability, contingency and instability from below is the most efficient way of confronting manipulability, contingency and instability from above. A strong politics of rights is a dual politics based on the dual management of legal and political tools under the aegis of the latter.
>
> The most intense moments of cosmopolitan legality are likely to involve direct action, civil disobedience, strikes, demonstrations, media-oriented performances, etc. Some of these will be illegal, while others will be located in spheres not regulated by state law. Subaltern illegality may be used to confront both dominant legality and dominant illegality.[13]

The Comaroffs have underscored that the burning critical theoretical issues of the Global South are, simply put, the burning critical issues that other nation states in Europe and the United States are facing. Their point is that we have an evolution of Euro-America to Africa, and I would add, South America. It is not surprising that we find the challenge to reigning hegemonic definitions of politics, law, ethics, and morality taking place in the Global South in a manner that is forcing those involved in the struggles there to rethink their fundamental categories, including the meaning of economic transformation and socialism. I have argued throughout this book that the relation between law, revolution, and on-the-ground struggles for socialism is complex indeed. But this complexity leads not to defeatism but to a demand to face it head on, and to find innovative forms of practice that include a profound respect for Afro-modernity and the ideals that have been developed within African Humanism. And so the struggle continues.

Notes

PREFACE

1. Jean and John L. Comaroff, "Liberalism, Policulturalism, and ID-ology: Thoughts on Citizenship and Difference," in *Theory from the South* (Boulder, CO: Paradigm, 2012), 65–90.

2. See Jean and John L. Comaroff, *Theory from the South*, 1–50.

INTRODUCTION: TRANSITIONAL JUSTICE
VERSUS SUBSTANTIVE REVOLUTION

1. For a searing discussion of both the organizational and military effort of the armed struggle, see Barry Gilder, *Songs and Secrets: South Africa from Liberation to Governance* (London: Hurst, 2012).

2. See also: Étienne Balibar, "Three Concepts of Politics," in *Politics and the Other Scene* (New York: Verso, 2002), 1–39.

3. See for instance, R. W. Johnson, *South Africa's Brave New World: The Beloved Country Since the End of Apartheid* (New York: The Overlook Press, 2010); Timothy D. Sisk, *Democratization in South Africa: The Elusive Social Contract* (Princeton, NJ: Princeton University Press, 1995); Donald L. Horowitz, *A Democratic South Africa? Constitutional Engineering in a Divided Society* (Berkeley: University of California Press, 1991); and Ruti G. Teitel, *Transitional Justice* (Oxford: Oxford University Press, 2000).

4. Sisk, *Democratization in South Africa*, 288.

5. Ibid., 299.

6. Marx famously used this slogan in his *Critique of the Gotha Program*, in *The Marx-Engels Reader*, ed. Robert Tucker (New York: Norton, 1978), 531. I changed the pronouns from "his" to "her."

7. See, for instance, Horowitz, *A Democratic South Africa?*, 124–62.

8. Ibid., 88.

9. Samuel P. Huntington, "Will More Countries Become Democratic?" in *Political Science Quarterly* 99, no. 2 (Summer 1984): 213.

10. Horowitz, *A Democratic South Africa?*, 89.

11. Teitel, *Transitional Justice*, 20.

12. "The problem of transitional justice arises within the distinctive context of transition—a shift in political orders. By focusing its inquiry on the stage of "transition," this book chooses to shift the terms of the debate away from the vocabulary of "revolution" often deployed by theorists to an analysis of the role of law in political change. Rather than an undefined last stage of revolution, the conception of transition advanced here is both more capacious and more defined. What is demarcated is a postrevolutionary period of political change; thus, the problem of transitional justice arises within a bounded period, spanning two regimes." Teitel, *Transitional Justice*, 5.

13. Sampie Terreblanche, *A History of Inequality in South Africa, 1652–2002* (Scottsville: University of Natal Press, 2002), 18.

14. See also Terreblanche, *Lost in Transformation: South Africa's Search for a New Future Since 1986* (Johannesburg: KMM Review Publishing Company, 2012).

15. I am well aware of the criticisms of Julius Malema as a provocateur who is inspiring a Schmittian political division between friend and enemy rather than an alliance on the ground that can truly fight for democratic socialism. Although Malema is the leader of the party, he is of course not the party, and many people who are joining are doing so in the name of a democratic and ethical vision of socialism, and not a return to a dictatorship of the proletariat or to one-party rule and the end of constitutionalism. I mention the EFF only to underscore how many people on the ground agree with Sampie Terreblanche that the transition and transformation has failed because of the ANC's capitulation to neoliberal capitalism, and that the only real alternative is a form of socialism.

16. Lourens W. H. Ackermann, "The Legal Nature of the South African Constitutional Revolution," in *New Zealand Law Review* 4 (2004): 633–79.

17. Hannah Arendt, *On Revolution* (New York: Penguin, 1990).

18. I return here to Étienne Balibar's three critical concepts of politics that would be fundamental to a radical or revolutionary political theory: emancipation, transformation, and civility. Balibar, "Three Concepts of Politics."

19. Comaroff and Comaroff, "Liberalism, Policulturalism, and ID-ology: Thoughts on Citizenship and Difference" in *Theory from the South* (Boulder, CO: Paradigm, 2012), 65–90.

20. Boaventura de Sousa Santos, *Toward a New Legal Common Sense: Law, Globalization, and Emancipation* (London: LexisNexis Butterworths, 2002), 81–82.

21. Hans Kelsen, *General Theory of Law and State*, trans. Anders Wedberg (The Lawbook Exchange, 2011).

22. See Ackermann, "The Legal Nature of the South African Constitutional Revolution." See also Drucilla Cornell and Nick Friedman, "In Defence of the Constitutional Court: Human Rights and the South African Common Law," in *Malawi Law Journal* 5, no. 1 (June 2011): 1–31.

23. See Karl Klare, "Transformative Constitutionalism and the Common and Customary Law," in *South African Journal on Human Rights* 26, no. 3 (2010): 403–509.

24. See Ackermann, "The Legal Nature of the South African Constitutional Revolution."

25. De Sousa Santos, *Toward a New Legal Common Sense*, 437.

26. Ibid.

27. See Drucilla Cornell, "A Call for a Nuanced Constitutional Jurisprudence: South Africa, uBuntu, Dignity, and Reconciliation," in Drucilla Cornell and Nyoko Muvangua, eds., *uBuntu and the Law: African Ideals and Postapartheid Jurisprudence* (New York: Fordham University Press, 2012), 324–32.

28. De Sousa Santos follows H. Kantorowicz in defining justiciability: "Justiciability is defined by H. Kantorowicz as the characteristic of those rules 'which are considered fit to be applied by a judicial organ in some definite procedure.' By 'judicial organ' Kantorowicz means 'a definite authority concerned with a kind of 'casuistry,' to wit, the application of principles to individual cases of conflict between parties.' As we can see, Kantorowicz uses the concept of judicial organ in a very broad sense or, as he puts it, in a very "modest and untechnical sense," since it includes state judges, jurors, headmen, chieftains, magicians, priests, sages, doomsmen, councils of tribal elders, kinship tribunals, military societies, parliaments, international institutions, areopagi, sports umpires, arbitrators, church courts, *censores*, courts of love, courts of honour, *Bierrichter* and eventually gang leaders." De Sousa Santos, "Toward a New Legal Common Sense," 100–1.

29. I originally intended to give a different title to the edited volume, *uBuntu and the Law*, namely: *Law in the uBuntu of South Africa*. However, some commentators felt it would be unclear to an Anglo-American audience, precisely because it was too radical of a challenge to Anglo-American conceptions of law. Drucilla Cornell and Nyoko Muvangua, eds., *uBuntu and the Law: African Ideals and Postapartheid Jurisprudence* (New York: Fordham University Press, 2012).

30. Comaroff and Comaroff, *Theory from the South*.

31. See www.theubuntuproject.org.

32. Boaventura de Sousa Santos, ed., *Voices of the World* (London: Verso, 2010).

33. De Sousa Santos, *Voices of the World*, x.

34. For instance, Wendy Brown, "All the Edge: The Future of Political Theory," in Wendy Brown, *Edgework: Critical Essays on Knowledge and Practice* (Princeton, NJ: Princeton University Press, 2005), 60–82.

35. De Sousa Santos, *Toward a New Legal Common Sense*, 234.

36. Comaroff and Comaroff, *Theory from the South*, 1.

1. IS TECHNOLOGY A FATAL DESTINY? HEIDEGGER'S RELEVANCE FOR SOUTH AFRICA AND OTHER "DEVELOPING" COUNTRIES

1. Amartya Sen, *Development as Freedom* (Oxford: Oxford University Press, 1999).

2. Martin Heidegger, "The Question Concerning Technology," in *Basic Writings*, ed. David Farrell Krell (San Francisco: Harper, 1993), 321.

3. Heidegger, "The Question Concerning Technology," 324.

4. Zakes Mda, *The Whale Caller* (New York: Farrar, Straus and Giroux, 2006), 8.

5. Ibid., 13.

6. Martin Heidegger, "Modern Science, Metaphysics, and Mathematics," in *Basic Writings*, 274–75.

7. Martin Heidegger, "Building Dwelling Thinking," in *Basic Writings*, 351.

8. Mda, *The Whale Caller*, 17.

9. Ibid., 16–17.

10. Ibid., 279–80.

11. Ibid., 2–3.

12. Ibid., 284.

13. Martin Heidegger, "On the Essence of Truth," in *Basic Writings*, 125.

14. Mda, *The Whale Caller*, 291.

15. Ibid., 297.

16. Ibid., 298.

17. Of course my own answer to that question in *The Philosophy of the Limit* (New York: Routledge, 1992) and in *Moral Images of Freedom: A Future for Critical Theory* (Lanham, MD: Rowman & Littlefield, 2008) is that we cannot know the answer to that question even in Heidegger's own terms.

18. Cf. Marx, *Critique of the Gotha Program*, in *The Marx-Engels Reader*, ed. Robert Tucker (New York: Norton, 1978), 531. I changed the pronouns from "his" to "her."

2. SOCIALISM OR RADICAL DEMOCRATIC POLITICS? ON LACLAU AND MOUFFE

1. Ernesto Laclau and Chantal Mouffe, *Hegemony and Socialist Strategy: Towards a Radical Democratic Politics*, 2nd ed. (London/New York: Verso, 2001).

2. Cf. the Poor People's Alliance, a network of grassroots organizations in South Africa that was formed in 2008. "Voices of the Poor Must Be Heard," *BusinessDay*, October 25, 2010.

3. Laclau and Mouffe, *Hegemony and Socialist Strategy*, 178.

4. Ibid., 188–89.

5. Ernesto Laclau, "Identity and Hegemony: The Role of Universality in the Constitution of Political Logics," in *Contingency, Hegemony, Universality: Contemporary Dialogues on the Left*, ed. Judith Butler, Ernesto Laclau, and Slavoj Žižek (London/New York: Verso, 2000), 53–54.

6. The Freedom Charter, as adopted at the Congress of the People, Kliptown, South Africa on June 26, 1955.

7. Laclau and Mouffe, *Hegemony and Socialist Strategy*, 189.

8. Étienne Balibar, "'Rights of Man' and 'Rights of the Citizen': The Modern Dialectic of Equality and Freedom," in *Masses, Classes, Ideas: Studies on Politics and Philosophy Before and After Marx* (New York: Routledge, 1994), 47.

9. The Constitution of the Republic of South Africa, as adopted on May 8, 1996, and amended on October 11, 1996, by the Constitutional Assembly.

10. Robert M. Cover, "Nomos and Narrative," in Cover, *Narrative, Violence, and the Law: The Essays of Robert Cover* (Ann Arbor: University of Michigan Press, 1995), 95–172. Seyla Benhabib, *Another Cosmopolitanism* (New York: Oxford University Press, 2006), 49.

11. See *Port Elizabeth Municipality v. Various Occupiers*, 2005 (1) SA 217 (CC) at para. 23.

12. Ernesto Laclau, "Subject of Politics, Politics of the Subject," in *Emancipation(s)* (London/New York: Verso, 1996), 57–58.

13. See, for example, Alain Badiou's argument as to how capitalism undermines the very idea of anything like a shared world in which people could meet one another as members of a demos. Alain Badiou, "The Democratic Emblem," in *Democracy in What State?*, ed. Giorgio Agamben et al. (New York: Columbia University Press, 2011), 6–15. See also Slavoj Žižek, "How to Begin from the Beginning," in *The Idea of Communism*, ed. Costas Douzinas and Slavoj Žižek (New York: Verso, 2010), 209–26.

14. Cf. Michael Hardt and Antonio Negri, *Multitude: War and Democracy in the Age of Empire* (New York: Penguin, 2005), 213: "This new common mode of life always forms in dialogue with local traditions and habits. Consider, for example, how the EZLN in the Lacadon jungle of Chiapas mixes elements of national history, such as the figure of Zapata and the legacy of peasant revolts, with local indigenous Tzeltal mythology and forges them together with network relationships and democratic practices to create a new life in common that defines the movement. The mobilization of the common gives the common a

new intensity. The direct conflict with power, moreover, for better or for worse, elevates this common intensity to an even higher level: the acrid smell of tear gas focuses your senses and street clashes with police make your blood boil with rage, raising intensity to the point of explosion. The intensification of the common, finally, brings about an anthropological transformation such that out of the struggles comes a new humanity."

15. Benhabib, *Another Cosmopolitanism*, 45.

16. The passage in *Hegemony and Socialist Strategy* most pertinent to this question, on 76–77, does not provide a clear response.

17. Rosa Luxemburg, *The Accumulation of Capital* (New York: Routledge, 2003). See also Drucilla Cornell, "Can There Be a People's Commons? The Significance of Rosa Luxemburg's *The Accumulation of Capital* for Politics in South Africa," in *The Intellectual Origins of the Global Financial Crisis,* ed. Roger Berkowitz and Taun N. Toay (New York: Fordham University Press, 2012), 191–98.

18. See Patrick Bond, Horman Chitonge, and Arndt Hopfmann, eds., *The Accumulation of Capital in Southern Africa: Rosa Luxemburg Political Education Seminar 2006* (Johannesburg: The Regional Office of the Rosa Luxemburg Foundation, 2006), http://ccs.ukzn.ac.za/files/RL%20Capital-africa.pdf.

19. "So comrades, today, I appeal to you, that what we need to do, is to conquer the capitalist system, because each second you turn your head, the capitalist system is there. We face electricity cut-offs, water disconnections, evictions and so on, because we cannot afford to pay." S'Bu Zikode, "The Shackdwellers Movement of Durban," in *The Accumulation of Capital in Southern Africa*, 165.

20. Slavoj Žižek, "Class Struggle or Postmodernism? Yes, Please!" in *Contingency, Hegemony, Universality,* ed. Butler, Laclau, and Žižek, 108.

21. Chantal Mouffe, *The Democratic Paradox* (London/New York: Verso, 2009).

22. Ernesto Laclau, "Universalism, Particularism and the Question of Identity," in *Emancipation(s)*, 35.

23. Drucilla Cornell, *Moral Images of Freedom: A Future for Critical Theory* (Lanham, MD: Rowman & Littlefield, 2008), 148–49.

3. DIGNITY VIOLATED: RETHINKING *AZAPO* THROUGH UBUNTU

1. *AZAPO and Others v. President of the Republic of South Africa* 1996 4 SA 671 (CC).

2. See the introduction to this book.

3. Costas Douzinas and Slavoj Žižek, eds., *The Idea of Communism* (New York: Verso, 2010).

4. Cf. Marx, "Critique of the Gotha Program," in *The Marx-Engels Reader,* ed. Robert Tucker (New York: Norton, 1978), 531. I changed the pronouns from "his" to "her."

5. Ernst Bloch, *Natural Law and Human Dignity*, trans. Dennis J. Schmidt (Boston: MIT Press, 1987), 20.

6. The Freedom Charter, as adopted at the Congress of the People, Kliptown, on June 26, 1955. Document can be found at http://www.anc.org.za/show.php?id=72.

7. For a fuller discussion of GEAR, see Sampie Terreblanche, *A History of Inequality in South Africa 1652–2002* (Pietermaritzburg: University of Natal Press, 2002), 72–93.

8. See Terreblanche, *A History of Inequality in South Africa 1652–2002*, for a full discussion of the history of unfree black labor in South Africa from the time of the initial colonization of the Western Cape until the present. Apartheid was only one organization of unfree black labor that built off centuries of previous exploitation.

9. See Mark Sanders, *Ambiguities of Witnessing: Law and Literature in the Time of a Truth Commission* (Stanford, CA: Stanford University Press, 2007).

10. Sanders, *Ambiguities of Witnessing*, 10–11.

11. John Dugard, *International Law: A South African Perspective*, third edition (Lansdowne, South Africa: Juta, 2005), 535–36. Dugard writes: "Article 1(4) of Additional Protocol I extends the application of the Geneva Conventions of 1949 to 'armed conflicts in which people are fighting against colonial domination and alien occupation and against racist regimes in the exercise of their right of self-determination.' To benefit from this provision, a national liberation movement (NLM) is required to deposit a declaration accepting the obligations under the law of Geneva with the Swiss Federal Council. Members of the NLM then become entitled, inter alia, to be treated as prisoners of war by the colonial/racist power (if it accepts Protocol I) and not as criminal rebels or terrorists. This controversial provision was directed largely at apartheid South Africa and Israel, the states then engaged in hostilities against NLMs. For this reason South Africa refused to ratify the Additional Protocols until 1995. Despite its controversial nature, which has resulted in both the United States and Israel refusing to sign Additional Protocol I, the practical impact of article 1(4) has been small. Indeed, it has yet to be applied."

12. *AZAPO v. President of the Republic of South Africa* 1996 (4) SA 671 (CC), para. 17.

13. Promotion of National Unity and Reconciliation Act 34 of 1995.

14. See Sanders, *Ambiguities of Witnessing*, 116–20.

15. Promotion of National Unity and Reconciliation Act, Art. 4 (c).

16. Art. 20 (7) (a) of the Promotion of National Unity and Reconciliation Act provides: "No person who has been granted amnesty in respect of an act, omission or offence shall be criminally or civilly liable in respect of such act,

omission or offence and no body or organisation or the State shall be liable, and no person shall be vicariously liable, for any such act, omission or offence."

17. Constitution of the Republic of South Africa Act 200 of 1993 ("Interim Constitution," repealed by the Constitution1996), chap. 3, sec. 22 ("access to court").

18. *AZAPO*, para. 25.

19. Epilogue to the Interim Constitution of 1993, cited in *AZAPO*, para. 3.

20. *AZAPO*, para. 36.

21. Ibid., 40. I am putting "truth" in quotation marks, because there has been much literature on what *truth* meant before the TRC, and wide recognitions that there were layers and layers of truthfulness implied in the testimonies that took place before the commission.

22. *AZAPO*, para. 41.

23. Charles Villa-Vilencio and Erik Doxtader, eds., *The Provocations of Amnesty: Memory, Justice and Impunity* (Lawrenceville, NJ: Africa World Press, 2004).

24. See Terreblanche, *A History of Inequality in South Africa*.

25. *AZAPO*, para. 43.

26. See Johan Snyman, "Thoughts on Dealing with the Legacies of Radically Unjust Political Behaviour," in *Law, Memory and the Legacy of Apartheid: Ten years after AZAPO v. President of South Africa*, ed. Wessel le Roux and Karin van Marle (Pretoria: Pretoria University Law Press, 2007), 3–10.

27. *AZAPO*, par. 44.

28. I am using my own Kantian understanding of degradation as I developed it in Drucilla Cornell, *The Imaginary Domain: A Future for Critical Theory* (New York: Rowman & Littlefield, 2008), 11–38.

29. *AZAPO*, para. 19.

30. Convention (IV) respecting the Laws and Customs of War on Land and its annex: Regulations concerning the Laws and Customs of War on Land. The Hague, October 18, 1907.

31. See Louis Henkin, *Human Rights* (New York: Foundation Press, 1999), 610–14.

32. Convention (IV) relative to the Protection of the Civilian Persons in Time of War, Geneva, August 12, 1949, art. 147. Contracting parties are required to enact "any legislation necessary to provide effective penal sanctions for person committing, or ordering to be committed, any of the grave breaches of those conventions." Ibid., art. 146.

33. Convention on the Prevention and Punishment of the Crime of Genocide, December 9, 1948.

34. Statute of the International Tribunal for the Prosecution of Persons Responsible for Serious Violations of International Humanitarian Law Committed in the Territory of the Former Yugoslavia since 1991, UN Doc. S/25704 at

36, annex (1993) and S/25704/Add.1 (1993), adopted by Security Council on May 25, 1993, UN Doc. S/RES/827 (1993).

35. UN Charter, chap. VII.

36. *State v. Makwanyane* 1995 (3) SA 391 (CC).

37. *AZAPO*, para. 30.

38. Ibid.

39. Nthabiseng Mogale, "Ten Years of Democracy in South Africa: Revisiting the *AZAPO* Decision," in *Law, Memory and the Legacy of Apartheid*, ed. Le Roux and Van Marle, 141–42.

40. Dugard, *International Law*, 542.

41. Ibid., 543.

42. *AZAPO*, para. 29, footnote 29.

43. Dugard, *International Law*, 543–44.

44. See Mogale, "Ten Years of Democracy in South Africa," 145.

45. International Convention on the Suppression and Punishment of the Crime of Apartheid, New York, November 30, 1973.

46. Sampie Terreblanche, *A History of Inequality in South Africa*, 316.

47. Steve Biko wrote: "Geographically, i.e. in terms of land distribution, bantustans present a gigantic fraud that can find no moral support from any quarter. We find that 20% of the population are in control of 87% of the land while 80% 'control' only 13%. To make this situation even more ridiculous, not one these so-called "Bantustan nations" have an intact piece of land. All of them are scattered little bits of the most unyielding soil. In each area the more productive bits are white-controlled islands on which white farms or other types of industry are situated." Steve Biko, "Let's Talk About Bantustans," in *I Write What I Like: Selected Writings* (Chicago: University of Chicago Press, 2002), 82.

48. Truth and Reconciliation of South Africa Report, vol. 1, 75.

49. For a longer discussion, see Albie Sachs, *The Strange Alchemy of Life and Law* (Oxford: Oxford University Press, 2009), as well as my forthcoming article, "Comrade Judge: Can a Revolutionary Be a Judge?"

50. Truth and Reconciliation of South Africa Report, vol. 1, 67–69. See also my discussion of just wars in Drucilla Cornell, *Defending Ideals* (New York: Routledge, 2004), chap. 2, "Worlds Apart: Perpetual Peace and Infinite War," 21–40.

51. Truth and Reconciliation of South Africa Report, vol. 1, 348.

52. See Richard Wilson, "The Myth of Restorative Justice: Truth, Reconciliation and the Ethics of Amnesty," in *South African Journal of Human Rights* 17 (2001): 531–62, and Darrel Moellendorf, "Amnesty, Truth and Justice: *AZAPO*," in *South African Journal of Human Rights* 13, no. 2 (1997): 283–91.

53. See Ronald Dworkin, *Taking Rights Seriously* (Cambridge, MA: Harvard University Press, 1978).

54. Thomas Nagel, "The Justice and Society Program of the Aspen Institute, State Crimes: Punishment of Pardon" (1988), 93.

55. Immanuel Kant, *The Metaphysics of Morals*, ed. Mary J. Gregor (Cambridge: Cambridge University Press, 1996), 105–6.

56. Immanuel Kant, "Toward Perpetual Peace," in *Practical Philosophy*, ed. Mary J. Gregor (Cambridge: Cambridge University Press, 1999), 326.

57. See Hegel, *Elements of the Philosophy of Right*, ed. Allan W. Wood, trans. H. B. Nisbet (Cambridge: Cambridge University Press, 2002), 119–32 (sections 90–104).

58. Steve Biko, "Black Consciousness and the Quest for a True Humanity," in *I Write What I Like*, 96–108.

59. Amartya Sen, *Development as Freedom* (Oxford: Oxford University Press, 1999).

60. Sanders, *Ambiguities of Witnessing*, 27.

61. Ibid.

62. Antjie Krog, *Country of My Skull* (Johannesburg: Random House, 1998), 278–79. Cited in Sanders, *Ambiguities of Witnessing*, 136.

63. Biko, "Black Consciousness and the Quest for a True Humanity," 108.

64. Mahmood Mamdani, "Reconciliation Without Justice," in *Southern African Review of Books* (November/December 1996).

65. See, generally, Sampie Terreblanche, *A History of Inequality in South Africa*.

66. Drucilla Cornell, Mahmood Mamdani, and Sampie Terreblanche, "Only Complete Reform of Economy Can Defuse Tensions," in *Cape Times*, May 28, 2008.

67. For a longer discussion of Khulumani's struggle for restitutional equality and a full program of reparations, see Tshepo Madlingozi, "Good victim, bad victim: Apartheid's beneficiaries, victims, and the struggle for social justice," in Le Roux and Van Marle, *Law, Memory and the Legacy of Apartheid*, 107–26.

68. I discuss this more fully in the introduction to this book.

69. See, for instance, Ruti G. Teitel, *Transitional Justice* (Oxford: Oxford University Press, 2000), particularly her chapter on "Administrative Justice," 149–90.

70. See also Jean Comaroff and John L. Comaroff, *Theory from the South, or, How Euro-America is Evolving Toward Africa* (Boulder, CO: Paradigm, 2012).

4. WHICH LAW, WHOSE HUMANITY? THE SIGNIFICANCE
OF POLICULTURALISM IN THE GLOBAL SOUTH

1. John Rawls, *The Law of Peoples* (Cambridge, MA: Harvard University Press, 1999).

2. Seyla Benhabib, *Another Cosmopolitanism* (New York: Oxford University Press, 2006).

3. See Mahmood Mamdani, *Citizen and Subject: Contemporary Africa and the Legacy of Late Colonialism* (Princeton, NJ: Princeton University Press, 1996).

4. Benhabib, *Another Cosmopolitanism*, 87.

5. Ibid., 75–76.

6. Ibid., 76–77.

7. We also need to make an addition to Rawls here, which is that the notion of individuality and even autonomy may not be a Western-European or an Anglo-American liberal idea. See Jean Comaroff and John L. Comaroff, "On Personhood: A Perspective from Africa," in *Theory from the South, or, How Euro-America is Evolving Toward Africa* (Boulder/London: Paradigm Publishers, 2012), 51–64.

8. Rawls, *The Law of Peoples*, 73.

9. John Rawls, "The Idea of Public Reason Revisited," in *Collected Papers*, ed. Samuel Freeman (Cambridge, MA: Harvard University Press, 2001), 594.

10. I am well aware that what is African is a political and ethical question, and not simply a question of geography. See V. I. Mudimbe, *The Invention of Africa: Gnosis, Philosophy, and the Order of Knowledge* (Bloomington: Indiana University Press, 1988).

11. Tzvetan Todorov, *The Conquest from America: The Question of the Other*, trans. Richard Howard (New York: Harper & Row, 1984).

12. See, generally, Jean Comaroff and John L. Comaroff, "Liberalism, Policulturalism, and ID-ology: Thoughts on Citizenship and Difference," in *Theory from the South*, 65–90.

13. Although the words "traditional leaders" do appear in the South African Constitution, the question of who does and does not have leadership within any particular ethnic, tribal, or national identity within South Africa is a hotly debated question, and the word *tradition* should not be defined in opposition to modernity. See Jean Comaroff and John L. Comaroff, "Nations With/Out Borders: The Politics of Being and the Problem of Belonging," in *Theory from the South*, 91–108.

14. See Drucilla Cornell, "Bridging the Span Toward Justice: Laurie Ackermann and the Ongoing Architectonic of Dignity Jurisprudence," in *Dignity, Freedom and the Post-Apartheid Legal Order: The Critical Jurisprudence of Justice Laurie Ackermann*, ed. Jaco Barnard-Naude, Francois Du Bois, and Drucilla Cornell (Cape Town: Juta Press, 2009).

15. Jean and John L. Comaroff edited an excellent book in which various authors challenge Western notions of civil society: *Civil Society and the Political*

Imagination in South Africa: Critical Perspectives (Chicago: University of Chicago Press, 2000).

16. Charles Taylor, *A Secular Age* (Cambridge, MA: The Belknap Press of Harvard University Press, 2007), 194.

17. Comaroff and Comaroff, *Theory from the South*, 77–78.

18. Ibid., 81.

19. Ibid.

20. Thandabantu Nhlapo, "The African Customary Law of Marriage and the Rights Conundrum," in *Beyond Rights Talk and Culture Talk: Comparative Essays on the Politics of Rights and Culture*, 136.

21. Nhlapo, "The African Customary Law of Marriage and the Rights Conundrum," 146.

22. Comaroff and Comaroff, *Theory from the South*, 85.

23. See Jean and John L. Comaroff's introduction to *Modernity and Its Malcontents: Ritual and Power in Postcolonial Africa*, ed. Jean Comaroff and John Comaroff (Chicago: University of Chicago Press, 1993).

24. Talal Asad, *Formations of the Secular* (Stanford, CA: Stanford University Press, 2003).

25. Nhlapo, "The African Customary Law of Marriage and the Rights Conundrum," 148.

26. See *uBuntu and the Law: African Ideals and Post-Apartheid Jurisprudence*, ed. Drucilla Cornell and Nyoko Muvangua (New York: Fordham University Press, 2012).

27. See, generally, Ebrahim Moosa, "Tensions in Legal and Religious Values in the 1996 South African Constitution," in *Beyond Rights Talk and Culture Talk: Comparative Essays on the Politics of Rights and Culture*, ed. Mahmood Mamdani (New York: St. Martin's Press, 2000), 121–35.

28. See Yvonne Mokgoro, "uBuntu and the Law in South Africa," in *uBuntu and the Law*, 317–23.

5. LIVING CUSTOMARY LAW AND THE LAW:
DOES CUSTOM ALLOW FOR A WOMAN TO BE HOSI?

1. *Shilubana and Others v. Nwamitwa* (CCT 03/07) [2008] ZACC 9; 2008 (9) BCLR 914 (CC); 2009 2 SA 66 (CC).

2. *Shilubana*, para. 35.

3. *Nwamitwa v. Phillia and Others* 2005 3 SA 536 (T); *Shilubana and Others v. Nwamitwa (Commission for Gender Equality as* Amicus Curiae*)* 2007 2 SA 432 (SCA).

4. *Shilubana*, para. 19, quoting from *Shilubana* (High Court) (note 3 above) 539B-E.

5. *Shilubana* (High Court) 544G.

6. *Shilubana* (High Court) (note 3 above) 546D–547D, 548E–H.

7. Ibid., 548E–H.

8. Ibid., para. 47.

9. Ibid., para. 49.

10. Ibid., para. 50–51.

11. Ibid.

12. Ibid., para. 51.

13. Ibid., para. 53–54.

14. Hans Kelsen, *General Theory of Law and State* (Cambridge, MA: Harvard University Press, 1945), 117.

15. Drucilla Cornell, "Bridging the Span toward Justice: Laurie Ackermann and the Ongoing Architectonic of Dignity Jurisprudence," in *Dignity, Freedom, and the Post-Apartheid Order: The Critical Jurisprudence of Laurie Ackermann*, ed. Barnard-Naudé et al. (Lansdowne, South Africa: Juta Press, 2009), 18–46.

16. *Shilubana* (note 1 above), para. 43.

17. Ibid., para. 44.

18. Ibid., para. 45–46.

19. Ibid., para. 47.

20. *Carmichele v. Minister of Safety and Security and Another (Centre for Applied Legal Studies Intervening)* [2001] ZACC 22; 2001 4 SA 438 (CC); 2001 10 BCLR 995 (CC), referring to para. 34–36.

21. *Shilubana* (note 1 above), para. 48.

22. *Van Breda and Others v. Jacobs and Others* 1921 AD 330.

23. *Shilubana* (note 1 above), para. 52, referring to *Van Breda* (n 22 above), 334.

24. *Shilubana* (note 1 above), para. 54.

25. Ibid.

26. Ibid., para. 55.

27. Jean and John L. Comaroff, "Liberalism, Policulturalism, and ID-ology: Thoughts on Citizenship and Difference," in *Theory from the South* (Boulder, CO: Paradigm, 2012), 65–90.

28. J. C. Bekker and C. C. Boonzaaier, "Succession of Women to Traditional Leadership: Is the Judgement in *Shilubana v. Nwamitwa* Based on Sound Legal Principles?" XLI CILSA 2008.

29. Ibid., 460–61.

30. Nomthandazo Ntlama, "'Equality' Misplaced in the Development of the Customary Law of Succession: Lessons from Shilubana v. Nwamitwa 2009 2 SA 66 (CC)" in *Stellenbosch Law Review* 20, no. 2 (2009): 333–56.

31. Ibid., 352.

32. *Shilubana* (note 1 above), para. 70.

33. Ibid., para. 72.

34. Ibid., para. 78.

35. Ibid., para. 76–77.

36. Ibid., para. 81.

37. Ibid., para. 88–91.

38. John Murungi, "The Question of an African Jurisprudence: Some Hermeneutic Reflections," in *A Companion to African Philosophy*, ed. Kwasi Wiredu (Malden, MA: Blackwell, 2006), 519–26.

39. Roger Berkowitz, *The Gift of Science* (New York: Fordham University Press, 2005), ix.

40. Murungi, "The Question of an African Jurisprudence," 525–26.

6. UBUNTU, PLURALISM, AND THE RESPONSIBILITY OF LEGAL ACADEMICS

1. Roger Berkowitz, *The Gift of Science* (New York: Fordham University Press, 2005).

2. I have endeavored to explain Cassirer's rewriting of the Kantian notion of schema in *Moral Images of Freedom: A Future for Critical Theory* (Lanham, MD: Rowman and Littlefield, 2008) and in Drucilla Cornell and Kenneth Michael Panfilio, *Symbolic Forms for a New Humanity: Cultural and Racial Reconfigurations of Critical Theory* (New York: Fordham University Press, 2010).

3. See generally Cassirer's *The Philosophy of Symbolic Forms* to note the ways in which symbolic forms ranging from myth to science are captured and illuminated through careful readings of the ways in which these symbolic forms of the larger world are explained in careful detail. Ernst Cassirer, *The Philosophy of Symbolic Forms, Vol. 1–4* (New Haven, CT: Yale University Press, 1953).

4. Chuma Himonga, "The Legal Culture of a Society in Transition: The Case of South Africa," in Roger Blanspain, ed., Law in Motion: *International Encyclopaedia of Laws*, World Law Conference, conference publication (The Hague: Kluwer Law International, 1997), 78–79.

5. A sangoma is variously described as a holy man or woman, a skilled diviner, or healer within the tradition of the Zulu and Ndebele people.

6. Berkowitz, *The Gift of Science*, ix.

7. Ibid., xii.

8. Kabir Bavikatte, "Spiritualizing the Law" (report on field work, on file with the author), 6.

9. Paget Henry, *Caliban's Reason: Introducing Afro-Caribbean Philosophy* (New York: Routledge, 2000), 11–12.

10. For a fuller discussion of African existentialism, see Cornell and Panfilio, *Symbolic Forms for a New Humanity*, 95–124.

11. *Port Elizabeth Municipality v. Various Occupiers* 2004 (12) BCLR 1268 (CC).

12. Ibid., para. 14.

13. Ibid., para. 32.

14. Ibid., para. 37.

15. *uBuntu Hokae*. Dir. Carl Houston McMillan (2009). Short film. Available online: http://theubuntuproject.org/documentary.php.

16. Bavikatte, "Spiritualising the Law," 16.

17. Hylton White, "Outside the Dwelling of Culture: Estrangement and Difference in Postcolonial Zululand," in *Anthropological Quarterly* 83, no. 3 (Summer 2010): 511.

18. John Comaroff and Jean Comaroff, "Millennial Capitalism: First Thoughts on a Second Coming," in *Public Culture* 12, no. 2 (2000): 299.

19. Thandabantu Nhlapo, "The African Customary Law of Marriage and the Rights Conundrum," in Mahmood Mamdani, ed., *Beyond Rights Talk and Culture Talk: Comparative Essays on the Politics of Rights and Culture* (Cape Town: David Phillip, 2000), 146.

20. Robert M. Cover, "Nomos and Narrative," in Cover, *Narrative, Violence, and the Law: The Essays of Robert Cover* (Ann Arbor: University of Michigan Press, 1995), 95–172.

21. Jean Comaroff and John L. Comaroff, "Liberalism, Policulturalism, and ID-ology: Thoughts on Citizenship and Difference," in *Theory from the South*, 77.

22. Tzvetan Todorov, *The Conquest from America: The Question of the Other*, trans. Richard Howard (New York: Harper & Row, 1984).

23. John Rawls, "The Idea of an Overlapping Consensus," in *Political Liberalism* (New York: Columbia University Press, 1996), 133–72.

24. This interpretation of section 10 arose in a discussion with Justice Ackermann.

25. Immanuel Kant, "On the Relationship of Theory to Practice in Political Right," in *Political Writings*, ed. Hans Reiss, trans. H. B. Nisbet (Cambridge: Cambridge University Press, 1991), 73–86.

7. RETHINKING ETHICAL FEMINISM THROUGH UBUNTU

1. On the concept of global apartheid, see Michael Hardt and Antonio Negri, *Multitude: War and Democracy in the Age of Empire* (New York: Penguin, 2004), 160–67.

2. Seyla Benhabib, Judith Butler, Drucilla Cornell, and Nancy Fraser, *Feminist Contentions: A Philosophical Exchange* (New York: Routledge, 1995).

3. Cf. most recently: Gayatri Chakravorty Spivak, "In Response: Looking Back, Looking Forward," in *Can the Subaltern Speak? Reflections on the History of*

an Idea, ed. Rosalind C. Morris (New York: Columbia University Press, 2010), 227–36.

4. Cf. Jacques Lacan, *Feminine Sexuality: Jacques Lacan and the école freudienne*, ed. Juliet Mitchell and Jacqueline Rose, trans. Jacqueline Rose (New York: Norton, 1985).

5. Cf. Frantz Fanon, *Black Skin, White Masks*, trans. Richard Philcox (New York: Grove Press, 2008).

6. Gayatri Chakravorty Spivak, *Death of a Discipline* (New York: Columbia University Press, 2003), 70.

7. Spivak, "Can the Subaltern Speak?" in *Can the Subaltern Speak? Reflections on the History of an Idea* (New York: Columbia University Press 2010), 237–92.

8. Judith Butler, *Precarious Life: The Powers of Mourning and Violence* (London/New York: Verso, 2004).

9. *Precarious Life*, 42.

10. Ibid., 33.

11. Judith Butler, "Restaging the Universal: Hegemony and the Limits of Formalism," in *Contingency, Hegemony, Universality: Contemporary Dialogues on the Left*, ed. Judith Butler, Ernesto Laclau, and Slavoj Žižek (London/New York: Verso, 2000), 11–43.

12. Spivak, "Righting Wrongs," in *South Atlantic Quarterly* 103, no. 2–3 (Spring/Summer 2004): 523–81. Cf. Drucilla Cornell, "The Ethical Affirmation of Human Rights: Gayatri Spivak's Intervention," in *Can the Subaltern Speak? Reflections on the History of an Idea*, 100–16.

13. Cf. Adam Ashforth, *Witchcraft, and Democracy in South Africa* (Chicago: University of Chicago Press, 2005), and Chantal Mouffe, ed., *The Challenge of Carl Schmitt* (London/New York: Verso, 1999).

14. Cf. Slavoj Žižek, *In Defense of Lost Causes* (London/New York: Verso, 2008).

15. Cf. Antonio Negri, *Goodbye Mr. Socialism: Radical Politics in the 21st Century* (New York: Seven Stories Press, 2008), 90–91.

16. Saba Mahmood, *Politics of Piety: The Islamic Revival and the Feminist Subject* (Princeton, NJ: Princeton University Press, 2004), 149.

17. *Bhe and Others v. Magistrate, Khayelitsha and Others; Shibi v. Sithole and Others; SA Human Rights Commission and Another v. President of the RSA and Another* 2005 (1) BCLR 1 (CC) and 2004 (1) BCLR 27 (C). Selections published in *uBuntu and the Law: African Ideals and Postapartheid Jurisprudence*, ed. Drucilla Cornell and Nyoko Muvangua (New York: Fordham University Press, 2012), 222–32.

18. Ibid., at para. 163.

19. Ibid., at para. 156.

20. Ibid., at para. 222.

21. Chuma Himonga, "African Customary Law in South Africa: The Many Faces of Bhe v. Magistrate, Khayelitsha," in *Recht in Afrika* no. 2 (2005): 163–83.

22. D. A. Masolo, "Western and African Communitarianism: A Comparison," in *A Companion to African Philosophy*, ed. Kwasi Wiredu (New York: Wiley-Blackwell, 2004), 483–98.

23. Mabogo P. More, "Philosophy in South Africa Under and After Apartheid," in Kwasi Wiredu, ed., *A Companion to African Philosophy*, 149 and 156–57.

24. V. Y. Mudimbe, *The Invention of Africa: Gnosis, Philosophy, and the Order of Knowledge* (Bloomington and Indianapolis: Indiana University Press, 1988).

25. Achille Mbembe, "African Modes of Self-Writing," in *Public Culture* 14, no. 1 (2002): 255.

26. Thomas Hobbes, *Leviathan* (New York: Norton, 1997).

27. Cf. Allen W. Wood, *Kantian Ethics* (Cambridge: Cambridge University Press, 2007).

28. Immanuel Kant, *Groundwork of the Metaphysics of Morals*, trans. Mary Gregor (Cambridge: Cambridge University Press, 1998).

29. Mabogo P. More, "Philosophy in South Africa Under and After Apartheid," 157.

30. Cf. the interview with S'Bu Zikode, the current president of the Shack Dwellers Movement, in *uBuntu in Everyday Life* (collective project, 2009), chap. 8, http://theubuntuproject.org/resources.php.

31. Cf. Virginia Held, *Justice and Care* (Boulder, CO: Westview Press, 1995).

32. Martha Nussbaum, "Capabilities as Fundamental Entitlements: Sen and Social Justice," in *Feminist Economics* 9, no. 2–3 (2003): 33–59.

33. Jean and John L. Comaroff, "Criminal Justice, Cultural Justice: The Limits of Liberalism and the Pragmatics of Difference in the New South Africa," in *American Ethnologist* 31, no. 2 (2004): 188–204. They have repeatedly made this argument in the uBuntu workshop on the naming and the status of customary law that was held at the University of Cape Town between 2007 and 2009.

34. Slavoj Žižek, *First as Tragedy, Then as Farce* (London/New York: Verso, 2009). I thoroughly agree with Žižek that the time has come to take communism seriously as a practical and philosophical task.

35. Drucilla Cornell, "Introduction: The Re-Cognition of *uBuntu*," in *uBuntu and the Law: African Ideals and Postapartheid Jurisprudence* (New York: Fordham University Press, 2012), 1–27.

36. See chapter, 4, "Sangomas and Traditional Leaders," in *uBuntu in Everyday Life* (collective project, 2009), http://theubuntuproject.org/resources.php.

37. Nkunzi Zandile Nkabinde, *Black Bull, Ancestors and Me: My Life as a Lesbian Sangoma* (Cape Town: Fanele, 2V008).

38. Ibid., 37.
39. Ibid., 38.
40. Ibid., 53.
41. Oyeronke Oyewumi, *The Invention of Women: Making African Sense of Western Gender Discourses* (Minneapolis: University of Minnesota Press, 1997).
42. Nkiru Nzegwu, "Feminism and Africa: Impact and Limits of the Metaphysics of Gender," in Wiredu, *A Companion to African Philosophy*, 560–69.
43. Ibid., 57.
44. Ibid., 131.
45. Ibid., 17.
46. Ibid., 38.
47. Ibid., 156.
48. Cf. the interview with S'Bu Zikode, the current president of the Shack Dwellers Movement, in *uBuntu in Everyday Life*.

8. IS THERE A DIFFERENCE THAT MAKES A DIFFERENCE BETWEEN DIGNITY AND UBUNTU?

1. *Dikoko v. Mokhatla* 2006 6 SA 235 (CC). I discuss this decision in "The Re-Cognition of *uBuntu*," the introduction to *uBuntu and the Law: African Ideals and Postapartheid Jurisprudence*, ed. Drucilla Cornell and Nyoko Muvangua (New York: Fordham University Press, 2012), 21–24.
2. Hans Kelsen, *General Theory of Law and State* (Cambridge, MA: Harvard University Press, 1945).
3. Kant writes: "The concept of every rational being as one who must regard himself as giving universal law through all the maxims of his will, so as to appraise himself and his actions from this point of view, leads to a very fruitful concept dependent upon it, namely that *of a kingdom of ends*. By a *kingdom* I understand a systematic union of various rational beings through common laws. Now since laws determine ends in terms of their universal validity, if we abstract from the personal differences of rational beings as well as from all the content of their private ends we shall be able to think of a whole of all ends in systematic connection (a whole both of rational beings as ends in themselves and of the ends of his own that each may set himself), that is, a kingdom of ends, which is possible in accordance with the above principles." Immanuel Kant, *Groundwork for the Metaphysics of Morals*, trans. Mary Gregor and Jens Timmermann (Cambridge: Cambridge University Press, 2012), 41.
4. Section 10 of the Constitution of the Republic of South Africa, 1996 reads: "Everyone has inherent dignity and the right to have their dignity respected and protected."
5. Kelsen, *General Theory of Law and State*, 117.

6. Allen Wood, "Human Dignity, Right and the Realm of Ends" in *Dignity, Freedom, and the Post-Apartheid Order: The Critical Jurisprudence of Laurie Ackermann*, ed. Barnard-Naudé et al. (Lansdowne, South Africa: Juta Press, 2009), 47 and 56–57.

7. Immanuel Kant, "On the Relationship of Theory to Practice in Political Right," in *Political Writings*, ed. Hans Reiss, trans. H. B. Nisbet (Cambridge: Cambridge University Press, 1991), 73–86.

8. Eva Feder Kittay, *Love's Labor: Essays on Women, Equality, and Dependency* (New York: Routledge, 1998).

9. Ibid.

10. Kwame Nkrumah, *Consciencism: Philosophy and Ideology for Decolonization* (New York: Monthly Review Press, 1964), 97.

11. Kenneth D. Kaunda, *A Humanist in Africa* (Nashville, TN: Abingdon Press, 1966), 22.

12. Julius K. Nyerere, "The Purpose Is Man," in *Freedom and Socialism: Uhura na Ujamaa* (Oxford: Oxford University Press, 1968), 316.

13. Nyere, *Freedom and Socialism*, 26.

14. Kaunda, *A Humanist in Africa*.

15. Ifeanyi Menkiti, "On the Normative Conception of a Person," in *A Companion to African Philosophy*, ed. Kwasi Wiredu (Malden, MA: Blackwell, 2006), 324–31.

16. D. A. Masolo, "Western and African Communitarianism: A Comparison," in *A Companion to African Philosophy*, ed. Kwasi Wiredu, 483–98.

17. John Murungi, "The Question of an African Jurisprudence: Some Hermeneutic Reflections," in *A Companion to African Philosophy*, ed. Kwasi Wiredu, 522–23.

18. Murungi, "The Question of an African Jurisprudence."

19. Immanuel Kant, *Religion Within the Boundaries of Mere Reason* (Cambridge: Cambridge University Press, 1999).

20. Roger Berkowitz, "Dignity Jurisprudence: Building a New Law on Earth," in *The Dignity Jurisprudence of the Constitutional Court of South Africa*, ed. Drucilla Cornell et. al. (New York: Fordham University Press, 2013), 74–80.

21. Hannah Arendt, *The Origins of Totalitarianism* (New York: Harcourt, 1994), ix.

9. WHERE DIGNITY ENDS AND UBUNTU BEGINS:
A RESPONSE BY YVONNE MOKGORO AND STU WOOLMAN

1. We have both written at length on dignity and uBuntu, and in many cases in conjunction with, or with support from, Professor Cornell. See, for example, Yvonne Mokgoro, "Ubuntu and the Law in South Africa," in *Buffalo Human*

Rights Law Review 15, no. 4 (1998): 15–24, republished in Drucilla Cornell and Nyoko Muvangua, *uBuntu and the Law: African Ideals and Postapartheid Jurisprudence* (New York: Fordham University Press, 2012), 317–23. Stu Woolman, "Dignity," in *Constitutional Law of South Africa*, 2nd ed., ed. Stu Woolman and Michael Bishop (Cape Town: Juta Press, 2005), ch. 36. Stu Woolman, "The Architecture of Dignity," in *The Dignity Jurisprudence of the Constitutional Court of South Africa*, ed. Drucilla Cornell et al. (New York: Fordham University Press, 2013), 73–123.

2. See Stephen Ellmann, "Marking the path of the law," in *Constitutional Court Review* 2 (2009): 97–145. Ellmann contends that emotional attachment, as opposed to detachment, plays a greater role in adjudication than even legal realists tend to posit and that the role of emotional attachment in the law ought, as a result, to be given greater recognition in the development of the law school curriculum, primarily in the form of an increased emphasis on clinical courses.

3. See Adam Smith, *The Theory of Moral Sentiments* (Cambridge: Cambridge University Press, 2002). See also Amartya Sen, *The Idea of Justice* (Cambridge, MA: Belknap, 2009); Amartya Sen, *Development as Freedom* (New York: Knopf, 1999).

4. See Drucilla Cornell, *The Imaginary Domain* (New York: Routledge, 1995); Cornell, *At the Heart of Freedom* (Princeton, NJ: Princeton University Press, 1998); Cornell, *Just Cause: Freedom, Identity, and Rights* (Lanham, MD: Rowman & Littlefield, 2000); Cornell, *Defending Ideals: War, Democracy, and Political Struggles* (New York: Routledge, 2004); Cornell, *Moral Images of Freedom* (Lanham, MD: Rowman & Littlefield, 2008). Cornell writes: "If we give Kantian dignity its broadest meaning, it is not associated with our actual freedom but with the postulation of ourselves as beings who not only can but must confront moral and ethical decisions, and in making those decisions, we give value to our world." Drucilla Cornell, "A Call for a Nuanced Constitutional Jurisprudence: South Africa, uBuntu, Dignity, and Reconciliation," in *uBuntu and the Law: African Ideals and Postapartheid Jurisprudence* (New York: Fordham University Press, 2012), 325. For an insightful overview of Cornell's oeuvre, see Karin van Marle, "'No last word': Reflections on the Imaginary Domain, Dignity and Intrinsic Worth," in *Stellenbosch Law Review* 13 (2002): 299–308.

5. *Pace* H. L. A. Hart, *The Concept of Law* (Oxford: Clarendon Press, 1960), Cornell writes: "Synchronization points us to the real problem. . . . How do we develop an institutional analysis which allows us not only to synchronize the competing rights of individuals, but also the conflicts between the individual and the community, and between different groups in society. The goal of a modern legal system is synchronization and not coherence. Synchronization recognizes that there are competing rights situations and real conflicts between the individual and the community which may not yield a coherent whole. The conflicts may be mediated and synchronized but not eradicated." Drucilla Cor-

nell, "Pragmatism, Recollective Imagination, and Transformative Legal Interpretation," in *Transformations* 23 (1993): 35–36.

6. Henk Botha, "Freedom and Constraint in Constitutional Adjudication," in *South African Journal on Human Rights* 20 (2004): 249.

7. Laurence H. Tribe, "The Futile Search for Legitimacy," in Tribe, *Constitutional Choices* (Cambridge, MA: Harvard University Press, 1986), 4–5.

8. *S v. Makwanyane* 1995 3 SA 391 (CC), 1995 6 BCLR 665 (CC), 1995 2 SACR 1 (CC), par. 308. In *Makwanyane*, Justice Langa writes: "*Ubuntu* captures, conceptually, a culture which places some emphasis on communality and on the interdependence of the members of a community. It recognises a person's status as a human being, entitled to unconditional respect, dignity, value and acceptance from the members of the community such a person happens to be part of. It also entails the converse, however. The person has a corresponding duty to give the same respect, dignity, value and acceptance to each member of that community. More importantly, it regulates the exercise of rights by the emphasis it lays on sharing and co-responsibility and the mutual enjoyment of rights by all" (para. 224–25).

9. Madoda Sigonyela, "On uBuntu and the Legitimacy of Our Constitutional Order," presentation given at "Is This Seat Taken?" colloquium, South African Institute for Advanced Constitutional, Public, Human Rights and International Law, August 29, 2010. Manuscript on file with the authors.

10. See *Khosa v. Minister of Social Development* 2004 6 SA 505 (CC), 2004 6 BCLR 569 (CC) (Mokgoro J), para. 74. In *Khosa*, the court goes beyond dignity as minimal respect and arrives at dignity as a collective concern. The Constitutional Court has discussed dignity as a collective responsibility in a number of its unfair discrimination decisions. See, for example, *Hoffmann v. South African Airways* 2001 1 SA 1 (CC), 2000 11 BCLR 1211 (CC), para. 43: "The interests of the community lie in the recognition of the inherent dignity of every human being and the elimination of all forms of discrimination." The Constitutional Court has written about dignity qua collective responsibility in the context of evictions and claims asserted under sec. 26. See *Port Elizabeth Municipality v. Various Occupiers* 2005 1 SA 217 (CC), 2004 12 BCLR 1268 (CC), para. 18: "It is not only the dignity of the poor that is assailed when homeless people are driven from pillar to post in a desperate quest for a place where they and their families can rest their heads. Our society as a whole is demeaned when state action intensifies rather than mitigates their marginalisation."

11. See, for instance, Thaddeus Metz, "African Ethics," in *International Encyclopaedia of Ethics*, ed. Hugh LaFollette (Malden, MA: Blackwell, 2013), 129–38. Metz maintains: "There are kinds of communitarian and vitalist approaches to morality commonly held by sub-Saharan ethical theorists that international scholars should take seriously as genuine rivals to utilitarian, Kantian, contrac-

tarian, and care-oriented outlooks that dominate contemporary Euro-American discussion of right action. . . . Many friends of sub-Saharan morality would sum it up by saying what is most often translated (overly literally) as either 'A person is a person through other persons' or 'I am because we are.' One encounters such phrases in a variety of societies, ranging from those in South Africa to Kenya in East Africa and Ghana in West Africa. While these phrases do connote the empirical or even metaphysical idea that one needs others in order to exist, they also convey a normative outlook. In particular, personhood and selfhood, in much African moral thought, is value-laden, meaning that one's basic aim as a moral agent should be to become a *complete* person or a *real* self. Or, using the influential term used among Zulu and Xhosa speakers in South Africa, one's fundamental goal ought to be to obtain '*ubuntu,*' to develop humanness or live a genuinely human way of life. Insofar as a large swathe of sub-Saharan thought takes one's proper ultimate end to be to become (roughly) a *mensch*, it may be construed as a self-realization morality, not unlike Greek and more generally perfectionist standpoints. . . . However, unlike the self-realization approaches that are dominant in the West, characteristic African versions are *thoroughly relational* or *communitarian* in the way they specify what constitutes one's true or valuable nature. That is, most Western accounts of morality that direct an agent to develop valuable facets of her human nature conceive of there being non-derivative self-regarding aspects of it, such as properly organizing one's mental dispositions (Plato's *Republic*) or understanding parts of the physical universe (Aristotle's *Nicomachean ethics*). In contrast, a large majority of sub-Saharan conceptions of self-realization account for it *entirely* in terms of positive relationships with other beings. In general, one develops one's humanity just insofar as one enters into community with others, particularly with other humans, but also with 'spiritual' agents who cannot be seen. Traditionally speaking, one's selfhood is partly constituted by communal relationships with God and ancestors, *viz*, elderly and morally wise progenitors of a clan who are thought to have survived the death of their bodies and to continue to interact with those in this world (the 'living-dead' as they are often called)" (129–31, citations omitted).

Metz's view of African ethics is not all sunshine and roses. See, for example, Metz, "African Moral Theory and Public Governance: Nepotism, Preferential Hiring and Other Partiality," in *African Ethics: An Anthology for Comparative and Applied Ethics*, ed. Munyaradzi Felix Murove (Durban: University Of KwaZulu-Natal Press, 2009), 335.

12. Rosalind English, "Ubuntu: The Quest for an Indigenous Jurisprudence," in *South African Journal of Human Rights* 12 (1996), 648.

13. A mainstay of the meta-theory of cultural anthropology and literary studies, relativism even managed to worm its way into the philosophy of science,

though it is fair to say that most scientists do not take such relativism seriously. Paul Feyerabend, *Against Method* (New York: Verso, 1993); Paul Feyerabend, *A Farewell to Reason* (New York: Verso, 1987).

14. As Donald Davidson writes: "So a theorem like 'Schnee ist weiss' is true in the mouth of a German speaker if and only if 'snow is white' has to be taken not merely as true, but as capable of supporting counterfactual claims. Indeed, given that the evidence for this law, if it is one, depends ultimately on certain causal relations between speakers and the world, one can say that it is no accident that 'Schnee is weiss' is true if and only if snow is white; it is the whiteness of snow that *makes* 'Schnee is weiss' true.'" Donald Davidson, *Inquiries into Truth and Interpretation* (New York: Oxford University Press, 1984), xiv (emphasis added).

15. Donald Davidson, "On the Very Idea of a Conceptual Scheme," in *Inquiries into Truth and Interpretation*, 183.

16. Davidson, *Inquiries into Truth and Interpretation*, 197.

17. 2005 1 SA 580 (CC), 2005 1 BCLR 1 (CC).

18. 2009 2 SA 66 (CC), 2008 9 BCLR 914 (CC).

19. See Tshepo Madlingozi, "The Constitutional Court, Court Watchers and the Commons: A Reply to Professor Michelman on Constitutional Dialogue, 'Interpretive Charity' and the Citizenry as Sangomas," in *Constitutional Court Review* 1 (2008): 63–76. See also S. Sibanda, *How Constitutional Democracy Has Blocked the Promise of South Africa's Liberation Movements* (PhD dissertation, in progress 2011, University of the Witwatersrand); Khoisan Chief Jean Burgess, "The Constitution Does Not Speak to Me or for Me," presentation given at a conference on "The Constitution and the Masses," South African Institute for Advanced Constitutional, Public, Human Rights and International Law (Constitution Hill, October 29, 2010). Chief Jean contends that not only does the Constitution's failure to recognize Khoi and San languages as official languages exclude Khoisan people from participation in South Africa's constitutional project, other laws that only permit persons who speak Khoisan languages to "speak" for Khoisan communities further marginalize Khoisan peoples. As a result, she argues that such a flaw in the basic law functions as a barrier to Khoisan acceptance of the legitimacy of the Constitution.

20. See Andile Mngxitama, "Introduction to Böhmke's The White Revolutionary as a Missionary," in *New Frank Talk* 5 (2010): 1.

CONCLUSION: UBUNTU AND SUBALTERN LEGALITY

1. For a fuller discussion, see my introduction to *uBuntu and the Law: African Ideals and Postapartheid Jurisprudence* (New York: Fordham University Press, 2011), 1–27.

2. Rapule Tabane and Ferial Haffajee, "Ideology Is Dead, Long Live ID-ology," in *Mail & Guardian* June 27–July 3, 2003. Cited in Jean and John L. Comaroff, "Liberalism, Policulturalism, and ID-ology: Thoughts on Citizenship and Difference," in *Theory from the South, or, How Euro-America Is Evolving Toward Africa* (Boulder/London: Paradigm Publishers, 2012), 65–90, 200n4.

3. Comaroff and Comaroff, "Liberalism, Policulturalism, and ID-ology," 67–68.

4. See Chapter 4. See also Comaroff and Comaroff, "Liberalism, Policulturalism, and ID-ology," 77.

5. Paget Henry, *Caliban's Reason: Introducing Afro-Caribbean Philosophy* (New York: Routledge, 2000).

6. "Revolutionary Ubuntu: The Shack Dwellers and Poor People of South Africa." http://www.eblackstudies.org/ebooks/ubuntu.pdf.

7. See "Unfree Black Labor: The Telos of History and the Struggle against Racialized Capitalism," in *Symbolic Forms for a New Humanity: Cultural and Racial Reconfigurations of Critical Theory*, Drucilla Cornell and Kenneth Michael Panfilio (New York: Fordham University Press, 2010), 125–50. Cf. Sampie Terreblanche, *A History of Inequality in South Africa: 1652–2002* (Pietermaritzburg: University of Natal Press, 2002).

8. Sampie Terreblanche, *Lost in Transformation: South Africa's Search for a New Future Since 1986* (KMM Review, 2012).

9. "The adoption of this Constitution lays the secure foundation for the people of South Africa to transcend the divisions and strife of the past, which generated gross violations of human rights, the transgression of humanitarian principles in violent conflicts and a legacy of hatred, fear, guilt and revenge. These can now be addressed on the basis that there is a need for understanding but not for vengeance, a need for reparation but not for retaliation, a need for ubuntu but not for victimization." Interim Constitution of South Africa, April 27, 1994, chapter 16.

10. Steven L. Robins, *From Revolution to Rights in South Africa: Social Movements NGOs & Popular Politics After Apartheid* (Pietermaritzburg: University of Kwazulu-Natal Press, 2008), 165.

11. See Mahmood Mamdani, *Citizen and Subject: Contemporary Africa and the Legacy of Late Colonialism* (Princeton, NJ: Princeton University Press, 1996), and Comaroff and Comaroff, *Theory from the South*.

12. Manuscript on file with the author.

13. Boaventura de Sousa Santos, *Toward a New Legal Common Sense: Law, Globalization, and Emancipation*, 2nd ed. (London: LexisNexis Butterworths, 2002), 467.

Index